Kindest regards of
Manly P. Hall

Manly P. Hall
All Seeing Eye
Book First
by
DARRELL JORDAN
Compiled and Edited

Athenaia.Co
Coeur D'Alene:
Printed and bound in the
United States, 2023

Manly P. Hall. All Seeing Eye – Book First. Compiled with graphics and edits by Darrell Jordan, Copyright © First Edition 2023. All rights reserved.

No part of this book may be reproduced in whole or in part without the written permission from the publisher, nor stored in any retrieval system or transmitted by any means, electronic, mechanical, photocopying, recording, or other, without the written consent of the publisher.

For bulk purchases, please contact the publisher.
Enquiry@Athenaia.Co

Library of Congress Cataloging-in Publication Data
Names: Hall, Manly P. | Jordan, Darrell
Title: All Seeing Eye – Book First by Manly P. Hall. / Darrell Jordan, MPS
Description: First U.S. edition. | Coeur D'Alene, Idaho: Athenaia [2023]
Identifiers: LCCN (pending) | ISBN 979-8-88556-040-5 (First Edition hardcover)
Subjects: OCC040000: BODY, MIND & SPIRIT / Hermetism & Rosicrucianism, | PHI013000: PHILOSOPHY / Metaphysics, | SOC038000: SOCIAL SCIENCE / Freemasonry & Secret Societies
LC record available at https://lccn. loc.gov

On the internet: Parallel47North.com/collections/esoteric-books

Managing Editor: Darrell Jordan
Original Author and Essay: Manly P. Hall
Executive Producer: Yuka Jordan
Book Cover Design by Darrell Jordan
Image Credits: Manly P. Hall's personal collection
Printed and bound in the United States

Publisher: Athenaia, LLC
2370 N Merritt Crk Lp, Ste 1
Coeur D'Alene, ID 83814
The United States
Enquiry@Athenaia.Co

Manly P. Hall
All Seeing Eye

Book First

by

Darrell Jordan, MPS
Compiled and Edited

CONTENTS

Introduction: 3

MAY 1923
NONSENSE AS A FACTOR IN SOUL GROWTH: 6
MUSIC: 10
CHINESE COSMOGONY: 11
THE BLUE KRISH: 13
WOULD MAN GAIN ANYTHING BY LIVING FOREVER IN ONE BODY? :   14
THE THIRD EYE: 14
THE BROTHERS OF THE SHINING ROBE - I: 22
MASONRY: "THE ROBE OF BLUE AND GOLD :   27
THE TRIANGLE ON THE MASON'S RING - I: 30
THE MAGICAL MOUNTAIN OF THE MOON - I: 32
ATLANTIS, THE LOST CONTINENT: 35
BOOKS AND THEIR PLACE IN OCCULTISM: 46
THE LIGHT OF ASIA: 50

JUNE 1923
THE MASTER: 52
HIGHBROWS AND LOW MORAL: 53
ART: 57
MAN THE HUMAN VIOLIN - I: 58
THE MAGICAL MOUNTAIN OF THE MOON - II: 65
A LITTLE EPISODE FROM LIFE - I: 68
BROTHERS OF THE SHINING ROBE - II: 69
OCCULT MASONRY: 73
ADAM AND EVE AND THE FLAMING SWORD: 76
THE MYSTERY OF INITIATION: 77
ASTROLOGY: 83
BROKEN DOLLS: 85
SHIPS THAT PASS IN THE NIGHT: 87
A LITTLE EPISODE FROM LIFE - II: 89

JULY 1923

MID NATURE'S CHARMS:	96
MENTAL HAZARDS VS. HEREDITARY FAILURES:	97
THE LAST OF THE SHAMEN:	104
THE BROTHERS OF THE SHINING ROB - II:	114
JUST LONELY:	119
EXPLANATION OF LAST MONTH'S PLATE:	121
OCCULT EUGENICS:	123
A LETTER FROM THE BROTHERS OF THE ROSE CROSS - II:	129
WHAT WILL THE HARVEST BE?:	132
THE DIVINE MASQUERADER:	135
ASTROLOGICAL KEYWORDS:	140
THE INDIAN SNAKE CHARM:	142

AUGUST 1923

FAITH:	146
EDITORIAL:	147
THE DOPE PROBLEM:	153
THE SPIRIT OF THE SNOWS:	155
THE BROTHERS OF THE SHINING ROBE - II:	160
BALDER THE BEAUTIFUL:	164
DESCRIPTION OF PLATE IN LAST MONTH'S MAGAZINE:	169
THE VEIL OF KRISHNA:	171
ASTROLOGICAL KEYWORD:	179
MAN THE HUMAN VIOLIN - II:	182
MASONRY:	185
AUTHOR AND MANAGING EDITOR:	189

Introduction

EDITOR'S NOTE

Manley Hall was born on 18 March 1901, in Peterborough, Canada, to William S. and Louise Palmer Hall. The Hall family moved to Sioux Falls, South Dakota, United States, in 1904. Manly Hall later settled in Los Angeles in 1919.

As a young man, he became interested in all forms of occult subjects. He subsequently joined a number of societies, among them the Theosophical Society, the Freemasons, the Societas Rosecruciana in Civitatibus Foederatis, and the American Federation of Astrologers.

In 1922, Hall wrote his first book: Initiates of the Flame and was collecting all form of esoteric/exoteric/mystical subject matter, in his own words: "late in the fall of 1922, the plan for a comprehensive work on the symbolism of western mystical societies began to take shape in my mind. It soon became apparent that research facilities for such a project were not available in Southern California... The only answer was to contact antiquarian book dealers and elicit their cooperation in the search for the items desired." In 1934, Hall founded the Philosophical Research Society, a research institute modeled on the ancient school of Pythagoras.

He was ordained a minister in 1923 to an occult/mystic congregation at the Church of the People in California. In that same year specifically in May 1923, Manly Hall began the membership/student based, not for sale magazine, all written, edited and published by Hall titled the "The All Seeing-Eye."

This Book series covers the first year of the All Seeing-Eye magazine for ease of reading. Bear in mind that Manly Hall at this time in 1923 was only 22 years old! Editing was minimal in terms of punctuation and spelling. In some cases, there are made-up words (or words that are no longer in use) in which case they were left spelled as is.

I'm sure that you will find, as did I, that Manly Hall was highly intelligent and possibly bordering on genius. Many of his stories that elucidate a particular subject were written in the first person. Whether or not this was the case, the stories demonstrate either a highly active imagination or perhaps he did, in fact, experience what he wrote in the first-person account stories or a combination thereof.

Suffice it to say, we are positive you will enjoy the many journeys Manly Hall takes you on.

MAY 1923

NONSENSE AS A FACTOR IN SOUL GROWTH

THERE ARE TIMES in the unfolding of human consciousness when the student feels and honestly believes that the entire weight of the Eternal Plan, the salvation of God, man, and the universe and the perpetuation of civilization, rests upon his shoulders. He feels that when he passes out, Truth will die with him and that his life must be so filled with duties that he has little, if any, time to demonstrate the qualities of the human race. Religion becomes such a weighty problem that he entirely forgets the necessity of humor and the value of mental and spiritual recreation, or, rather, we may say that lack of use has caused his sense of humor to atrophy.

The inevitable result of losing the ability to laugh and to relax the tension of massive thought and incessant labor is unbalance and ultimate spiritual crystallization, commonly known in the world of affairs as freakishness and crankism. The ability of the philosopher to forget his philosophies and the mystic to lay aside his religion and smile with the world over some hopelessly trivial bit of nonsense is the sign of true superphysical greatness and spiritual balance.

All students of symbolism know that for ages a long face has been considered symbolical of religion and that the sadder you appear and the more dejected your countenance, the holier you are and the closer you are to a God who has long foresworn laughter. This idea is based on an entirely erroneous concept of life. The appreciation of humor is a divine faculty, the quick wit that it develops may be used for much deeper works, while the inevitable radiation of cheer which accompanies the happy person is just as important to the growth of humanity as the philosophical concepts which we expound and the problems of compound ratio.

There are those known in the world as "wet blankets," "gloom dispensers" and "Aunty-dolefuls" who in the name of God take all the cheer from life and with their blankets of pessimism totally eclipse the sun which might otherwise send to our hearts at least a solitary ray. If there be an exceptionally high spot in Heaven, a brownstone front in the Great Beyond, we shall undoubtedly find it reserved for those mystics and philosophers, sages and seers, who have not only made man think and pray but have taught him how to laugh.

The world is filled with trials and worries, with long faces and hopeless souls which must be met along the weary road that leads to Light, but the Powers that be have seen fit to bring laughter into the world to cheer the weary hearts of striving men and women and to make this gift doubly sure have supplied a special set of facial muscles for its expression, and it is the duty of every student not only to promote aestheticism but also to bring into faces furrowed with care and hearts frozen in endless snows the happy smile which is indeed the greatest boon of the gods.

All the greatest philosophers have been noted not only for their quickness of mind but for their sharpness of wit and in truth there is nothing which shows the depth of thought and knowledge of life more than an original joke which has something really funny in it. There is an art in jesting which can only be appreciated after a suffering mortal has listened to what the world calls humor. This art should be listed with the seven immortal arts and sciences.

Let us remember the words of an ancient philosopher who said, when referring to the court jester of a king, "It takes the brightest man in all the land to make the greatest fool." The kingdoms of suffering humanity must have that court fool but few of our so-called religious lights will allow their faces to relax for fear that their dignity may be affected, and their congregation dwindle away.

When we laugh from the depths of our soul, relaxing for a moment the nerves and muscles that have so long been at a tension in fighting the battle of life, it is like a gymnasium exercise for the body and a tonic for the soul. The lungs fill with air, the liver receives its "daily dozen," and the face beams with a greater joy because for one moment the purely human has been given expression in a way which can injure none. Even those people who are unconsciously ridiculous will never realize nor be accredited with the honor that is due them from the fact that they have made others laugh, for while their personality is hurt and is many cases their noses are seriously cracked still that laughter will reach to the ends of creation before its last echoes die away at the very footstool of divinity.

It is said that the Christian theology is the only one that has not at least one laughing god in its train, and we cannot but feel that there has been a serious omission. The laughter of the gods sounds through all nature, which is filled with cheer. It is the sorrows and discouragements of life which turn all things to a leaden gray. Those who radiate this soot-colored expression of life are never popular, never happy, seldom useful, and always a bore. The laughter of children is music in the ears of the Almighty and all living things are children who cry one moment and laugh the next, and of those moments which comes closest to the divine, the joy or the tear? All human beings are like little ones crying over broken dolls and the toys which have fallen to pieces in their hands, but their sorrows are short-lived and soon the bursts of merry laughter shroud the sorrow in forgetfulness. But there are some who cannot forget, and it is the duty of all to cheer them on their way, for every heart is filled with sadness and when we, too, are sad it but brings back memories which do not help but always surround us with thoughts of bitterness or remorse.

It is said that animals do not smile, but it seems that they do, for every horse and dog and even the old cat purring on the hearth rug have a contented, smiling appearance concealed somewhere about their faces. Even the fowls of the farmyard with all their stateliness and dignity have a certain twinkle in their eyes and a certain upward curve at the corner of their bills which is often missing from the human physiognomy, and their dignity is all the greater because of its absurdity while man's absurdities are always greater because of his dignity.

There is a psychology in humor, a moral effect upon all with whom we come in contact. It makes us friends; we are invited to call again in a voice which means it; it brings us closer to the hearts of others; it tries us more tightly to the truly human; it tears down the barriers of creed and caste and gives us a footing in the hearts of others.

There is no greater power which man can evolve than that of seeing all Nature smiling, every plant and flower wreathed in merriness, smiling because his own soul is laughing, filled, and overflowing with that exuberance of spirit which marks the true expression of spiritual growth. To see the laughter in nature, the joy in living, the good concealed beneath the ever painful, is a thing not always easy to do. One must have within himself this Fountain of Mirth, which would have lengthened the life of Ponce de Leon had he not shortened his career by the seriousness of his search, which sees in everything not only the deep and mystical but the divinely and sublimely ridiculous.

When our hearts are about to overflow with sorrow, if we could but see with the eyes of the gods, we would smile at least. When we are about to be offended by the words and actions of others, if we could but think a moment, we would probably make matters much worse for it would be a Herculean task to restrain the laughter which would bring with it the wrath of our opponent.

You may say what you will. It is better far to see the ridiculous in life than the ever sordid; it is better far to laugh at the mistakes of man than to curse the decrees of God, and those who go around brewing cups of hemlock and radiating avalanches of gloom should indeed be listed with the false prophets and the blasphemers of God. The man who cannot find something pleasant to say no matter where he may be, how unpleasant the experience, how uncongenial those around him, or how contrary to his taste the incident in question, should never claim even the first degrees of spirituality. The mystic knows that in the last analysis all opposites blend, tragedy and comedy are one, and their apparently diverse ways are united at the doorway, which leads to heights immortal.

So, laugh and list among the benefactors of humanity those who often with hearts filled with sadness have realized the sweetness of a smile and the gloriousness of mirth and who have been the fools to make their brothers laugh, their only reward being the realization that for a moment at least a few hearts have forgotten their sorrows and a few lonely wanderers have seen the sunny side of life.

There is nothing more contagious than joy and nothing more infectious than gloom. These two inseparable companions of mankind walk side by side, gloom noted for its length, joy for its breadth, and their eternal battle for mastery one over the other must be played out in every human heart.

Acid temperaments make acid bodies, and the world is filled with intellectual alkalis which seem to stunt all the glories of nature. The reward of gloom is dyspepsia, ankylotic joints, rheumatism, and sour stomach. Those who cannot smile ferment all the world and spoil a glorious crop by their own tiny apple and too often they do this in the name of God. There are thousands whose motto for life is, "If ye smile upon the Sabbath, ye shall weep ere Monday dawn," and other equally sentimental concepts of God's demand of man.

Let us rather use as our motto "A smile a day keeps the doctor away," and the more smiles, the more "undesirables" are excluded from the aura of our association. There are glooms of all kinds revolving in their orbits around us, but until the wet blanket enters our own hearts, we are master of them, and if our own lives are sunny, the spirits of negation have little chance of entrance there.

One thing about the Devil that we always admire is the fact that he has a most resounding laugh and in spite of all his villainies there is a certain refreshment which comes over us even as we are chilled by his hilarity. He does the most miserable things in the most jovial and likeable way and can even damn us with a smile upon his face, while many of our friends cannot even say "Good morning" without looking like a heavy storm.

Occultists and occult students must realize that when they forget how to be jovial, they lock the door of Heaven and throw away the key.

MUSIC

THERE IS NO POWER that holds so great a sway over the hearts and souls of living things as the charm of music. From the earliest dawn of time when the primitive civilizations of the world were in the making to our modern and apparently more ethical day, the life of man has been softened, his expressions molded to nobler ends, and his emotions raised to more lofty heights by the power of harmony and rhythm. In the early days of the world the children of the earth learned to imitate the eternal music of Nature, the singing of the birds, the moaning of the winds, the swishing of the waves on rock-bound shores, the night cries of bird and beast, all of these blends into a mystic cadence which we may call in truth the endless symphonies of Nature. The powers of creation are eternally musical, their mystic cadences swell from star to star with note divine. All nature, seen and unseen, formed and unformed, listens in rapt awe to the endless symphonies of the Great Unknown.

Then there is another music, the song of Life, the beating of human hearts, the peals of merry laughter, the broken sobs of sorrow. All these blends into a mystic orchestra, ofttimes unheard, which swells in note invisible through eternity to the very footstool of the Divine. Man's nature pours forth from his being with the expression of living music. The old organist allows his fingers to slip over the keys in an apparently unconscious, mechanical way but the very emotions of his soul pour out in divine harmonies from the instrument that registers and seems to live the innermost thoughts of the musician, the innermost symphonies of his soul.

The deep, wailing notes of the violin seem to speak of the master's touch and the very heart of the musician expresses itself in the harmonies that he plays. The heart that is broken in sorrow sends forth sweet melodies that touch the heartstrings, while the ponderous clashes of massive themes speak of the weighty minds that bring them forth.

All life is musical, for it is a language universally understood. Its strange discord speaks of human hate, its harmony of mutual understanding. Upon the seven-stringed lyre of its own being, the human soul plays its harmony celestial; each thought and action are but a note of living music. When we live askew and our natures are unbalanced, the instrument is out of tune because the hands of the master do not rest upon the keys. The Stradivarius is dead until the soft fingers of the violinist draw from its latent soul the mystic yearnings of his own heart. So, the bodies of man are like instruments in the hands of master musicians. The spirit within each living thing plays upon its bodies, seeking to build them into more glorious instruments for its own expression that its notes may swell the harmonies of cosmos.

When man's life is a sham, when his heart is cold, all the sounds from his living keyboard are inharmonious and discordant, the keys are out of tune; the strings are broken, and the hands that would play them are shackled by the things of earth. But those who have labored long and suffered much are mellowed like old violins. The ages of sorrow and suffering have brought out the greatest that is in them, and they are masterpieces in a master's hand. Each year the tones grow more mellow and the hand that draws the bow brings more perfect harmonies from its hallowed instrument, until at last in the hands of the Great Musician they pour forth in cords and symphonies sublime, each wondrous melody the reflection of the genius of the soul.

Music is a wonderful thing. It melts the hardened heart, softens the stern lines of the face, brings peace to those who long have suffered, and like the child drifting into sleep, lulled by the soft notes of a lullaby, the soul of man finds rest in the music of his own soul and the divine harmony of Nature's plan.

CHINESE COSMOGONY

KHEEN OR SHANG-TE is the great Prince or model man; He is the Great Father of Gods and men; He is Heaven, or the Kosmos animated by a mind or soul and hence He is a sphere or circle; that being the most perfect figure. All parts of the Kosmos, therefore, viz., Heaven, Earth, Man, Sun, Moon, Stars, Mountains, Rivers, Birds, Beasts, Insects, Reptiles, Trees, Vegetables, etc., are all His parts and members and these are all pervaded and animated by the "One Mind" or Soul of Heaven or Shang-te.

In the state religion, Shang-te is worshiped in all His parts, beginning with His triplication Heaven, Earth, and Man.

This philosophy is evidently founded upon the Confucianist idea of man transferred to the universe; as man is composed of mind and body, so Heaven or the Kosmos is supposed to be composed of mind and matter, and the mind in each is one and the same, therefore Shang-te designated God or the Divinity within. Hence Confucius states that this Heaven or Shang-te is a gigantic Man, also this Shang-te is a sphere containing the whole universe within Himself and is the highest Numen.

From the "Classic of Chance," By the Rev. Cannon McClatchie, M.A. This sidelight into the mythology and cosmogony of china shows how closely it is correlated with the teachings of the Hebrew Qabalah and the alchemical and theosophic concepts of life. This Shang-te, the All Prevading manifesting in its multiplicity of forms, is called by many names in many lands but is the same wherever found. This cosmic Being who made man in His own image and whom we honor as the Creator of our universe has been known and studied for hundreds of thousands of years by the ancient peoples of the eastern countries.

Students who analyze religion soon realize that there is but one to analyze and that the most heathenish concept in the world is to believe in heathens.

The ancients of the western world have symbolized the Grand Man as a great figure twisted backward until His head and feet touch, forming a great sphere. There is little doubt that the ultimate form of all things is spheroid and that the planets which we see in the sky, the sun, etc., are all of them organisms not unlike our own with intelligence, circulation, and consciousness but instead of, like our bodies, being peopled with cells and corpuscles these bodies are peopled with flora and fauna of evolving life.

A true understanding of the mystic philosophies depends upon the willingness of the student to credit all things with intelligence, and to realize that as mind and body expand, they eternally express themselves in new environments which are the expressions of need, and that at various times during our growth the forms of our vehicles change.

Man is a universe is himself just as complicated upon a miniature scale as the heavens which unfold around us. Within him are the planets, the great powers of light and darkness, and millions of evolving lives. Some have estimated six septillions in the human body. Thus man as he raises his hand to Shang-te, the Father of Light, and the globe-shaped Spirit of Creation, within whose Being we live and move and have our being, must also realize that he himself is Shang-te and that the universe wonderful beyond conception which expresses itself as his bodies is in truth built in the image of the Father, and that he himself is not only a God in the making but is already a great spiritual power to the millions of lives seeking expression through his extension of consciousness.

THE BLUE KRISH

ON PICTURING the Christ Child of India, Shri-Krishna, the Blue Lotus, we find He is always painted as having a blue skin. Now let us consider briefly the reason for this rather unusual symbolism. Why the Lord of Love playing upon His flute with Radha in the woods is always colored with this bluish light has caused considerable speculation among students of occult philosophy.

The reason for this is said to be that blue is the symbol of the Father, the highest of the three primary colors. All great spiritual workers are said to be under the protection of the Father, or, as the East would say, enfolded in the cape of Brahma. This blue spiritual wall which divides the Great Ones from men is symbolized by the Oriental by coloring the body of Krishna, the incarnation of Vishnu, the second principle of the Indian Trinity, a pale blue color.

Briefly, it is said to mean that between that soul and the world there was forever a wall, and that while Krishna came to the world, He was not of the world but belonged in the home of the Gods. This beautiful symbolism applies to the problems of life. There are many who are in the world, and while apparently, they are one with us, still they know, and we often feel that there is a wall between us. This is the wall of spirit, the wall of greater light and truth, which spiritually divides the living from the dead. Those who come to us from behind the veil still wander with us, but the blue veil of spirit conceals them, the blue light of spirit shines out from their being, and while they labor with us, they are concealed forever behind the blue veil of immortality.

Each will one day step behind this veil and the blue folds of the Father's cape will stand between us and the world as protection and relief. Then we too shall labor in the world concealed forever and divided from mortal man by the blue veil of Krishna, the Blue Lotus of India.

WOULD MAN GAIN ANYTHING BY LIVING FOREVER IN ONE BODY?

AS SOON as the average student realizes that there are certain powers which transcend material things or apparently do so and discovers that there are those who remain for indefinite periods in one body, the student immediately desires to do the same thing because, after all, living and dying appear as very inconvenient phases in the evolution of man. Perpetual life seems to be a novelty which has attracted a number of people who should have much better sense and the fountain of eternal youth is sought for as earnestly now as in the days of Ponce de Leon. But let the student always remember that these great things are effects and that the only cause which can bring them about is mastery and Adeptship. Until he lives right, thinks right and becomes master of those lower desires and passions and emotions which wreck his life he can never hope to lengthen it by spiritual powers.

There are many lessons for man to learn besides those of this plane of nature and in other worlds he learns and studies while the stage is being set here for the next great step in his unfoldment and if he was forced to remain here age in and age out with no one that he knew and the incessant monotony which to him now seems a novelty he would soon pray for death as now he prays for life. But when he has learned to be of use through the ages, when he has completely given up all desire to live for himself alone, when he has become so useful in the Great Plan that he is needed every moment for the good of all, then he will be able to live forever and to do useful works in many worlds to come.

THE THIRD EYE

BANG! The shot sounded through the hotel like a clap of thunder in the dead silence of the winter night. A moment later there came a dull thud as if something was falling and the loose fixtures in the hotel room shook. Then came the soft patter of footsteps in the hallway, a woman's half broken sob, then all was still again.

The sound of the shot aroused everyone in the building, doors opened, and frightened faces appeared in the frames of light.

"What has happened?"

"Is someone killed?"

"Was it a shot?"

"I don't know, do you?"

From mouth to mouth, the questions flew along the hallway like wildfire, but no one could be found who seemed in a position to answer them.

It was then that with a tremendous gust of personality Mr. Jeremiah Johnson, the house detective, appeared upon the scene with a glorious blue-green dressing gown draped over pink-striped pajamas. In one hand he carried a revolver while with the other he endeavored to make his scanty attire cover as much ground as possible, not forgetting to brush the nickel-plated star which he fastened conspicuously on the blue-green background of his bizarre attire.

"Where did the shot come from?" he demanded in a booming voice as he scuffed his way in bedroom slippers to the center of the hall and gazed around.

"That is precisely the information with which we desire you to supply us," answered a distinguished-looking gentleman, dressed in an iron-gray Vandyke and blue nightshirt, as he gave the house detective a careful inspection through gold pince-nez and then vanished in the direction of his wardrobe.

The detective looked along the hall at the opened doors and startled faces; registering professional poise and then his eyes fastened themselves upon two portals side by side at the extreme end of the corridor.

They were the only two on the entire floor that had remained closed during the excitement. Many pairs of eyes followed the rather Bohemian figure of Jeremiah as he laid his course on these doors. In a second, he was pounding on one of them; he waited a second and knocked again, but no answer sounded from within. He tried the door but found it locked, so turned his attention to the other. He rapped upon this also, but silence alone rewarded his effort. Trying this one and finding it unfastened, Jeremiah opened the door and stepped inside. The portal screen closed behind his back.

About a minute slipped by, although it seemed much longer to the watchers in the hall. Then the door reopened, and the detective stepped out, but it was with a look of horror on his pale and drawn face that Jeremiah Johnson half staggered into the hallway leaning upon the wall for support.

"What was it?" all asked in one breath.

"Yes," reiterated the gentleman with the Vandyke who had reappeared upon the scene, a necktie and smoking jacket added to his wardrobe, "we would be-ah-much obliged if you would elucidate this perplexing problem."

"Murder," muttered the detective, as turning he locked the door with his pass-key, "go back to your rooms everyone and remain there until the inspectors arrive."

And without further word, Jeremiah Johnson disappeared a trail of pink and green in the direction of the elevator.

"I wonder who the dead person is?" asked a kindly appearing old lady halfway down the hall.

"I don't know," came a shrill voice from across, "but I think it's just too romantic for words!"

"Brrrrrrrr," muttered the distinguished gentleman with the Vandyke as his knees shook together, "really if they must murder in this hotel, I would certainly consider it a favor if they would turn on the steam heat first. This is a most undesirable moment for a crime."

As no one could cast any light upon the mystery, one by one the doors closed until the only sound breaking the stillness was a whisper now and then which trickled through some keyhole. An hour later, four very puzzled men stood in the center of the room where the tragedy had occurred. Before them on the floor, illuminated by a reading lamp, lay the dead man fully dressed with a bullet hole in his back. There were no signs of weapons or apparent motive for the crime, nothing had been touched in the room and as usual, the officers could not find the clue upon which to base their further investigations. One of the detectives turned to the hotel inspector. "Have you been able to secure any information concerning the murdered man?"

"Very little," replied Johnson. "the name he signed on the hotel register was Professor Amos Martin. I hear he is a scientist and a globetrotter. I have also gathered from my examination here that he is an author and connected to research work with several well-known universities. He is just back from several years in the Orient. On the table, you will find the beginning of the latest book that he was writing. It was to be called "The Third Eye" and is apparently of a very scientific nature. He seems to base it on some Eastern sacred writings or something of that sort. So far as I have been able to discover, he was not married, has no relatives, and is a long way from his original home. He appears to be well fixed financially and has been in the hotel three days short of a month."

At the word "Orient," the detectives pricked up their ears and looked at each other in a significant way. "You say he was just back from the Far East? That is a very important point. Do you know whether there are any Orientals in this neighborhood at the present time, especially stopping at the hotel?"

"Oh, yes! Why didn't I think of it before? There is a Chinaman here who came soon after the Professor's arrival who is supposed to be assisting him in the completion of his great book. He may have been with him last night."

"Where is his room?" asked one of the detectives.

"Wait a minute and I'll find out," replied Jeremiah, as he slipped quickly from the room. While awaiting the return of the house detective, the other three walked over to the desk upon which lay a great mass of typewritten manuscripts. One of them picked up a sheet and read:

"The Third Eye is a small ductless gland in the brain, known to modern science as the pineal gland. In India, China, Thibet I have come across great scientists who have so developed this gland, which is much more powerful than the physical eye, that they can see through solid walls and into the very secrets of the human mind."

"Humph," muttered the detective, scratching his head. He then took a long breath and continued,

"Few people realize the powers which work through this eye when it is awakened. If they did, greater attempts would be made to revivify this partly atrophied organ of cognition. This is only possible, according to those who have awakened this power, through the turning upward of the forces playing through the segments of the spinal canal. These forces dilate the gland, which then becomes a super organ of sense orientation. In the eastern countries, much time has been spent in the awakening and training of this very important gland and the purpose of my book is to show the western world the value of this little-known organ."

The detective looked at his companions, then down at the dead man on the floor, a rather peculiar expression playing on his face, then shrugging his shoulders he held the paper under the light and continued:

"There are certain superphysical powers known to the ancients which the western world little understands, but these secrets are still in possession of certain priests and eastern scientists whom I have met during my travels. It is of those mysterious ones that I would write. They are found most frequently in Northern India, Burma, and China, and among the Llamas of Thibet. They have powers of sight far beyond those of the average individual. Their lives as aesthetics and hermits and their self-sacrifices and rigid purification have given them powers over their own being and also over others, which are perfectly uncanny to those unacquainted with the hidden side of human nature and the powers of the universe."

"Oh, tommyrot!" laughed the officer as he threw the paper back among its fellows. "Some people are getting dippy over this sort of stuff nowadays. And he looked like a nice, sane, sensible sort of man," and the detectives gazed down on the face of the murdered professor. "But this is the way they all get when they delve into these things. They either go insane or get killed or something."

At the same instant the house detective returned, apparently quite excited, "Why," he exclaimed, "it's all clear now. That Chinaman had the room right next to this one. I hear he spent nearly all of his time with the Professor and was here with him up to a late hour last night. There's no use talking, boys. When we get him, there'll be another feather in the cap of this department." Jeremiah brought his fist down on the big table, his excitement registering through the blow and sending the papers of the late Professor's book skidding around in a mad frenzy on the floor.

"My, but I'd like to get my hands on that Chink now!" As Jeremiah Johnson expressed the thoughts flooding his innermost soul, there came a soft knock at the door which the house detective swung open and then stepped back giving a gasp of amazement.

In the doorway stood a tall Chinese dressed in a long Mandarin gown of sober color but rich in texture. On his massive head was a tiny black cap while a glorious peacock feather hung down his back. In his hand he carried a beautiful fan inlaid with mother-of-pearl which was closed and which he used as a pointer. It was his face, however, which caused the amazement and that uncanny feeling which seemed to pour out from him wherever he went. He had the dome and brow of a philosopher and his eyes, while almond, were wide apart and of such great size and brilliance that they could be but poorly hidden by the dark shell-rim glasses that he wore. Under his drooping mustache his mouth was fixed in a true oriental smile, a pleasant but absolutely blank expression which hinted many things but never committed itself.

He spoke in a soft, purring voice, English worthy of a college-bred man, "My honorable friend expresses a desire to see me, so I take great pleasure in coming. It is an honor to have important persons such as house detectives and you worthy gentlemen of the police desire my presence."

Some way the thought came into the detectives' minds that this Oriental was deliberately ridiculing them, but his tone was so exemplary and his manner so polite that there was no chance of taking offense, even though Jeremiah fancied he saw the upper lip of the Chinaman quiver slightly at times although this might have been only his imagination.

"Are you S_____?" asked the hotel inspector in as sharp and brisk a tone as he could with a sense of a certain personal discomfort and an inexplainable feeling of smallness which had crept over him since the entrance of this gifted Chinese.

The Oriental bowed low. "Ah, the honorable gentleman has taken the pains to learn my unworthy name. So much attention overwhelms me, and I can only reply by saying that I shall pray to my ancestors for your eternal salvation and the extension of your labors."

"Save your prayers for yourself," muttered the detective, "I believe you're going to need them worse than I do in the near future."

"Ah, most honorable gentleman, refuse not the prayers of thy lowly servant," and the Chinese bowed again, "for in my country prayers returned are often needed by those who give them back." At the same instant, his eyes fell on the murdered man for the first time.

"Ah," he exclaimed, and the almond eyes became mere slits, "Murdered?" he turned to the detective, "Oh, so many times I have warned him to be more careful and told him what the immortal Confucius, the giver of all wisdom, said, but it was of no avail it seems."

"Of what did you warn him?" The Chinese tapped his jade thumb ring with his fan and bowing low took the liberty of picking a small white thread from the inspector's coat sleeve before making a reply, "Oh, only this, that he had certain weaknesses of which I was aware and I have told him often that some day these little indiscretions would most likely cost him his life, and," the Chinese twisted his foot and gazed at the toe of it as it protruded from his Mandarin cape, "and," he repeated, smiling blandly, "it appears to have done so."

"Um-m," muttered one of the detectives, "so our deceased client was subject to indiscretions?" he turned to the Chinese and bowed sarcastically. "Will you please be a little more explicit?"

The Chinese merely shrugged his arched shoulders and, with long, slender fingers, picked up a sheet of paper from the table. It was the title page of the professor's book.

"I should advise my honored friends of the detective force to secure a copy of this most esteemed work should the Gods decree that it ever be finished, for I am seriously afraid that this useful organ is not properly developed in the brain of our most worthy friend, the hotel inspector."

The detectives looked at each other, not quite sure how to act with this Oriental who it now seemed was also slightly unbalanced. But as they themselves had nothing to work on in the form of information they mentally decided that they could not be any worse off so concluded to allow the Chinese to go on.

"Do you know who murdered him?" demanded all in one voice of the Chinese.

"No, no, no," answered the Oriental as he opened his glorious fan to blow away some of the smoke from Jeremiah's none too select cigar, "but I think I can find out for you if you wish me to do so."

The detectives looked at each other and then one of them spoke. "Go on, but remember, whatever you say here will be used against you."

"Oh, I don't think so," replied the Oriental, "for this is a matter between honorable friends and as gentlemen, I am going to ask you to forget what I have said when I go. In fact, to make this easier, I shall even assist you in the forgetting." The Oriental walked to the center of the room and removing his black cap with its glorious peacock feather, he hunched his shoulders and bent his back until the dome of his massive head was pointing directly at the dead man.

The officers then saw that the top part of his head was shaven clean for a piece about the size of a silver dollar and that on this spot, a small green snake was traced in a dark pigment. With his eyes closed and the crown of his head pointing first in this way and then in that, the Chinese noiselessly slipped about the room and finally spoke in his soft, musical voice.

"It was precisely as I feared. A lady called upon the Professor, my esteemed friend, last evening. How many times have I warned my worthy brother of letters, even going to the extremity of presenting him with a beautiful book of proverbs by Lao Tze and underlining in red those pertaining to his indiscretions? It was not the first visit of the fair lady, but she had married and came to tell the Professor that their friendship was at an end. My honorable friend was so unwise he could not understand the warnings that I gave him, although I have prayed to my ancestors to preserve him. He and the lady had a little misunderstanding, shall we say, there was a slight struggle which would not have occurred had he been a Chinese gentleman. My worthy friend, losing his temper, knocked the lady down with an undue expression of western energy, unpardonable in the East, and turned his back. Now it seems that the lady's husband, being out a great deal of the time, had loaned her one of his revolvers to be used in case of burglars or another emergency. She had brought this with her and when my unfortunate friend turned his back, she shot him and dropping the revolver with a scream ran from the room."

"That's a very pretty story," muttered one of the detectives, "but you forget one thing, Chinky. Where's the gun?"

"It is still in the room," answered the Chinese, and the Oriental turned his head first in a general circle which he steadily decreased in size until it stopped on Jeremiah Johnson, the house detective.

"The revolver is in the upper pocket of this gentleman's coat where he has hidden it. He concealed it because upon entering the room for the first time, he recognized it as the one he had given his wife."

The hotel inspector collapsed. "How did you know?" he gasped. The Chinese bowed himself towards the door, the smile still playing around his mouth.

"I should advise our friends, the honorable detectives, to carefully read that little book of tommyrot which my late friend will not now be able to complete upon the interesting subject of "The Third Eye."

He slowly closed the door, saying as he passed out, "I do not think any of you will use the information I have given you against me, but should that be your intention I can only pray to my fathers for assistance."

The four detectives stood alone, blank expressions on their faces.

"What happened?" asked Jeremiah Johnson as he looked down at the revolver in his hand.

"I don't know," replied the other three.

"Say, was that Chink in here or not?"

"I don't know."

"Then where did the gun come from? Whose is it?"

The oldest of the four detectives scratched his head and turned to the other three.

"What have we been doing this last half hour? It seems like I've been asleep. I can't remember anything."

"It is the same with me," answered one after the other, in turn. They looked down at the dead man.

And there, upon the ground beside him, lay the title page of his book. In the meantime, the Chinese, his hands crossed in his sleeves, shuffled slowly down the corridor, his face set in the placid satisfaction of the Oriental.

"I really do hope that these honored gentlemen will not use anything that I have said against me. In fact, I very much believe they will not be able to do so, for my good brothers in the western world have short memories of problems of this nature. Poor Professor, if he had only developed that Third Eye a little himself, he might have been spared by the gods to complete that honorable work!"

THE BROTHERS OF THE SHINING ROBE - I

Chapter I
The Temple of Caves

WHY I CAME into the world with this deep-seated wanderlust, I have never been able to explain. Relatives and friends said that it was the blood of ten generations of soldiers and fighters for the British crown, but I have always believed that these things are not inherited but rather result from peculiar phases of individuality, the true explanation of which has only come to me in later years. Suffice it to say by way of introduction that I have been a wanderer upon the face of the earth, from the South Sea Islands to the great salmon fisheries of Alaska and Columbia, from plague-stricken Burma to the Deserts of Mexico, from Tartary to Algeria, from the blue lagoons of Venice to the domes and mosques of Constantinople, I have wandered in an endless search.

I came into this world with a larger fortune than is good for most, the younger son of an Earl. None of the responsibilities of my family worried me for it seemed improbable, with two elder brothers, that the cares and problems of an estate would ever descend upon my shoulders. So, year after year, I wandered over three-quarters of the known globe. At last, one sultry evening I found myself standing on a point of rock jutting out from the sides of a great cliff, before me unrolling in majestic grandeur rose the snow-topped glaciers of the Himalayas. Straight in front the sheer crest of Mt. Everest shot heavenward and the rays of the fast-setting sun bathed it in purple and rose shadows so that its glacial peak gleamed, like the diamonds in the crowns of Emperors.

The strange land of the East had always held a fascination for me, and now I stood looking out at this great expanse of natural majesty hundreds of miles from the nearest white man merely as the result of fancy. During my wanderings in Northern and Central India, which had occupied some five years I had come closer to a true understanding of the Oriental mind than many white men. I had eaten with them, slept with them, prayed with them, tended, with practical knowledge, which is the inherent right of the western world, their sick, read their books, loved them, and hated with them, and as the result I believe I can honestly say that to some degree at least I know the East.

While talking one day with one of their learned and holy men, he told me a little with the trust of many months of friendship, of the center ground of their faith, pointing to where the blue haze of the sky was broken by the line of mountains, in a voice filled with awe and reverence he told me of the sacred Temple of the Caves. He said that there lived in this ancient monastery, a very wise man beloved of God and the mouthpiece of Brahma. Then he became silent and would say no more, but my inquisitiveness was aroused, and I asked many learned Brahmans to give me more details of this sacred temple, but all shook their heads and despite their high regard either knew nothing or refused to reveal that which they did know. It was that short legend, those few involuntary words of the old mendicant, that changed the destiny of my life, for with the impetuosity which remained with me even after the days of my youth, I decided to wander these hills and mountains until I myself found the Temple of the Caves and spoke with this great wise man whom legend told me lived there.

My readers would suppose that a simple thing like this was of small importance, but to a mind like mine which knew nothing of the responsibilities of one phase of life the mere carrying out of a desire was all important.

As evening fell on the day in question, I stood on the crag of rocks overlooking the valley in whose dark and gloomy depths a fine mountain stream fed by the glaciers flowed on in silence to spread later and be lost in the marshlands below. Five months I had climbed through the mountains, among the caves of the holy men, through cities long deserted, through jungles and among broken rocks, and like many other searchers who had gone before found no trace of the thing I sought. At my feet on the boulder lay a heap of human bones. Some other wanderers had ended his pilgrimage where I had but started mine. Slowly the beautiful view vanished in the haze of night and a pale blue light from the waning moon took the place of the sun, and slowly turning I descended again to the plateau some fifty feet below.

As I did so, my eyes wandered upward past a great cleft of rock where I had been standing. Walls of granite and stone rose nearly a thousand feet in rough, broken grandeur. But as I stood gazing out and up, a strange feeling possessed me. I do not know whether you have ever felt when alone that someone was standing behind you looking at you, but this feeling suddenly swept over me and in the eerie stillness I felt I was not alone, and yet as far as I could see in the pale moonlight no living thing was visible.

Suddenly, over the rough ground at my feet, a dark shadow passed as though a great bird had soared over the cliffs and rocks, but the shadow was not that of a bird. It was that of a tall human being passing silently somewhere between me and the moon. Looking quickly to the top of the cliff, I was in time to see a stately, white-robed figure with long gray beard and white turban pass the field of vision between me and the light and vanish between two great rocky boulders.

Around this figure hovered a number of flashings, dancing lights of shining white and after he had gone for several seconds, the opening gleamed and glowed as though by some hidden fire. Then even that vanished.

I cannot explain the reason, but the thought crossed my mind in a flash that this figure was in some way connected with the place I sought, and regardless of tearing my hands and clothing I climbed as rapidly as possible upward and in some ten minutes stood where the shining one had been. I found that I was in a natural hallway of rock, which reminded me of the roofless temples of Karnak. On each side massive pillars of natural stone rose from thirty to fifty feet above me to be lost in the shadows of night, and the tiny, winding path led straight into the side of a lofty hill invisible from below.

I hesitated for I realized that it is not always safe to enter the temples of the East, but my hand closing over the hilt of my revolver reassured me, and with the bravado which shows a lack of better sense I took a hitch at my belt and started up the mountain. I must have gone nearly a mile in gloom which grew ever deeper before I realized that the walls had closed above me and that I was no longer in a great canyon or cleft but was in a cave. There was no sign of human beings and save for the narrow path, it seemed that no living thing had ever entered there. My matches had been given out, but I had taken the precaution of picking up a broken stick which I had lighted and with this firebrand I kept on my way. The ruddy light of my torch made each outcropping rock appear to be a living thing.

Suddenly I stopped, another light was added to that of my torch. Outlined against the smooth stone wall was a lighted doorway reflected from some angle invisible from my present position and in the doorway was the silhouette of a tall, thin figure whose hands seemed clasped upon his breast. Drawing my revolver, I started to advance and suddenly a cold chill ran up and down my spine, I could not move my eyes, my hands and feet could move but I could go neither forward nor backward. As far as I could see, there was nothing to prevent me, but when I tried to take a forward step, it seemed that I struck a wall which no power of mine could pass through. Then, slowly, a strange numbing sensation passed over me. My revolver dropped from a hand that could no longer hold it, and my firebrand struck the ground with it. I could do nothing but gaze at the red shadow outlined on the wall, a shadow which told by its flickering motion that it was caused by a blazing fire.

Slowly the figure moved and around an elbow of the rock there appeared a solitary being, the strangest that my eyes have ever looked upon. The man was nearly six and a half feet tall, robed from head to foot in a glistening, shining, pearl gray garment which in the moonlight outside I had mistaken for white. Around his head was a turban, one end of which fell upon his shoulder. His age none could tell, but he appeared to be beyond the prime of life, for his full black beard was flecked with gray, as was his hair that fell contrary to custom on his shoulders from under the edge of his turban.

As I looked at him, it seemed that my eyes too were paralyzed for in spite of all the efforts that I made, I could not take them from his face. His eyes, though large and piercing, still held in them a look of gentleness and kindness. The feeling of fear changed to a strange attraction, and warmth and comfort surrounded me the moment he turned his face to mine. All around his body, which seemed powerful but spare, strange flickering shadows seemed to twist and turn. I felt in spite of myself and my disregard for heathen ideals that if I had not been paralyzed, I would have been on my knees before him, for there was something in that cave which no words of mine can express.

He slowly came forward and, taking me by the hand, motioned me to advance. As he did so it seemed that the metal fetters and bonds dropped from me, my consciousness and power of locomotion returned, and with perfect ease I followed him where before I could not go, and passing through an arch of natural stone I entered into one of the strangest rooms I believe that human being was ever in.

(To be continued)

"THE SACRED MAGIC OF THE QABBALLAH"
By Manly P. Hall

In this work, the study of numbers and the Hebrew alphabet is taken up in a way never before undertaken. No system of numerology or cabalism is promulgated but a few underlying principles are given here useful to all students of mystic, occult, and cabbalistic philosophy. The work is divided into three parts, as listed below:

Part One .... The Key to the Sacred Wisdom.

A Study of the flaming letters of the Hebrew alphabet, the creation of the Sacred Name, the mystery of the vowel points and the unwritten books of Moses.

Part Two .... The Origin and Mystery of Numbers.

Under this heading are grouped the natural laws as they are expressed in numbers from 1 to 10, and the application of these laws to the problems of daily living.

Part Three .... The Power of Invocation and The Science of the Sacred Names.

In this part of the work, transcendental magic is completely unveiled and the ancient rituals of calling up spirits is exposed, and the true meaning of transcendentalism and the finding of the lost Word is presented to the student, including the invocation of Christ. A most unique and unusual document containing over fifty pages, neatly bound in an art cardboard cover. This work should be in the library of all occult students, not to be believed, but to be considered.

As is the case with our other publications you must fix your own price for the work, not to cover your share of the responsibility but that the entire work may go on and you and others may be in a position to receive the work which we are putting out.

MASONRY: "THE ROBE OF BLUE AND GOLD

THREE SILENT BEINGS hidden in the depths of the Unknown weave eternally the thread of human fate, three sisters known to the world as the Norn's or Fates incessantly twist between their fingers a tiny cord which is one day to be woven into a living garment, the coronation robe of a king. Under many names, this garment is known among the mystics and occult students in the world.

To some it is the simple yellow robe of Buddhahood, by the ancient Jews it was symbolized as the robe of the High Priest and the garment of glory unto the Lord, while to the Masonic Brother it is the Robe of Blue and Gold, the Star of Bethlehem, the wedding garment of the spirit. Three Fates weave this living garment and man himself is the creator of his fates. The triple thread of thought, action, and desire binds him when he enters into the sacred place or seeks admittance to the Lodge, but later this same cord is woven into the wedding garment whose purified folds shroud the sacred spark of his being.

We all like to be well dressed and robes of velvet and ermine seem to us symbols of rank and glory, but many an ermine cape has covered an empty heart while many a crown has rested on a tyrant's brow and many a velvet cloak has gowned an empty void. These symbols are earthly things and in the worlds of matter are too often misplaced. But the true coronation robe, the true garments of the Mason, are not of earth, for his robe of glory tells of spiritual growth. The garments of the High Priest of the Tabernacle were but symbols of the bodies of men, which purified and transmuted glorify the life within, and the little silver bells tinkled with never ending music from the fringe of his vestments, their silver note telling of a harmonious life while the breastplate reflected the gleams of Heavenly Truth from its many-sided gems.

There is one garment without a seam which was worn often by the Masonic Brothers of old, in the day of the Essenes when the monastery of the lowly Nazarenes rose in gloomy grandeur from the steep sides of Mount Tabor to be reflected in the silent waters of the Dead Sea. This one-piece garment woven without a seam is the spiral thread of human life, which, when purified by right motive and right living, becomes a tiny line of golden light which weaves eternally the purified garment of regenerated bodies. Like the white of the lambskin apron, it stands for the simple, the pure, and the harmless, the requirements of the Master Mason, who must give up forever the pomp and vanity of this world and seek to weave with his own soul that simple one-piece robe which marks the Master.

We can still see the lowly Nazarene in His spotless robe of white, a garment no king could buy but worthy of a god. This robe is woven by the daily actions of our lives, each expression weaving a thread, black or white, according to our actions and the motives which prompted them.

As the Master Mason labors in accordance with his vows, he slowly weaves this spotless robe out of the transmuted expressions of his energies. It is this white robe which prepares and sanctifies him for the robe of glory, which can only be worn over the spotless, seamless garment of his purified life.

Now comes the moment when the candidate, purified and regenerated, begins to radiate the life powers of the divine. From him pour forth streams of light and a great aura of many-colored fires surrounds him with its radiance. This wonderful garment of which all earthly robes are but symbols is built of the highest qualities of human nature, the noblest of ideals, the greatest of aspirations, the purification of bodies, the unselfish service to others. All these things build into the Mason spiritual powers, which radiate as a wonderful body of living fire. This is the Robe of Glory. This is the garment of Blue and Gold, which shining out as a five-pointed star of light heralds the birth of the Christ within. Man is then, indeed, a Sun of God pouring out through the tubes of his own being the life rays which are the Light of men.

This spiritual ray, striking hearts that long were cold, raises them from the dead; it is the living light which illuminates those still buried in the darkness of materiality; it is the power which raises by the Grip of the Lion's Paw; it is the Great Light which seeks forever the spark within all living things and finding it awakens again dead ideals with the power of the Master's word. Then the Master Mason becomes, indeed, the Sun in Leo and reaching downward into the darkness of crystallization and materiality raises his murdered Builder from the dead by the grip of the Master Mason.

As the sun awakens the seedlings in the ground, so this Son of Man, glowing with the Light divine, pours out from his own purified being the mystic spears of redeeming light which awaken the seeds of hope and truth and nobler lives in others where discouragement and suffering have too often brought down the temple and buried beneath its debris the true reason for being and the true motive for growth.

It is this robe which enfolds all things, warming them and preserving them with its light and life as the glorious robe of the sun, the symbol of all life, bathes and warms all things with its glow. Man is a god in the making and on the potter's wheel he is being molded as in the mystic myths of Egypt. As his light shines out to lift and preserve all things, he accepts the triple crown of godhood and joins the throng of Master Masons who in their garments of glory, the Robes of Blue and Gold, are seeking to illuminate the darkness of night with the triple light of the Masonic Lodge.

Ceaselessly, the Norns spin the thread of human fate. Age in and age out upon the loom of destiny are woven the living garments of God. Some are rich in glorious colors and wondrous fabrics, others are broken and frayed before they leave the loom. But all are woven by the Three Sisters, thought, action, and desire, which in the hands of the ignorant build around them walls of mud and bricks of slime, while in the hands of the pure of heart this living thread is woven into raiment's celestial and garments divine. Do what we will. We cannot stop the nimble fingers that twist the threads, but we can take the thread and use it as we will. The wool may be red with the blood of others, it may be dark with the uncertainties of life, but if we will, we may restore its whiteness and weave from it the seamless garment of a perfect life.

※※※※

> Blessed are they that know and know
> that they know, for they are wise; blessed
> are they who know not and know that they
> know not, for they can be instructed;
> cursed are those who know not and know
> not that they know not for they are foolish;
> cursed are they who know and know
> not that they know, for they are asleep,
> and who shall awaken them?

THE TRIANGLE ON THE MASON'S RING - I

ALL CREATED THINGS express themselves through a trinity as the Yod, the Eternal Flame, manifests through the triangle of differentiation. The triangle is used in practically all the Mystery Schools, representing the three outpourings of the Unmanifest. The triple scepter and the threefold crown also symbolize the same general principles. Radiating out from man, the equilateral triangle symbolizes:

First side —
Mastery of the celestial world-Heaven.
Second side —
Mastery of the material world-Earth.
Third side -
Mastery of the demoniacal world-Hell.

Taking the three general divisions of Heaven, Earth, and Hell, as they are played out in nature, we find them symbolical in the religions and philosophies of the world of the following principles:

Heaven, the superior:	Earth, balanced:	Hell, the inferno:
Above	Center	Below
God	Man	Demon
Spirit	Mind	Matter
Sulphur	Mercury	Salt
Brain	Heart	Procreative System
Fire	Eart	Water
Altruism	Balanced	Egotism
To be raised	Equilibrium	To be lowered
Ligh	Firemist	Darkness
East	South	West
Vitalization	Vitalized Matter	Crystallization
Oxygenation	Blending	Carbonization
Regeneration	Generation	Degeneration
Light	Shade	Darkness
Thought	Heart Sentiments	The Strength of Hand

THE TRIANGLE ON THE MASON'S RING - I

The Great Triangle of human existence consists of the powers that bring in, the powers which preserve, and the forces which take out. These three form the Trinity of religious thought and have been personified as three phases of the Godhead, namely:

The Fathe	The Son	The Holy ghost
The Creator	The Preserver	The destroyer
Brahma	Vishnu	Shiva
Odin	Balder	Thor
Blue	Yellow	Red

These three are expressions of God whose color is indigo and who manifests in this world through His Three Witnesses, which we know as the Triangle. To a Mason the triangle is symbolical of balance. It teaches him that as a student of the mystic and the occult; it is his duty to balance and harmonize all of these series of extremes, each one of which is dependent upon the others. All opposites are dependent one upon the other for existence and the Initiate is one who has blended and unified all diversity. These three sides of the triangle represent the three kings of the Masonic temple glorifying their God, but they also become murderers and prison walls when they are perverted through human ignorance and the animal tendencies.

(To be continued.)

THE MAGICAL MOUNTAIN OF THE MOON - I

From the Rare Work, "Lumen de Lumine" by Eugenius - Philalethes, London, 1651
Concerning the Invisible Magical Mountain and the Treasure Therein Contained

THE MAGICAL MOUNTAIN OF THE MOON - I

EVERY MAN naturally desires a superiority, to have treasures of gold and silver, and to seem great in the eyes of the world. God, indeed, created all things for the use of man that he might rule over them and acknowledge therein the singular goodness and omnipotence of God, give Him thanks for His benefits, honor him and praise Him. But there is no man looks after these things, otherwise than by spending his days idly, they would enjoy them without any previous labor and danger, neither do they look for them out of that place where God has treasured them up who expects also that man should seek for them there and to those that seek will He give them. But there is not any that labor for a profession in that place, therefore these riches are not found, for the way to this place and the place itself has been unknown for a long time and it is hidden from the greatest part of the world. But notwithstanding, it is difficult to find out this way and place, yet the place should be sought after. But it is not the will of God to conceal anything from those that are His, and therefore in this last age, before the final judgment comes, all these things shall be manifested to those that are worthy: As He Himself (though obscurely, lest it should be manifest to the unworthy) has spoken in a certain place; there is nothing covered that shall not be revealed and hidden that shall not be known. We, therefore, being moved by the spirit of God, do declare the will of God to the world which we have also already performed, (a) and published in several languages. But most men either revile or condemn that our manifesto or else waving the spirit of God they expect the proposals thereof from us, supposing we will straightway teach them how to make gold by art or furnish them with ample treasure, whereby they may live pompously in the face of the world, swagger, and make wars, turn vultures, gluttons, and drunkards, live unchastely and defile their whole life with several other things, all which things are contrary to the blessed will of God. These men should have learned from those ten Virgins (whereof five that were foolish demanded oil for their lamps from those five that were wise) how that the case is much otherwise. It is expedient that every man should labor for this treasure with the assistance of God, and his own particular search and industry. But the perverse intentions of these fellows we understand out of their own writings, by the singular grace and revelation of God; we do stop our ears and wrap ourselves as it were in clouds to avoid the bellowings and howlings of those men, who in vain cry out for gold. And hence, indeed, it comes to pass that they brand us with infinite calumnies and slanders, which notwithstanding we do not resent, but God in His good time will judge them for it. But after that we had well known (though unknown to you) and perceived also by your writings how diligent you are to pursue the Holy Scripture and seek the true knowledge of God; we have also above many thousands thought you worthy of some answer, and we signify this much to you by the will of God and the admonition of the Holy Ghost.

There is a mountain situated in the midst of the earth or center of the world, which is both small and great. It is soft also above measure, hard and stony; it is far off and near at hand, but by the Providence of God invisible. In it are hidden most ample treasures which the world is not able to value. This mountain by envy of the Devil who always opposes the glory of God and the happiness of man is compassed about with very cruel beasts and other ravenous birds which make, the way thither both difficult and dangerous: and therefore hitherto because the time is not yet come the way thither could not be sought after nor found out but now at last the way is to be found by those that are worthy but notwithstanding by every man's self-labor and endeavors.

To this mountain you shall go in a certain night (when it comes) most long and most dark and see that you prepare yourself by prayer. Insist upon the way that leads to the mountain but ask not of any man where the way lies. Only follow your guide who will offer himself to you and will meet you in the way, but you shall not know him. This guide will bring you to the mountain at midnight when all things are silent and dark. It is necessary that you arm yourself with resolute, heroic courage lest you fear those things that will happen and so fall back. You need no sword nor any bodily weapon, only call upon God sincerely and heartily. When you have discovered the mountain, the first miracle that will appear is this: a most vehement and very great wind that will shake the mountain and shatter the rocks to pieces; you shall be encountered also by lions and dragons and other terrible beasts but fear not any of these things. Be resolute and take heed you return not, for your guide who brought you hither will not suffer any evil to befall you. As for the treasure, it is not yet discovered, but it is very near. After this wind will come an earthquake that will overthrow those things which the wind has left and make all flat but be sure that you fall not off. The earthquake being past there shall follow a fire that will consume the earthly rubbish and discover the treasure, but as yet you cannot see it. After all these things and near the daybreak there shall be a great calm and you shall see the day star arise and the dawning will appear and you shall perceive a great treasure. The chiefest thing in it and the most perfect is a certain exalted tincture with which the world (if it served God and were worthy of such gifts) might be tinged and turned into the most pure gold.

This tincture being used as your guide shall teach you, will make you young when you are old, and you shall perceive no disease in any part of your body.

By means of this tincture, also you shall find pearls of that excellency which cannot be imaged. But do not you arrogate anything to yourselves because of your present power, but be contented with that which your guide shall communicate to you? Praise God perpetually for this His gift and have a special care that you use it not for worldly pride but employ it in such works which are contrary to the world. Use it rightly and enjoy it so as if you had it not. Live a temperate life and beware of all sin, otherwise your guide will forsake you and you shall be deprived of this happiness. For now, this of a truth whosoever abuses this tincture and lives not exemplary, purely and devoutly, before man shall lose this benefit and scarce any hope will there be left ever to recover it afterwards.

This letter was written by the Brothers of the Rose Cross to Eugenius Philalethes and appears in his work now rare and out-of-date Lumen de Lumine, published in London, 1651, and in next month's issue we will consider the occult and Rosicrucian interpretation of this symbolical letter.

ATLANTIS, THE LOST CONTINENT

Very few people know of this wonderful land now one with the land of forgotten things for today there is very little to remind us of this ancient continent that was once so fair and greater even than ours in glory and beauty, a land filled with happy homes, with peasants, statesmen and philosophers, and all those things which we now think of in connection with the highest and greatest phases of life.

This great continent now lost, the great land of Atlantis, is now somewhere miles beneath the ocean and over it passes our great ocean liners and sailing ships. Strange sea creatures now play through the pillars of its ancient temples, weeds and mosses are twined around its ancient gateways, its libraries containing the sacred tomes of ages have vanished from the light of day and are now known only to the finny denizens of the deep, a land of desolation miles under the surface of the sea-blue waters, its wondrous arches thick with coral and its statues deep beneath the shifting sands of the ocean bottom.

In truth, it is a continent that is gone, a land forgotten, saved by a few poets whose ancient songs tell of its vanished glory. Can we say that it is lost? No, nothing in nature can be lost, but great changes have come in the eternal program of divinity. As a land, it is no more, but as a memory, it will remain forever in the soul of the mystic, while the wondrous lesson that it teaches is well worth the glory that is gone.

Nature is like the changing surface of the sea and the waves that come and go. Today the thing is, tomorrow it is no more, but somewhere in the endless vistas of the infinite, the thing that once has been shall always be. In a new environment, in settings changed, its life goes on manifesting the powers of the Creator. The broken flower is gone, not dead; it has vanished but is not lost. Somewhere mid stick or star, it will bloom again. In other lands, it will carry on its work of charming the eyes of the world and building ever more stately mansions and more complex organisms to give greater expression to its tiny life; its message is eternal, and its life is without an end.

In order to understand the sublime message and the wondrous mystery of Atlantis it is necessary to realize the indestructibility of all things, and while its continent now lies beneath the ocean its work still goes on, its memory remains, its fingerprints are on the marble slabs of eternity. Its work is never done but when it needs new fields for its endeavors, nobler channels for its expression, it goes on to other worlds, to other lands, to other beings, and its empty, broken shell molds from the sight of men.

Let us picture for a moment this lost continent inhabited by a strange race, a few broken remnants of which still wander the earth, tottering slowly towards the veil of oblivion. Here and there still walks a Red Man, the remnants of a dying person. The ancient Egyptian of the Pharaohs is gone and now there lives in his place another people; the glory of Egypt is crumbled to the dust and the Temples of the Rising Sun are buried beneath its desert sands. The ancient Red Man is fast vanishing from our midst, he is no more. His last great stronghold in the Western Americas has been broken and as a dying wanderer, he passes silently into the eternal West. Many are they who have hastened the day of his destruction. Many are there today who have upon their hearts and hands the blood of these ancient people. But the law works eternally and, those who have helped to bring about the destruction of even the least of these ancient people shall live to see their own land in ruins, and the time will come when the white race shall lie down in an endless tomb to be listed with the forgotten, to be laid side by side with the mighty kings of Atlantis. But that does not concern us at the moment.

Let us picture the Red Man in the days of his glory. A few remnants of broken temples on the Peninsula of Yucatan, a few deserted altars amid the snow peaks of the Andes, here and there a lonely pyramid rising from a desert waste, a sphinx of stone that never speaks, a handful of dried bones, a few old philosophies and heaps of broken stone, are all that is left to tell us of an ancient civilization upon whom the wrath of the gods was loosened and whose annihilation is practically complete. They had brewed their cups of poison, which they themselves drained to the dregs.

Their iniquity overflowed, and they vanished, as all must do.

Let us pass again, back through the ages to the dawn of human thought. Let us read again their record of the living powers of nature. As we gaze into the eternal mystery, we see great mountains rise from the blue waters of the Atlantic; great plains clothed in verdure glorious appear from the darkness of the tomb; wondrous cities with twisting spiral minarets rise upward to the sky; colleges and universities paved in marble dot the fairest of all lands; great coliseums and amphitheaters, which modern man has never sought to build, rise out of the mists and bring back memories of days gone by. A beautiful land stretches before our eyes, a continent that blossoms as a rose, which extended all over that great area where now the mighty Atlantic rolls.

Far up in Iceland and Scandinavia, from Nova Scotia and Labrador, through banks of ice and snow, great mountains rise, peopled with strange, wild beings. Further South the beautiful lands of the temperate zone rise out of the deep, from the British Isles to the coast of the United States, a great host of phantoms rise from the forgotten past, a mighty race of copper-colored beings. Down through Egypt and South Africa, they pass in steady streams; even through South America they wandered amid fertile fields which they tilled and over wondrous mountains that they climbed. A mighty race of happy, laughing people, strong of arm, great of heart, glorious in ideals. They were the Red Men that are now fast disappearing in the setting sun.

There amidst them great nations were established, princely governments were built, great universities spread knowledge to the corners of creation, kings, and emperors in robes of silk and gold, in jewels and diamonds the heritage of gods, ruled over mighty peoples as numberless as blades of grass.

Here there came into being the Priest Kings of ancient times; the divine servants of the gods with the snakes upon their brows ruled Atlantis in the days of its glory, for it was not a land as we know it but a world of demigods, a land of masters. Life as we know it now was very different in the world in which they lived. Their civilization was wild, massive, and grand. The ignorance of many, but the divine wisdom of a few, marked the civilization of that ancient empire.

During those days, great giants labored on the earth. Man was no puny being as he is today but stood rather like the one-eyed Cyclop gods of Homer and the strange beings of the Odyssey and Iliad. There the Frost Giants of Scandinavia walked the earth in the millions of years that are past. And the glorious, grand, and wonderful truth is, that these giants are not dead, the Hercules of myth still lives, the bodies have changed but so surely as these ancient peoples wandered the earth in the dawn of this day of creation so surely; we are those peoples.

You and I have wandered amid the temples of Atlantis. The City of the Golden Gates has opened its portals that we might enter. We are the ones whose footsteps sounded on its streets of marble in the days of the greatest race that yet has been. Row after row of pillars, mile upon mile of fluted columns, millions of domed roofs, marked the civilization of Atlantis. Then the pyramids were in their glory and the casing stones had not yet known the vandalism of neglect. On ancient tablets now lost, in languages forgotten, were engraved the history of mighty things, of the world in its making, of the glory of gods and sages that walked with men.

You and I were there in the ages listed with the dead, we wandered through the pillars of the ancient temples, in the robes of glory we stood before the altar fires, we gazed down from the mountain tops in pride and glory upon the works of our hands. Stone by stone, we built the city of the Golden Gates. We were the Atlanteans who raised temples on the mountain peaks to the glory of our gods. Through the ages we labored, as slaves we have known the master's whip, as kings we have held the scepter, and today we are living the things we once were as we raise our eyes and gaze into the future as of old from the mountain peaks of Atlantis.

In order that we may appreciate the civilization of the ancients, it is necessary for us to accept the great fundamental principle of the continuity of life. Those unwilling to accept this principle can never learn the mysteries of Atlantis, they can never know why that continent came and vanished again. In order to find the true reason, we must gaze back to the things we were and realize again how the altar fires in the temples burned low and dying buried beneath them the nations of the dead.

Let us try to picture one of the great Atlanteans, his massive frame, his glorious brow, his eyes filled with the luster of primitive life, unhampered by the ties which bury races, unbroken by the millstone of today's affairs, which in this land of ours are grinding human hearts to feed ambition. They had many things that we have lost; we have many things they never knew.

The reason for it all is that man must grow along many lines. If it were only necessary for him to have a glorious body and strength divine, then the world would have ended with Atlantis or its end might have come in the days of classic Greece and the work would have been well finished, but there were other things to do.

Today, we are the fifth great race of beings that have inhabited our world. The Atlanteans were the fourth; they lived their day and now have passed on to endless sleep, but the spirit continues its march eternal. Man has not yet reached the grandeur of Atlantis in the new civilization with which he works, but one day in the mystic future he will pass beyond anything that ever was before, and, having reached the heights of all, the white race will draw its shroud around it and vanish to make way for other peoples and other works, but the same spirits will remain.

Let us learn the lesson of Atlantis and build again in the mirror of the mind the things that brought about its grand destruction on the seventh day of its creation. We are the breakers of new ground but 'ere we go on we must review the old, we must live again that great power of concrete thought which was the crowning genius of Atlantis, we must remember its philosophies and sciences. Then shall we be crowned with a new power to which end all races are striving, the power of creative genius, the power of abstract thought, the power to unite, and that spiritual eye which sees the oneness of life and the brotherhood of man.

The keynote of Atlantis was the survival of the fittest. Its great ones were great because the weak were weaker, but in our day a new power is being added. We have not yet reached the glory of the Aztec king before the coming of the white race, but we will reach it and pass beyond it with the great power of compassion crowning us more gloriously than ever, but, in passing, let us learn the lessons on the way. Our world today stands as Atlantis stood, our buildings rise upward, their many towers pointing to the skies, our libraries are filled with ancient wisdom, our scientists and philosophers are exploring the mysteries of nature, again we fly through the air and under the sea, again we walk the path that Atlantis walked, but we must go on, we must survive to the glory of a greater work. The great birthright of every person is to labor with new things. This new world has dreams which Atlantis never dared to conceive and possibilities undreamt of by the men of old. But to do great things, we must have the courage of conviction and the power to pave the way.

You see, we have other work to do in other ways. For a day, we have forgotten the things we were doing. A veil conceals the past so that we may learn the new thing in a different way. We are unfolding new powers, building new faculties, mastering new arts, creating new ideals.

The old soul, its years measured by the labors it has done, is now confronted with a great problem. It is our duty to take the best that Atlantis had to give, to learn the mysteries that Lemuria, now lost beneath the waters of Australasia, gave us in times more ancient even than Atlantis, and use them as steps to build upon their top a new temple based upon the foundations of the old. To go higher, to reach ever heavenward, is the age long cry of the mysteries. It is the same cry that sounded through the temples of Atlantis. It is the fulfillment of this inner urge that makes necessary new experiences, that bring new worlds out of the waters and causes others, their labors finished, to vanish from the sight of men.

In Atlantis, many of the things we call sublime would have formed but kindergarten classes amid those ancient philosophers. White-domed temples of education filled Atlantis. Every city no matter how small was crowned by its universities and colleges and in the City of the Golden Gates, were the divine sources of learning which initiated those who came out of the world into the way of the gods. We have taught many things they did not know, but they taught things which today we cannot remember but still have hidden in our souls to be used again when the moment arises. Or mayhaps, we were thoughtless then as we are now, and today we little realize life because we never lived or studied it then. Therefore, we wander through the mazes of religion, our spiritual teachers contradict each other eternally, and when we read the mysteries of Revelation, we believe the writer must have written for himself alone. We wander betwixt sacred philosophies and moral ethics, which are sealed truths that mean nothing to our souls. We were the drones amid the hives of learning as ofttimes we are today, so now we know what we learned then and tomorrow we shall be known by what we learn today.

We can tell the world how to live, but we cannot make them live it. Those who were told but did not practice today know not the lessons that they might have learned.

There was in the City of the Golden Gates a temple dedicated to the worship of Light, the divine principle of human knowledge. This Light was served by the priestcraft, it was served also by the legislator; it was honored and adored by all the powers of that ancient land. From between the pillars of this temple came forth the Priest Kings. Here humbly before the altar they prayed that the divine light from the seven stars might come down to them, but the years went by and materiality took the place of spirituality. Then came the handwriting on the wall, the stars in their courses upon the heavens penned strange, celestial words upon the blue field of eternity, and the priests raising their crucifixes, cried, "Behold! the Sun-God is murdered, the Light is passing over into darkness!"

Then the great cataclysms came that shook these mighty people to the very foundations of their world. The savages from the North and South fought with the civilized people who tried to enslave and defraud them. They were driven back but the debt of blood was upon the hands of Atlantis and the priests of the ancient temples cried in the marketplaces, "With the spilling of blood Atlantis has sealed its doom!"

Its high spiritual ideals were buried beneath materiality, death and pestilence walked in its ways, degeneracy and lust overran its people, and its nations were drenched in blood.

There are many kinds of blood. There is that which comes from broken hearts. There is the lifeblood that pours from the soul. There is the blood of our fellowmen, and all this was loosened by the falling peoples of Atlantis. Again, the warning of the gods broke upon it. Its nations were split and torn, but more and more the black light took the place of the white. Slowly the divine Priest King lost his touch with God, his connection with divine powers which mold the destiny of worlds was broken, the priestcraft lost its sacred word, the name of the Living God; the light went out upon the altars; magic and sorcery took the place of the sacred mysteries and from the gods no longer flowed the life which makes nations live.

A new person was born out of the land of darkness to carry the dying fires and the Shekinah's glory out of the lost land. All glorious things, it seems, must sometime wither; all the flowers that bloom must one day fade. Blessed are those who know that the fading flower but marks the passing of a life to a more glorious work, for man need not be always in the trough of the sea, but may step from the crest of one wave to the crest of the next. So, a new race was born to take charge of those who were true, and the Great White Brotherhood slowly formed a new people amid the falling temple pillars of the old, and the sacred Ark with the Cherubim sacred to the Lord passed slowly onward to the West. Around them gathered the faithful ones and the Great Light went out in the land of darkness, which again was shattered by mighty cataclysms. Its people were torn by an unknown fire; none knew what that fire was, or they had not read the handwriting on the wall; they had not heard the warning which the white-robed priests had spoken to them from the housetops nor the sacred words which were chanted from the temple steps for their ranklings and dissensions had drowned its note.

But the voice had sounded from the temples of Atlantis, saying, "Thou art weighed in the balance and found wanting." The Great White Brotherhood worked on, however, in a mysterious way and a new continent was unrolled for the chosen peoples, a great pathway was made in the waters and those who still served the noble and true, passed onward into the promised land.

All that was left of the Continent of Atlantis was a single island. At last, about 9000 B.C., or a little later, this dying remnant of Atlantis sank and in less than twenty-four hours, millions of souls were freed from their molds of clay.

Now comes the problem. With all their arts and sciences, crystallization crept in, which is the end of all that lives, the crystallization of thought, vitality, and growth. Nothing has to crystalize, but all things do that stagnate. Today we face the same problems that brought about the destruction of Atlantis in the ages that are past. Our lands stretch out in peace and plenty and we too feel secure. Nothing, surely, can happen to us! Yet the moment no man knoweth. But one thing we do know, either the work must be done and done well, either the soul must learn its lessons or else new environments are necessary to make completion possible.

When we allow the fires upon our altars to die out, when we allow our higher beings to starve, then we are failing in the great work. Then again, will the thunderbolts of Jove be loosened, and the eternal scythe reap in its harvest?

Let us consider some of the causes that brought about the destruction of Atlantis. The first was blood. All those who live by the sword shall perish by the sword and with the first drop of blood that man sheds comes the price. His own must flow. Blood feeds the flames of passion and when the animal in man is fed, he becomes as a ravening wolf and the Four Horsemen ride forth again on their journey of destruction. Only peace can bring peace and that must come from man himself. We are all the body of the Father; we are all the Christ in flesh, and when each of us does as he should things will prosper, not with the transcending prosperity that rises up and then disappears like a comet but with the slow, gradual growth that marks the spreading oak. Unless man learns the ways of peace, the day is not far off when the blue waves will break over his homes and the Light will go on to other lands.

The second necessity of man is to find the lost art of beauty. Probably you do not know what beauty means, for beauty is a mystic thing. We can look at a man like Lincoln, as homely as the fence rails that he split, and yet there is beauty there. We can look around us and many are there whom we call handsome, but beauty is not there. There is much prettiness but little beauty. As we look at the gods of Greece and Rome, we find what the world has long called beauty, but when you look at the eyes, you will find a blank for the sculptures did not fill them in. Few realize what beauty is or how subtle are its ways. None know it who has it; none realize who really possesses it. It is something that shines out and molds man into an expression of itself. Gold trinkets, ribbons, and a powderpuff are not the secrets of beauty. Beauty is of the soul, and we need more of it. We must have more of that beauty that molds form into the ideal. The eyes of form see the beauty of form alone, but the true mystic realizes that the source of beauty is not the form, it is the soul that shines within. We may look over the world at those who are now judged as the beautiful, the handsome, the distinguished, and yet always there is something missing, and it was the loss of that something that sank the Continent of Atlantis. We must have more beauty and the world must realize more and more that "Beauty is as beauty does." Never mind how perfect the form if the soul and mind are not there. It is an empty shell. It is a dead thing without a reason for its being. The beauty of harmony based upon strength, the beauty of peace strong on the foundation of compassion, the beauty of purity supported by knowledge, is missing. It was missing with the later Atlanteans and if we would not follow in their footsteps, we must find it again today.

We must mold our lives into that divine glory we seek under the name of Christ, into the grandeur that was found in the temples of the ancients where a beautiful life molded a body worthy of a Greek god. The beauty of compassion, of love, and of spiritual thought is sadly missing in the world today. It is the first to go. We hardly know when it goes; slowly it fades away and with it fades the strength of a people. Long before the inharmony breaks forth as a ravenous flood, this subtle something vanishes in the night. It is the handwriting on the wall, a warning to all who live, for when beauty goes with it goes the strength of a person. We can bring it back, this elusive thing, this Psyche, floating over the marshlands, veiled in a mystic haze, something unseen but felt. It must come back if our age is to reach the goal it seeks.

There is something else also that must return, the universities of Atlantis must be built again. We must raise again the schools of learning, by learning how to live, for the ignorant are dead and there are none so ignorant as those who will not learn, there are none so blind as those who will not see. Yet we forget, but let this thought be in our minds. Those who forget shall be forgotten. Our world is filled with forgetful people who forget by habit. They have forgotten so long that now they cannot remember, but in some way, they must be helped to learn. We must understand the meaning of education, educo, to draw forth, not to cram in, to bring out that which we have already built within. From the heart of our beings blaze forth the fires of Atlantis, in our souls is the history of peoples as we have lived it. We must remember it, we must draw forth that knowledge, for the great things we would build can only be raised upon the things we know. If we are to create dream castles in the ethers, we must bring back again the power of dreaming. We cannot imagine that which we have never known or think of that which we have never been, therefore education means to draw forth and profit by the things that we have been and the lessons that we have learned.

This world must learn. If it learns as Atlantis did, it will die, but if it profits by the lessons of Atlantis it will live, and each of us were the Atlanteans and have studied the lessons that can save our lands. It is no longer a problem of what we want to do; it is what we should do; it is what the duties of nature demand of us. In the name of the gods, we must act. Let us remember the blood that sank Atlantis. Blood is heat, strife, and confusion. It is the life force of the universe; it is the Lamb of God slain for the sins of the world; it is the power of a people. We must take the golden chalice and, catching in it the lifeblood that now we waste, return it to the altar of our God.

Then too we must have beauty, beauty of thought, glory of ideal. The loves of men must give place to the loves of God, the passions of our age must be transmuted into the compassions of the gods, form must give place to spirit, or again we shall be numbered with the dust.

We must have education. If we do not, we shall find out to our sorrow that the strength of a person depends upon the knowledge that it applies; not upon hopes, wishes, or the willy-nilly blowing of concepts, but upon the solid rock of truth, must our nations stand.

Man is a slave of his fears, a servant of ignorance, and a groveling wretch at the feet of the Unknown. He must rise and taking his light explore the recesses of each mystic cave. Each individual, if he does not know how to live, to eat, to think, must find out; the gods will never tell him unless he hears the voices of the gods in the wisdom of his fellowmen. The way of knowledge, brotherhood, and service, the way of purity and truth, alone can liberate us from the wheels of birth and death. We may talk of our shortcuts, backdoors, second stories, patent medicine spirituality, canned religion, just-as-goods, etc., to say nothing of the advanced spiritual teachings which transcend common sense, but unless we live the life to which we aspire, we shall be numbered with Atlantis.

It is more important to know these things by far than rounds and periods, for upon them rests life itself. We are governed by the laws of cause and effect and today we are building the causes which sank the Atlantean world, and we can expect nothing better for ourselves. We must realize that the earth beneath our feet is indeed the Son of Necessity born that man may live. It will mold itself into the needs of man, but his needs are seldom his wants. Humanity needs a good housecleaning but they do not want it, and it must either come about through our loving service and labors with our fellowman or the thunderbolts of love.

Let the spiritual fires of our universities rise from the planes of matter, let the grandeur of ancient Greece be ours, let us so live that we shall be a credit to creation and to the plan that brought us into being. As Luther Burbank converted the cactus with its prickly thorns into a nutritious food product by removing the sting, so let us transmute the powers of the people that they may rebuild and recreate. It is far more important to help someone who is not able to help himself than to have been cloistered for hours with the sages. We warn all occultists and true students that their place is in the world working and not in the temple praying, that their duty is to make the world their temple, to don the white armor of purity and ideals, and armed with the greatest of all weapons, which leaves no sting, the sword of truth, knowledge, and light, to go out and labor for the right.

We cannot escape the sorrows of the world, but we can go out and change its tears to laughter and be in a happier world that we ourselves have made.

So as we stand on the cliffs of lost Atlantis and see the restless sea breaking upon the shore and hear the dark waves which are like the surging of a lost people, let us realize that they are our own broken lives and that our own voices speak to us from the depths of the waters salty with the bitterness of the tears of millions who allowed black magic to replace the true mysteries, even as we do today. Black magic means the perversion of things. When we use energy to destroy, when we tear down the dream castles of those we love, when we fill our lives with sordidness, we are black magicians. When we take the powers of God and use them to deceive our fellowmen, when we use the powers, God gave us to free our souls, to cast down, then we are black magicians who have not learned our lesson from the sinking of Atlantis.

Let us open wide the gates, let the gates of brass swing open and man come forth. Let the tombstones be rolled away and the divine in man be released from the shackles that now bind him, let the divine in us be liberated, and Christ call unto the lower man, "Lazarus, come forth!" Let our ideals be gleaming lights upon the hilltops. We must tear up the thistles and briars before it is too late and plant flowers in their place and dedicate our lives to helping, serving, lifting, purifying, and glorifying, mentally, physically, and spiritually, all with whom we come in contact. We shall then be listed with the white-robed Brothers, who, carrying the sacred relics, pass with them into the promised land.

A new race is to be born. Who will be its parents? There are few on earth who are ready to give the new land a proper birthright. Let us remember once more the three things which bring with them the loss of all, the price of blood, the loss of beauty, and the perversion of education which sank an Empire greater far than our own, and that the same power will sink this continent unless in each individual peace and brotherhood takes the place of blood and hate, beauty of spirit replaces sordidness of life, and that great eternal light, knowledge, supplants human ignorance.

BOOKS AND THEIR PLACE IN OCCULTISM

OF ALL THE THINGS in the universe which mold themselves into the expression of individual likes and dislikes, there are none with such elastic consciousness as books for regardless of our feelings or the conditions which have colored the day, we always find something congenial in the pages of a good book. There are no truer friends than volumes whose treasured contents have become etched into our souls. The average individual's idea of a friend is someone who will agree with them, and a book is the most obliging of all. If you feel lazy, the book will be most uninteresting, if you feel mean, meanness gleams from every page, if sarcasm holds you in its grasp every word of the author seems a satire, while if you feel hungry for a certain line of information the book is eager to give it to you.

Those who have found joy in reading and bringing into play upon their lives the wisdom of past ages as it is immortalized in ancient times have reached a great point in the growth of their being. But, above all, if we realize that the book gives to us that which we have given it, we then understand that mirrored in its pages are the thoughts and ideals of our own lives.

In reading ancient books we see pass before our mind's eye the thoughts of others brought down to us through the ages from races and cultures now extinct, yet to all of them we must give understanding through the light within our own soul and with the keys of our own being unlock their sealed pages.

There is no more wonderful place in all the world than the bookstores such as we find in the old countries, with rows and rows of musty volumes, where stepladders lead up to shades unknown, and ancient tomes some of which have slept upon their shelves since the days of Cromwell line the walls as far as the eye can see. The hands that wrote them are long since laid to rest and many an aged philosopher has put them aside to wander in some distant land, yet the thoughts, ideals, and aspirations of thousands live again for posterity through the words in their books. They are dead and yet they live eternally in their thoughts and these thoughts live on through the ages in the leaves of their books.

We feel a certain reverence and awe as we enter one of these hallowed spots, the curiosity shops of the human mind. We can feel that the shades and shadows of author and poet hover still around the children of their genius. A subdued hush falls upon our being as we stand before a mighty book, for it seems that we are in the presence of a great and superior thing. Before us stands a throbbing brain stored with information, and its old bindings seem to enfold the massive brows of philosophers.

As we go to various parts of these ancient shops, we find many wondrous things, beautiful books illuminated with glorious faces and flowered letters by monks in their meditation, when lives were spent in the writing of a single work. Some are in ancient parchments, others in old block bindings, while a few here and there have been desecrated by the hands of man and their torn and tattered pages speak of the vandalism of human nature.

These old books bring back to us the days that are past and tie the breathing, living today to the yesterday's numbered with the dead. All these wondrous relics of thought recall sacred memories as they stand like silent headstones on the drooping shelves, for in truth bookstores are graveyards of the human mind. As cemeteries are filled with the children of men, so these old bookstores conceal in their numberless niches, shrouded in darkness, the children of human thought. But the thoughts live on eternally and within the rude coffins of their ancient bindings, they wait to be liberated by those who love them.

Let us roll away the stones which mark their resting place and, with the light of our own thoughts and the vision of our own lives, carry on these beauteous truths. Many of them are the dying bequests of those who have given all for man, written at a time when every pen stroke was a hardship, when to express a thought or an ideal was to court destruction at the stake or wheel. These books stand as living testimonials of the courage of great souls, for they are the last word to the world of poets and mystics, the dreamers of the ages who have suffered much and given all that their dreams might survive to posterity.

Good books, indeed, are treasures for the very soul of the author, who speaks through the pages that he wrote. Today, alas, books with great ideals and noble thoughts are few, but in those days, they were the labors of a lifetime, and their every word was illuminated by the blood of the author. Every book has behind it a quaint pathos which are irresistibly fascinating to those students who have developed organs of veneration. Why should man not feel reverence as he clasps in his hands the life work of another human being who now lies silently in some little churchyard while the thing for which he gave so much rests undusted on the shelves?

If the clairvoyant could but go there, he would see lives and wars, hates, and fears, loves, and sorrows, living again among the lives around him, speaking again from the silent walls while loving hands behind the veil still fondly guard the children of their souls.

There are many reasons why we should love to wander among these old bookstores and digging into the past bring forth these treasured writings, for in some mystic way they seem to whisper of the libraries lost in the darkness of the human soul. Among the mystics there are those who spend their lives in doing nothing but preparing and preserving ancient writings, and far from the sight of our ordinary lives these great souls have dedicated their beings to the transcribing again from the akashic records of nature the mystic truths now lost to mankind.

The average individual does not know how to read a book. If he did, he would not read so many. Reading is an art and there are few indeed who know how to glean the treasures from the printed page. Books have to be read as they were written, thought for thought, spirit for spirit, and to know the works of philosophers we must ourselves be philosophers. To understand the meaning of ancient truths, our minds must be attuned to the souls who wrote them. One who really reads belongs to the realms of the immortals, for every sentence is something to be lived for years, every thought a child entrusted to our care. Few, indeed, ever learn the mystery of the wondrous lives immortal concealed beneath their broken covers. An old book is an oracle which not only gives forth the thoughts of the author but whispers in the voice of the age in which it was written the living story of human progression.

The rows of ancient books that fill the curiosity shops of Europe sink into oblivion beside the cosmic library of human consciousness, the lost libraries of the human soul. Up in the dusty attic of the human brain is a room filled with ancient heirlooms, memories of a forgotten day, and in this room a library is stored away. It is not seen by everyone and even its existence is dreamed of but by few, but there you will find under the cobwebs of time the rare occult tomes of other days, the sacred books of mystery and magic, philosophy, and art, which are missing from the bookshelves of the world. In this little room, stored away, are the lost library of Alexandria, the sacred books of the Incas and the Aztecs, and the mystic scriptures of the ancients. All these are the rightful possessions of every living soul. If only man would break through the dust of ages and enter once more that little room! This is the great library of thought, immortal in the human mind, and books are merely thoughts put on paper.

Each day we inscribe in the great Book of Life the history of our world as seen through the eyes of the soul, each life we turn a page and store away the ancient manuscripts somewhere in the darkened attics of the past. As we walk the path that leads to greater understanding and the light within shines forth more brightly, we find ourselves amid these ancient rooms, surrounded by these mystic tomes, and if we would read, we have but to take them from their shelves and within their dusty pages is the history of our being. In the brain of man is an inexhaustible fund of knowledge and truth hidden away and accessible only to those who have found the knock that will open the door. Millions of years man has been writing this library, tracing its letters in flames and tears. Some wonderful day we shall find this little room and they're surrounded with the ideals of the past we shall know again the things that we have done and the powers that we have had. Then we shall realize that our labors have never been lost for in this great domed library of our own consciousness on records of living ether is stored away our every thought and action, and like the ancient volumes on the bookshelves we have but to take them out and read again the message they contain.

THE LIGHT OF ASIA

THERE IS no more beautiful character in the world than that of Buddha, immortalized by Arnold's wonderful poem, "The Light of Asia." As the Christian worlds, divided by so many barriers from the East, seek to walk the path that leads to Light, they ofttimes overlook this great Light which has shone on over half the known world and the wonderful message which he has given out to the children of men.

God works in many ways, through many vehicles, in many lands, but if there ever was one through whom the Almighty labored, it was the Prince Siddhartha, the Compassionate Lord of the Lotus. His teachings filled with truths divine in no way to combat the principles of Christianity but rather give to the western world keys with the aid of which it may labor more successfully.

To this Great One we owe our greatest understanding of the doctrine of Reincarnation, one of the fundamental principles of spiritual growth. This hypothesis is generally neglected not because of its improbability but because it is so different from the accepted concepts which we have. There is no real reason for our disputing it; nowhere in our sacred Scriptures are there any words against it but in many places, it appears that an understanding of this law was taken for granted.

Reincarnation is the only concept of life which is universal in opportunity, personal in responsibility, impersonal as to environment, and all-promising in its possibilities. The accepting of this law, while it does not bring Heaven closer, forever dissipates the concept of Hell eternal, the bugaboo of the Christian religion. It gives noble incentive to greater labors; it promises sure rewards for work well done; it is socialistic in its concept, and the entire doctrine of Reincarnation as it has been presented by Buddha, the great Oriental educator and non-radical socialist, can be stated as follows: The doctrine of Reincarnation teaches equal opportunities for all and special privileges for none, success being the reward for work well done and failure the result of indolence. Buddha, in giving to man this law, has presented the only concept of life which could be acceptable to a just Creator and still explain the inequalities of human consciousness.

Therefore, we are grateful to the bearer for the Light which he has brought, who brings it matters not, for the Light is of Heaven. And as these concepts of life become universalized, we shall recognize the Light of Asia as one of the Lights of the world.

JUNE 1923

THE MASTER

Alone mid the throng that surrounds him,
    A figure silent and meek,
While the battle of life surges round him,
    Still he walks in the ways of the weak.
    A soft, sweet look from tender eyes,
        The clasp of a comrade's hand,
    A word of hope from a world of sighs,
        A heart that can understand.
By this he is known in the world of men
    As one of that mystic band
Who has turned back to trod again
    Life's ever-changing sand.
Where he walks the world seems brighter,
    Better for his having trod,
While sorrowing souls grow a little lighter
    For having felt their God.
    With never a fear, he walks the way
        That leads to the heights above
Where the light of Truth holds perfect sway
        Mid the selfless hearts of love.
    This is the way that the Masters go
        To the light through a battle won,
Far up from the shade in the depths below
        On the path of the Rising Sun.

EDITORIAL

HIGHBROWS AND LOW MORAL

DURING THE COURSE of human events, it has come under our personal observation that a certain Mr. Belshazzar Jinx, whose intellectuality and power of analytical reasoning is of international repute, was arrested last night by Officer Murphy who found him intoxicated rushing up and down the main street of a small town with a revolver in each hand shooting wildly. Such a thing came as a wonderful surprise to us, for we had fondly believed Mr. Jinx to be the soul of spirituality and learning. To be more explicit as to his strong qualities, he is one of our leading paleontologists, a university man draped with sheepskins and with so many letters after his name that he requires a six-inch calling card, while his small frame seems bent under the weight of honorary degrees. He had been dean of this, honorary president of that, and somebody or something else of the other, and is considered one of the most promising of our men of renown.

We had placed Mr. Jinx on a pedestal and pointed him out as one of the most blossoming of our scientific possibilities. When we heard that he was in for thirty days without bail, our idol was shattered into a million pieces, and we felt for a short time at least that the world would come to an end. The very idea that Mr. Belshazzar Jinx with his colossal, philosophical dome and his superlative education being so hopelessly lacking in self-control, and our ideas of social decency tore forever this man of letters from our list of speaking and thinking acquaintances.

As we were slowly recovering from this amazing revelation, we received another shock. Mortimer J. Highbrow, Jr., one of our leading religious lights, wonderfully balanced between mystical theology and Chaldean archaeology, whose knowledge was of a nature most complete, and in whose inspiring sermons we had reached heights where our souls had never dared to tread on account of the rarified atmosphere of the high altitudes, had been called into court as the leading light and star of a divorce suit in which he was being sued by a mere member of the ignorant society for alienation of affections. This thunderclap was almost too great to be endured. That Mortimer J. should have done anything like this was beyond the wildest dreams of his worst enemy. Even Mortimer J. himself seemed to be a little amazed at his own audacity, but when we visited court the next morning, we found him a most dejected-looking individual fighting in a sort of dazed way for liberty against insurmountable evidence.

We went away shaking our heads and sad beyond expression only to meet a good friend, one of those human broadcasting stations, who was running over with a still later bit of news. One of our famous occult teachers, whose knowledge of rounds and periods was something terrific and who had worked out by trigonometry the length of a Night of Brahma, had just vanished from the light of men for ten years as the result of a bootleg still being found in his cellar.

Our heads were spinning around as one after the other the world's highbrows apparently demonstrated their low morals, but the capping of the climax occurred when Miss Algernida DuBarry, one of the sweetest exponents of Divine Love, was sued for divorce by her doting spouse as the result of having fractured his skull with a bootjack during a friendly argument.

We left the sight of men for several hours and within the darkness of our own sanctum sanctorum sought an answer to this inexplainable problem which has undoubtedly confronted a large percentage of mystic students who have seen their idols collapse ignominiously at some unexpected moment. After many hours of deliberation, we reached a solution which relieved somewhat the ache of our soul. You know this is not only a problem of the worth of a teacher but from a very personal standpoint it is quite a blow to our dignity to witness the weird and woozy actions of those whom we hold up as scintillating examples of human erudition. One after another we have seen our patron saints un-haloed, run out of town on rails, or tarred and feathered in the public square for some surpassing bit of inexcusable villainy, or else we found them sneaking out of the backdoor of certain unsavory places with their hats down over their eyes and their collars turned up. And slowly a peculiar feeling comes over us which clutches us in a grip of terror, we begin to fear that we may become a genius ourselves some day and be found sneaking into the second story of a church to steal the prayer books or cutting the stones out of the stained-glass windows.

Practically every genius that we know occasionally demonstrates individual eccentricities or else someone whom we know informs us of their failings. Several of our leading religious shrines are raided occasionally and many an illuminated one has been brought up before the police court to plead not guilty of doing something, which it is proved they did. What is the answer to this soul-perplexing, heartrending problem? These are the conclusions we have reached:

Science has now proven that genius is a mild form of insanity or at least tends in that direction, and we have never found a person yet who could be too long-headed without being hollow somewhere along the line. When they get too broad, they get shallow and mud-flats border the stream, when they get too deep they get narrow and fall into ruts, and when they get too high, they cease to watch their feet and soon slip over some philosophical or sentimental banana peel and are hurled headlong flaming from the ethereal skies. If they get too deeply immersed in their problems and only an occasional bubble comes up to the surface, a seismic cataclysm usually follows. When they get too deeply wound up in rare specimens, Latin verbs, or split infinitives, and too busy analyzing the embryonic life of a strombolis gigantis, about that time some other man sues them for something, they wake up with some weird domestic problem, or else they come out of their lethargy long enough to realize they murdered someone in the night or have robbed the leading bank.

There are two reasons for this strange condition, it seems. The first is the unequal development of mental faculties and the fact that the energies which have been drawn to a certain point to feed a brain center, which is being heavily used while certain scientific or philosophical work is being carried out, flood back again to other parts of the body when this work is discontinued. When there is no other legitimate channel for its expression the body does not absorb this energy in a well-balanced manner, and it breaks out through some part of the being not under control and usually results in some unwise and unbalanced action. If Balshazzar could have cut wood as well as he talked Latin, he would not now be making little ones out of big ones at the county jail; if a well-known lawyer in a small town had played golf as well as he argued, he wouldn't have knocked the court clerk over the judge's stand when a certain trial was over. But these one-sided people do not realize the ebb and flow of energies within themselves, which, when they have only one thing they can do, must in time burst out somewhere along the line.

Then, Mrs. G. talking to Mrs. F. over the back fence will say, "I just know he's been that way for years and we didn't know it, the hypocrite, but I always knew he was crooked underneath, he had such a mean look in his eye," et cetera, when in truth the individual disgust is a good, kindhearted, well-meaning, and hard-working individual, Professor of Bacteriology in a leading university until they found him one morning rolling moth-balls around his room, playing dolls or drunk. Sometimes one of our leading lights in scientific circles is found in a dope den for no other reason at all than that his unbalanced nature as the result of his unnatural life had mastered him through his own disorganized energies.

When a man is mastered by an art or science, he is insane and there are few masters of philosophies and religion who are not in truth slaves to their concepts until finally their religion runs them amuck, or, as it was said on the Western plains during the early days, they got "locoed" and we find them doing all kinds of things which they should not do and working up scandals generally.

The need for balance is one of the greatest considerations for the occultist. It is the easiest thing in the world to get so twisted up in theory and argument, science, or theology, that the individual becomes mildly insane and hopelessly irresponsible.

The second reason for the degeneration of reputation and complete ruination of celebrities is that compendium of Christian charity which is turned upon them by their loving and sincere disciples. Mr. and Mrs. Buzzzzz are always with us and will probably remain until the last great dawn of eternity folds them in its sable mantle, and their last words will be, "M'dear, did you hear about buz-buz-?" If anyone can remain thirty days famous without someone making him infamous, if he can boast a reputation for one month in philosophy, religion, or politics, there is but one explanation. It is the direct result of the fact that so much has been found out about him that his doting followers do not know what to say first. Of course, if by chance he happens to be a little short of scandals, it only requires a few hours to produce them. The rocking-chair and smoking-room brigade specialize in this work and the record at the present time is two hundred scandals per rock.

A reputation is one of those peculiarly subtle things which, like your appendix, you do not know you have until you lose it, and strange to say it is taken from you by your nearest and dearest beloved. It is usually a loving friend, a helpful and accommodating relative, or one of these illustrious individuals noted for religious inclinations or leanings whose tongue being hung in the middle and wagging both ways strips you of every vestige or respectability and leaves you shivering before the world, the perfect picture of dejection and misery.

Therefore, between these two evils, your weak points and your strong friends, there is very little chance for a highbrow to keep both ends of his reputation above water. As fast as he gets his philosophy up, either he or someone else pulls his private life down until finally he lands in a padded cell where he remains counting sunbeams and praying to the Lord with Abraham Lincoln to deliver him from his friends.

Of course, these may seem exceptional cases, but the principle remains, and we cannot be too careful not only of our own lives but in our thoughts and actions with others because each is fighting a great battle, and many a great soul has been completely broken by the harsh words and thoughtless actions of others, when its own battle against the powers of unbalance was as much as it could shoulder.

ART

THERE IS NO POWER that holds a greater sway over the hearts of men than the subtle mystery of color. Who has not stood before the child of a great master and seen on the canvas before him the creation of the master genius? Raphael, Murillo, Titian-their souls have left on mortal canvas traced by the endless motion of their subtle fingers, visions from somewhere behind the veil of human consciousness.

Few there are who have the power to know the heart of the master painter whose pictures are not of earth but are the rapt visions of seers illuminated by the great Light brought close through years of dreaming and hours of meditation. As we gaze upon some hallowed painting, a Madonna, or some face of Rembrandt, it seems to live, to speak to us from the depths of its gilded frame. We cannot help but feel that art is not of man but of God, that a power unseen works through the master's fingers, a hand unknown mixes the pigments of the pallet. There is no power but God, no creator but the One Divine, who can blend colors into these mystic harmonies which touch the strings of the soul, and it must be true that God made artists to picture Him.

There are few old masters today who like the ones of centuries gone by have beheld with broader vision the grandeur of the universe and whose skilled fingers have placed upon canvas and carved into stone the visions that filled their souls. They were the master artists who bowed in reverence before One who with colors no mortals ever used, with the artist's eye far greater than human sense, the hand more skilled than any earthly fingers, paints eternally in colors indescribable life and all living things. He is the Genius and all that mortal artists can hope for is to reproduce His art but never to excel it. Who on earth can paint with the colors of the sunset? What artist of mortal school can discover the wondrous pigments that shade the autumn leaf? Where is the hand of skill consummate? Where is the eye which divines the perfect blending?

There is but one great Artist and He is the Master of the human school, and above all mortal instructors there is one true Genius of living art. Today, this Master lives incarnate in the creations of His students. Through brush and pen He lives for His heart is ever filled with a mystic harmony which has been expressed by few of this world as it is revealed in the brush strokes of Guidio Rene, in the massive marbles of Michelangelo, or in the simple Angelus of Millet.

But there is a more glorious art within the soul of man which paints anew all things of nature. There is a master school which paints not on canvas that perishes but on the living background of the human soul. There are fingers that with the deft touch of the true genius paint again with bright color cheeks that have long been paled. There are souls who bring sunshine again to the dark clouds of sorrow. There are master painters who dry the eyes that weep and, with the brush of love, remove furrows from the souls of men.

Here and there is a great genius who comes to the world to paint that one eternal masterpiece of the gods. In colors rich with light and truth, he takes away the shadows from the canvas and, with the inspired touch of genius, paints all life in living colors. These are the Master's immortal, the truly great artists, who are pupils of that one great Genius whose nameless paintings are the basis of all human aspiration.

MAN THE HUMAN VIOLIN - I

ALL existing things divide themselves into two general classes, objective and receptive. For all times the outpouring, vitalizing power or that expression which is the source of light, power, and motion we call spirit, the divine Father, the positive expression of existing things. It is called positive because it expresses mentally, physically, or spiritually animated qualities; it is called the spirit that goes forth and that which goes forth has always been symbolized as positive and is known as the Father-ray. Opposed to this principle is the divine negative element. This negative element represents a cessation of animation for it is the basis of matter, and matter is spiriting the rate of vibration of which has been slowed down by one of two reasons, either obstruction to the passage of spirit or else the rates of vibration have so far to go before reaching the end of their wave that the slowing of these rates produces matter. In other words, so-called matter is a crystallization of energy which crystallization inhibits its expression. Matter is a globular substance in which the latent life germ is incapable of expressing itself through the walls of negation or not-being. This negative element depends upon the vitalization of external energy for the liberation of its own latent life. Therefore, matter is said to be divinely receptive and is referred to by the ancients as the divine Mother principle. For ages life and the fiery sun globe have represented the fierce, blazing Father while the verdant, liquid sustained earth, the reposing place of the spirits of life has been referred to as the moist and harmless receptive principle of nature which is known to all students as the Mother of spirit. All matter enfolds within itself a germ of life; thus, matter is the incubator which protects and, like a wall or shell, surrounds latent life qualities with protecting substances. Matter, being life asleep, is incapable of individual self-expression while in latency, consequently it depends upon the life within it for its expression, and matter manifests the state of growth reached by its indwelling, central, flameborn consciousness. For this reason, the spirit has been symbolized as self-expressing force, which striking against the walls of negation is thrown back from these, as are the notes of music from the sounding-board of a violin.

All the way down through the ages the Wisdom Teachings have taught that the unfolding of the body is necessary to the clearness and beauty of the notes of spirit, which as rates of vibration and spirited substance in motion strike this natural sounding board. In other words, we may symbolize spirit as the divine musician, which, in the intelligent kingdoms of nature, is incessantly playing upon and expressing itself through the medium of harmonies which depend for their sweetness upon the quality of matter and its arrangement as it expresses itself in bodies.

The same rates of vibration vary in physical expression in accordance with the quality, shape, and size of the instrument which is played. The same rates of vibration do not produce the same sound on all instruments, the same spiritual influx which makes one man a saint leaves another a sinner. The same thing which produces divine harmony will produce divine discord if the instrument is not what it should be.

Life expresses itself in the world of affairs in many ways, but its beauty is always limited by the quality of the instrument through which it is manifesting. We cannot see vibration, neither can we see spirit which expresses itself through vibration, but spirit manifests in the world of affairs as thought, action, and desire, and we are either charmed or irritated not by the ideals of the musician but upon the registering of these ideals in the world of concrete things, and this is only possible through a material vehicle of expression.

Our daily lives are visible, tangible, comprehensive evidences of things unseen and unknown which can be wholly felt or believed only on the abstract planes of consciousness. The most beautiful thoughts are often unrevealed because the thinker has no words to express them; most glorious melodies are lost to the world because the one who feels them is incapable of expressing them musically.

Man's vehicles of expression must always limit the life and while he may dream on forever beautiful dreams, if he does not properly attune his instrument, he dreams for himself alone, and ofttimes he cannot even formulate clearly within his own mind the dreams which fill his soul.

Vibration is caused by the animation of substances and the setting of air or ether in motion. Every word that comes out of our mouths is toned by the mouth. It is changed and often ruined by the shape of the teeth, the position of the tongue, and the quality of the sound-box at the back of the mouth. As the rates of vibration pass out of the throat into the various chambers of the head and chest, they produce the various tones which we admire or dislike.

Wherever there is an impediment in the natural expression of vibration we have the so-called nasal tone, which is out of tune because it isn't nasal, and the passages being stopped up inhibits the flow of the vitalized energies. The results of developing the cavities in the head and chest are the building of resonant tones which striking the eardrum in a harmonious way we recognize as melodies and harmonies, and every known tone is the result of air in motion passing through chambers differing from each other in two things. First, size, shape, and location; second, the quality of the material forming their walls.

In the beginning it is said that man was created through the out-breathing of God, who, as He out pours the vibrations from the celestial soundbox of cosmos, becomes the great Father principle of creation for He is sending forth the sparks of life from His own mouth. These strike matter and the various combinations of these two forces produce the differentiation in form, shape, and quality. All the varying expressions of life in the form of which we can conceive are the result of motion striking the lack of motion, the result being spiritual, mental, or physical harmonies or sounds, which are tuned according to the sounding board of cosmic root substance upon which these harmonies strike in their search for expression.

The same sound wave we hear in a cornet passes also through the bass horn, but the notes of the latter are heavier and deeper and, in many ways, different, the only cause being that the general form, magnitude, and orifices of the two instruments are different in size and shape. The same setting in motion of atmosphere takes place, and the same noted energy is used in drawing the bows of both a cello and a violin, but the result of the action differs on account of the difference in the instruments.

In the spiritual things of life, the same principle is true. Man is completely limited by the quality of the instrument upon which he is seeking to play the celestial harmonies. There are no two individuals who ever have been or ever will be exactly the same in their thoughts, desires, and actions, and these in turn mold the instrument of matter into an expression of their own quality which results in the distinct individuality of specie. In spiritual things, we find a perfect analogy, for the spiritual waves of living substances in motion are molding eternally their own keyboard into an expression of themselves and this keyboard is, in turn defining and limiting the expression of its own creator.

Spirit or God is an intelligent force which being creative itself bequeaths the power of creation upon everything which expresses it. Man is a creator every time he animates substances, and he animates certain substances with every expression of active energy, mental, physical, or spiritual. Whenever he speaks or even thinks the result is a chain of vibratory waves which on the various planes of nature mold the vehicles of man into expressions of their own intrinsic vibratory power. These vehicles in turn are the concrete expressions of man's innermost ideals, and the spirit, I Am, manifesting imperfectly through the not-self or what are called the spiritual centers of the body, is hampered in turn in its own expression by the limitations which its thoughts, actions, and desires place upon the unfoldment of its bodies.

The sounding board makes the instrument. Thought, action, and desire to create the sounding board and the sounding board limits the expression of the divine in man. Our bodies are the sounding boards and as vehicles of consciousness the three bodies are under the control of individual intelligences. Each of these intelligences is twofold in its expression: selfish and selfless. When each body strives for individual mastery then we have unbalance in people whose thoughts, actions, or emotions run away with them and who cannot control their own bodies. When this condition is present, it means that the sounding board is being limited by bodily intelligences, which are in turn limiting the spirit of man, which should be served by these intelligences.

If, on the other hand, the body consciousness centers of thought, emotion, and action are selfless in their expression and governed wisely and selectively by the spiritual consciousness and used always to build more stately mansions for the soul, then the sounding board is limited only by the spiritual consciousness itself and quickly responds to every note which strikes it, and harmony will be the eternal result for if the body is married to the spirit, their union being unimpeded by expression of individual bodies, the result is that each body becomes a pen in the hand of a ready writer which will always be in harmony with itself if not interrupted by inharmonious relations between centers of sense consciousness.

The true musician realizes that quality does not depend upon pedigree alone, neither does harmony depend upon commercial value, but that the value of a violin is in its tone. Our bodies are violins upon which the spirit plays varying harmonies and discords until finally they attune themselves with the music of the spheres. As the violin depends for tone upon the quality of the materials composing it and the harmony depends upon the tone, so the bodies of men depend for their quality upon the things which are incorporated into them mentally, physically, and spiritually. Man's most valuable asset at this time is the tail appendage of consciousness, which he calls the physical body. If it be poorly constructed the individual who inhabits it will never be a functioning genius for, he will always be limited in some way by the organic quality of his vehicles, and the result will be a series of squeaks and rasps which grate not only upon the ears of the musician but upon the whole world which hears consciously or unconsciously his discordant expressions.

The centers of the four bodies within us can be called the strings of the instrument and the spiritual consciousness within our being plays upon these centers, and they in turn through their vibratory qualities produce in the finely evolved individual the same spiritual, bell-like tones that physically sound out from a master's violin. Two things are absolutely necessary to the full of genius and the instrument worthy of a master. The result of this combination is divine harmony. But if you take a genius and give him a cheap instrument, though his technique is perfect, he will never be satisfied either with the instrument or with himself. In fact, a truly great musician would refuse to play on a cheap instrument. It would grate against his soul. Then, again, take a Master of Music and give him a cheap violin and there will be within him a repugnance, he is disgraced, for with the soul of genius there comes something else, and although he is blindfolded and not allowed to touch the strings, the master musician will feel the quality of his instrument. Then let us look at it in another way. Suppose you take an instrument worth thousands of dollars and give it to someone who cannot play. Does the value of the instrument make him a musician? No. In all nature, two things are needed, the instrument and the player. These are the basis of all expressions, and, in nature, they are called spirit and matter. The existence of either means struggle until there is a mutual harmony and an agreement of quality between the two. A good body in the hands of a sleeping spirit is like a grand violin in the hands of an amateur; a beautiful soul in a shapeless body filled with inharmony and discord is likened to a master with a cheap instrument. The result is always inharmony.

Many instruments look alike but they are not, for many lack the soul of the maker. There are two ways of making instruments. There are those just made to sell, maybe turned out at the rate of fifty a day, they look just like the greater instruments that it has taken a lifetime to build, but they are not the same. Then there are the instruments made by those who loved their craft, who labored for the joy of building, and who raised these children of their souls with the same tenderness and care that loving parents bestow upon their children, for the great musicians love their instruments and the great makers feel that they have built gods.

In the same way, there are two kinds of people living in the world. There are those who work as fast as they can to get things done. They do not care whether they build well, if they get through it's all right. They labor because they must eat. And there are others who get spiritual because they believe it is the only way to escape work and hard knocks. They are just like the people who build instruments to sell. The soul is missing that, in some mystic way, adds beauty to its tone. Then there are those who do not care how much they labor for they serve for the joy of serving, they build for the joy of building, to them their labors are divine, they almost worship the creations of their hand, to them their creations have a soul-their soul. And though the workmanship may be unskilled, often the instrument is more beautiful than some mechanically made masterpiece.

It is the same with our bodies. There are bodies thrown together, pressed together, crammed together and there are bodies that are gathered through ages of experience, the sublime desire of the spirit to unfold the godhood within itself, not just to get through but for the joy of the building. All these considerations play their part in the making of the master's instrument, and every student must realize that the most glorious work is not to unfold the spirit but to unfold bodies through which the spirit may speak for the spirit can never be greater than the temple where it is enshrined. There can be no soul where there are no bodies, no life where there is no shape, no color where there is no substance. Remove the worlds of material things and you will leave just the life itself which cannot even know itself, for in taking away matter you have removed the brain through which mind thinks, you have removed the mind which is also a thing of matter through which spirit speaks, for this is a great truth: If you remove not being, being can never know itself.

Let us picture for a moment a great and wonderful violin, one of those master instruments which have come down to us through the ages. Many a broken heart has wept alone clasping it to his breast, many a lone life has whispered its innermost dreams through the strings of an ancient instrument, for it is beloved by its user and worshipped by its maker. It is said that Stradivarius, probably one of the greatest known violin makers, expressed himself in the following way: "God made Antonio to make violins." It is sad to think how few love the living temple of their own body as the old musician cherishes his beloved violin. It is said that Antonio Stradivarius made his greatest violins from the bell-post of an old church and that the wood was many years old when it was cut down, for it is known that great violins are made out of wood that is seasoned. Whenever there is water or moisture in the wood, the tone is injured, and the master's instrument must be made of seasoned wood.

All musicians know that a violin grows sweeter with age. People do not realize this fact, but it is true. The tones of these instruments, which have lasted hundreds of years, are far sweeter than any made today. For the tone changes, every hour it grows mellower and sweeter, and the old violin weighs much less than the new one for it has dried out until it is merely a shell devoid of self-expression, it is nothing but a sounding board which registers each fine vibratory tone.

Now, the spiritual consciousness of man is a very peculiar thing. Every expression of the bodies is sharp and harsh until finally, with age, the spiritual consciousness of man becomes master of the selfless body. It is experience, growth, sorrow, the things with which man battles through the ages which mold the body and the mind into the more seasoned and spiritual instrument. All the outside contacts of life build certain qualities in man and as he wanders through the ages, the instrument of his body grows sweeter and sweeter, as in spiritual powers as he grows older and older. The soul and the body of man are mellowed through the ages like great violins. The rough edges, the false tones, the selfish phase of the instrument, the great I Am, are nothing more or less than a drop of water in the wood, a bit of resin which is the sour note all through the ages, until at last after experience and growth and bitter sorrows the self-part goes forever, and the soul is all that is left. The bodies have gone and from them has been born a wondrous, selfless thing-the true companion of the self-and this is the divine instrument of the master genius and upon the strings of its selfless sounding board he plays the harmonies celestial.

The world is filled with people who grate upon us and who seem unsavory. The explanation is this; the instrument is new, and it has not been mellowed. The same deft fingers are trying to play it, the same sweet spirit tries to express itself, but it cannot, for the depth of tone is not yet there. We should not feel that our brothers are below us for their violins when mellowed may be wonderful instruments and they have not been laboring as they might, maybe, and then again, we all have a sour note somewhere. Everyone has a flaw in his being which injures the tone of his instrument, but as the ages go by these flaws seem to disappear and for some unknown reason the violin that was sour when new is sweet and mellow when old. Many an instrument has been discarded by its maker as of no use and many, many years later, hundreds perhaps, it was taken out and found to have a master tone.

There is a wonderful lesson in this for everyone. You and I are like Antonio. The Lord has made us to make violins. Like Antonio, God has given us the work of making bodies, each complex organism is a master's labors through the ages, it is the eternal problem of spiritual consciousness and some day in the mystic future we shall learn to make a perfect instrument. Many people do not think, ofttimes they do not want to think, they do not like to feel the responsibility of creation rests upon them. And yet it does. It is our duty and each of us must build a master instrument which is to give perfect expression to the genius within his own soul.

Then comes another great consideration. Take a great violin and crack it and the sound is gone until it is repaired and often then it is more beautiful than before. It is the same way we take an individual, a child for instance, and abuse and break that instrument, or not being strong enough for the battle it is damaged by the blows of life and the sweetness is gone, ofttimes it is many ages before the soul can repair the break caused by the thoughtless actions of others.

(To be continued.)

THE MAGICAL MOUNTAIN OF THE MOON - II
A Letter From the Brothers of the R. C. to Eugenius Philalethes (Continued)

IN LAST MONTH'S EDITION of this magazine, we published the letter from the Brothers as it is found in the original edition of "Lumen de Lumine," and now it is well to consider what Thomas Vaughan, who uses the pen-name of Philalethes, has to say concerning this mystical and magical Mountain of the Moon. On page 24 of his book, published in 1651, we find the following statement: "This is the emblematical, magical type which Thalia delivered to me in the invisible guiana. The first and superior part of it represents the mountains of the moon.

The philosophers commonly call them the mountains of India on whose tops grow their secret and famous Lunaria; it is an herb easy to find but that men are blind, for it discovers itself and shines after night like pearls. The earth of these mountains is very red beyond all expression, it is full of crystalline rocks which the philosophers call their glass and their stone: birds and fish say they bring it to them. Of these mountains speaks Hali the Arabian, a most excellent, judicious author. Vade fili ad Montes India ad Cavernas suas, accipe exeis lapides honoratos qui liquefiunt in Aqut, quando commis centur eis. Go, my son, to the mountains of India and to their quarries or caverns and take thence our precious stones which dissolve or melt in water when they are mingled therewith. Much indeed might be spoken concerning these mountains if it were lawful to publish their mysteries, but one thing I shall not forbear to tell you. They are very dangerous places after night for they are haunted with fires and other strange apparitions, occasioned (as I am told by the Magi) by certain spirits which dabble lasciviously with the sperm of the world and imprint their imagination in it producing many times fantastic and monstrous generations. The access and pilgrimage to this place with the difficulties which attend them are faithfully and majestically described by the Brothers of R. C. Their language indeed is very simple and with most men perhaps contemptible, but to speak finely was no part of their design, their learning lies not in phrase but in the sense and that is it which I have proposed to the consideration of the reader.

After having read this slight introduction by the renowned alchemist and mystic, it would be well for the reader to consider again the letter which was published in last month's edition and then let us study the general symbolism of the entire work.

Among all the ancient people, mountains were held sacred and the points most sacred to every land were its lofty hills. Among the ancient Greeks the temple of their gods was upon the top of Mount Olympus where far above the clouds the gods dwelt and labored with man, coming down occasionally into the valley to sojourn with and direct the energies of their children. Among the Scandinavians, we find Asgard, the home of the twelve gods, far upon the top of a magical mountain which was symbolized as the highest point of the world. We are all acquainted with the sacred mountain of the Jewish people, Mount Sinai, where the Lord spoke to Moses, and Mount Moriah, over the brow of which Hiram Abiff, the Masonic hero, was buried. Among the Orientals, we have Mount Moru, and the world still turns in awe to the shadowy heights of the Himalayas, where many people yet believe the gods to dwell. The knights of the Holy Grail had their castle far up among the crags of Mount Salvart in ancient Spain, and among the Andes of the western world we still find the ruins of massive altars at the very top of pyramids and mountains.

The entire story of the magical mountains is based upon the analogy between the world and man. Each individual is a universe, a god, a planet, an infinitesimal bit of something all in one. We find the human body to be the plan of the temple; it is undoubtedly the symbol of Calvary, and where the head of man is in the ancient churches, there were steps leading up to an altar. There are three worlds of human consciousness in which man is particularly interested. There is

Hel, the land of darkness and dissolution, the land of dead things, lighted only by the fires of perversion; then there is the middle garden of the earth-world which man knows, the world of purely human affairs; then far up on the heights of a lofty mountain is the heaven world of man with the skull as its dome. Now, all the powers which man really uses are centered upon the top of the mountain of his body in the domed temple of his own head. It is within this superior world of which the lower is a counterpart, for all the functions of the human body and its organs are duplicated in the brain, that the treasure of great price is concealed. The path that leads to light is the path taken by the consciousness of man up through the red mountain of his own body into the superior, mystical world concealed upon its top. The twelve convolutions of the brain are the twelve disciples or gods who govern and regulate the destiny of human affairs, and it is the passing of the spiritual consciousness upward through the thirty-three segments of the spinal column that constitute the path of initiation up through the Magical Mountain of the Moon. It is known to alchemists and all students that the world is divided into two general divisions: the sun and the moon. The sun has to do with spiritual things while the moon affects material things, and here it is important to note that the magical mountain of the bodies forms the living throne upon the very crest and in the very heart of which is concealed the "quintessia vitra," the philosopher's elixir. The passing upward of the consciousness of the individual through regenerated thought and action is by means of the mastery of things. He grows through mastery, and initiation is the mastery of certain elements by the consciousness or spiritual power within.

It is stated above in the letter that the path which leads to this mountain is beset with many dangers, and any student who has attempted to walk the spiritual path realizes that this is true. The terrible beasts, dragons, and reptiles represent our own lower natures which are ever between us and the path that leads to higher things. There is, as it is said, but one weapon with which we can fight them, and this is the weapon of truth, light, and non-resistance. The only way of overcoming evil is through the boycott system, as the student will discover before he reaches the goal he seeks.

Three tests confronted the candidate according to this allegory, three great natural elements were called into play, a very mighty wind, a terrific earthquake, and a consuming fire. These may very briefly be explained as thought which along spiritual lines breaks up the rocks of crystallization, this thought being symbolized by air which blowing the clouds across the sky was symbolized by the ancients as the ideas of man in the blue dome of the skull. As the result of this thought there is the expression of physical action and the action of physical bodies, which are commonly listed under the heading of earth conditions and are symbolized as the earthquake, which, more spiritually interpreted, represents the -changes which take place in the physical organism when the candidate begins his active, spiritual work. The fire is the spiritual power generated by the previous processes which loosened upon the individual by his thoughts and actions immediately burns away whatever is not fit for its own works, the alchemy of transmutation within its own soul.

The rising of the day star symbolizes the extension of the soul, which has been referred to as the "star body" by the ancients. Through the rising of the Light, the spiritual center of consciousness within him, after having passed through the three grand initiations of the Father, Son, and Holy Ghost, air, fire, and earth, man is then enabled to see within himself the Magical Mountain of the Moon and the wondrous treasure that is contained upon its top. These treasures are entirely of a spiritual nature and have nothing to do with material things, the gold and precious stones referred to symbolizing the awakened centers which are jewel-like and the streams of transmuted vital energies which the ancient's called gold, and it is this gold which is said to pave the streets of the New Jerusalem.

In next month's magazine, we shall continue the consideration of this mystic message of the Magical Mountain of the Moon and the mystery of the Magi referred to by Philalethes in his wonderful book.

A LITTLE EPISODE FROM LIFE - I

IN EVERY LARGE CITY of the world, we see those solitary figures which whisper of life's tragedy. On almost every street corner, we find someone sick, blind, or poor, asking for the consideration and kindness of others. Among the eastern peoples we hear the eternal cry, "Alms! In the name of Allah!" and in our western world there are many who hold out their hands asking those who have to aid those who have not. In every land there are those for whom the battle of life has been too severe and one after another they sink down beside the way and ask our aid that they may live. The Master expressed a great truth when He said to His disciples, "The poor ye shall have with you always."

Huddled on the street corners we find them and while some no doubt use these methods to evade honest labor, still there are many broken souls who if it were not for the coins of the passersby would find life cold, indeed, and we should remember the bond of brotherhood that ties all living beings together, for it is better by far to give to a dozen who do not need than to miss the truly worthy one. There is a little drama played out here as in all things of life, a little story that should etch itself into the soul, and I want to tell you of one little drama witnessed on a street corner just a few days ago.

In a darkened doorway away from the passing throng a little old lady sat on a broken stool, her face was tired and worn, pinched with suffering and poverty, and while many may seek in the road of begging sympathy and easy money this little soul bore the stamp of sincerity. She had an accordion on which she was playing and a little tin cup for the coins of thoughtful people. She was playing old-fashioned tunes, and it is to be admitted that she did not play them well nor was the little broken voice in tune with the squeaky notes of the cheap accordion, still there was a certain pathos, a certain sweetness and softness which spoke of sorrow and suffering and disappointment. Who can say what stretched behind in the years that had passed? Who can tell of children now in other parts of the world, maybe dead, possibly only thoughtless? Who can know the shattered hopes, the broken idols, the crushed ideals, hidden away beneath that tattered shawl of camel's hair? And still there must have been hidden beneath that broken body, the star of hope which, even in the cold desolation of life, still shines eternally in the human heart. This little figure whispered of better days, of years more filled with joy than those which stretch before her. It may be in truth that she should be in the home for the old; very possibly her present position was the result of her own mistake, in some way it must have been, but that is not the drama with which we are interested.

As we stood there listening to the plaintive wail of the cheap accordion, we watched the throngs go by as the drama played itself out. First comes a stout (Continued)

BROTHERS OF THE SHINING ROBE - II
Chapter One
The Temple of Caves, (Continued)

I CREDIT MYSELF with being in a position to know, for I have been in the Catacombs of Rome, through the dungeons of the Coliseum, in the Palace of the Doges, and through the vaulted chambers of the Pyramids. So far as the eyes could see, the room stretched on in avenues and rows of natural pillars carved into gigantic elephants holding up with raised tusks and trunks the ceiling above. On one side of me was a great god with hundreds of arms and whose hundreds of heads gazed down from the vaulted archway. On the other side sat the Elephant God upon a couch of lions.

In the center of this great room stood a massive stone bowl, the pedestal of which was a great green cobra carved from marble. In the bowl blazed a fire of many colors, the light of which I had seen reflected on the wall without. Around the edge of this great room which grew dimly visible as my eyes became accustomed to the darkness, I saw twelve great doorways leading into recesses which I could not fathom, and at once the thought came into my mind, one which I hardly dared to believe myself, that I was in the Temple of the Caves cut from the heart of a living mountain.

There was no one in sight save my lonely guide and he led me silently across the great room and along the temple pillars to where a great shrine opened in the wall and here three great mysterious Beings looked down from recesses which had no end. You might call them gods or idols in the outer world, but they did not seem such here and to this day, I do not know whether they were made of stone or of strange living substances. If they were stone, they were of some other kind than that which is known in the world for they glowed and gleamed and seemed never still, not with the reflected light of the fire but with a glow and blaze from within themselves.

The Three together supported a great frame which seemed of solid gold and around the frame great serpents twined and within was a strange, bluish, transparent haze of unknown depth.

My curiosity, which was of true European type and incapable of the stoic attitude of the East, overcame me and in spite of what might be the result of my actions, I stepped forward to examine the relics and reaching out my hand sought to touch the mirror, for that was the only thing which it seemed to resemble in my mind.

Then a smile came over me, a smile, however, filled with terror and awe. I had sought to step forward, but I had not moved, I had tried to raise my hand, but it did not lift, and I realized that I was in a place unknown to the outer world and that the laws which govern ordinary man were not effective here.

My companion now broke the silence for the first time, and although I spoke both Hindustani and Sanskrit, he addressed me in flawless English.

"Well, my friend, this is the first time that you have seen me, but it is not the first time I have known you. A strange series of apparent coincidences have occurred, not only within the last short span of years but in the ages that are past. All things work as the gods decree and before the coming of the Compassionate Ones, when these great stone walls had not yet had the builder's hand upon them, the work which we do today was ordained. Look back over your life and its restless wandering and can you not see the hand of Destiny which is molding you, has molded you, until today you stand within the shrine of the living god in the Temple of the Caves? Forever, there has been between you and man the blue veil of the gods and the restless wandering of your own soul must have whispered that you were not as other men. Some great reason yet unknown you must realize has been the potent factor of your being. I have been watching you and in this silent room have guided you in the ways of light. I have been near you in loves and fears, preparing a great way that later you shall walk. In this strange mirror, not of glass but of living ethers, I will show you the reason for all things, the labors that have stretched behind, the works to come, how you are fulfilling vows you made when worlds were in the forming, and why now you have been called out of the multitudes of men, for I put the words in the mendicant's heart that led you here. You do not know us or believe in the sacred ways and yet before this body returns to the earth from which it came, you shall be listed with the Compassionate Ones."

CHAPTER TWO
THE MIRROR OF ETERNITY

I LISTENED with close attention while my strange companion made the remarks which concluded the preceding chapter. I was not a religious man; I did not understand nor particularly care about the spiritual things of life. From the time when I first entered the world, I had been told that I was supremely selfish, and all the conditions of my childhood tended to bring out my egotism, self-aggrandizement, and laziness, and I felt that I had been pretty true to my early teachings.

Still at his words I felt a tugging at some invisible cord within my own being and in spite of myself, my eyes turned to the strange, blue haze which filled the frame supported by the three gods.

In the old guide, I recognized the great saint referred to by holy men, and I remained silent as he continued his discourse.

"I know, my son, that you do not understand, or rather that you fail to remember the things which I am telling you, therefore be very attentive to my words. The fact that you alone out of all the holy men of India are the first in nearly forty years to find this sacred place proves beyond all words that a great reason lies behind your coming, and in order that you too may understand all that lies around you I shall tell you of this sacred mirror.

"In the days now gone by when the gods lived with men, when the great devas from the higher plane and the Manu himself walked the earth in flesh, he built himself in a single night this wondrous temple and left in it his most precious gifts of which this wondrous glass which reflects the worlds invisible to the eyes of men is not the least. From the ever-changing substances of nature, this glass draws forth each hidden secret and is indeed the Mirror of Eternity. For, know you, that there surrounds and interpenetrates the world which we know other worlds that we do not see, and this mirror while of this world is sanctified in other worlds and shows to those who look the records of Brahma's Day preserved within the living beings of earth. Look!" and he pointed at the fathomless depths.

As he spoke, great swirling, twisting clouds appeared in the bottomless abyss of the sacred mirror. I looked and before my eyes there slowly formed out of the whirling clouds a strange world that stretched into the infinity of darkness. It was a world of broken things, great, twisted, gnawed trees of types unknown, their trunks blackened as though by fire, raised their branches like supplicating arms. Great cloudy, smoldering flames burst forth from cracks and crevices in the rocks and in the air great banks of sulphureous smoke tinted by the flames formed into twisting clouds of oily red. In my ears were the moaning and sighing of the winds and the dashing of the waves upon a broken shore.

I tried to recall from somewhere out of the past this strange scene but nowhere, even among the volcano and lava beds of Vesuvius and Etna, had such clouds of smoke ever gathered.

"What is this strange scene?" I asked my guide.

"That, my son, is called the Land of the Lonely Ones," answered the Oriental. "Although the eyes of mortal cannot see it, what you now behold is built of the thoughts and desires of the people of earth. You are now gazing at the home of men as it has been seen by the Compassionate Ones. From this strange land of death and dissolution there pour forth the spirits of the flame, the demons of war, the miseries, strife, and contention which fill the world. It is here that the work you are to do begins. It is, here in the world of Causes that the Compassionate Ones labor for their brothers."

I gazed at the picture again and a strange chill came over my being. It was so cold, so cheerless, so dead, and yet from within came the echo of an accusing voice, and although I was loath to admit it I realized that beneath the life I lived my own being wandered in a wilderness as gloomy and desolate as the scene I beheld.

As I watched, I saw a tiny, golden star shine out through the darkness. Wherever its beams fell the broken, confused mass of ragged rocks melted away with its glow and the deep, angry red of the smoldering fires turned golden with its warmth. As I looked more closely, I saw that this little star was carried in the form of a lantern by a strange, mystic figure which walked, or rather floated, over the scene of desolation.

"Who is that?" I muttered under my breath.

"Watch," answered my strange companion.

(To be continued)

OCCULT MASONRY
THE SHRINE

AMONG THE MASONIC CRAFTS there are many wonderful degrees, but none has a deeper or more beautiful sentiment than the Mohammedan Shrine. Let us drop for the present the social side of Masonry, for it is only an accessory which means nothing to the true art and science of the active craft. The Mason is a builder throughout eternity, and in the beautiful degree of the Shrine a wonderful thought is given to him which should assist him to better thinking and better living, otherwise its profound significance in Masonry is lost to the craft.

Let us go back to the ancient peoples where practically all of the modern symbolism had its origin, and here we find many wonderful facts concerning the mystery of the Shrine.

Man is eternally a worker, but to what end? That is a question which only mystics and philosophers can answer. What is the great reward for years of sorrow and labor? What is man's recompense for his works and his life? The answer is that man is a builder of Shrines.

From the beginning of time to the end of eternity, man is building a wondrous altar piece for his living temple; he is fashioning a wonderful and glorious decoration to adorn an empty niche. In other words, with thought, action, and desire, through his thousands and millions of years of growth, he is laboring consciously or unconsciously to a single end. This end is the preparation of a holy place to be the dwelling of the Most High. Therefore, in spirit and in truth man is a Shriner, a builder of shrines.

Now, in many ways man carries on his appointed destiny, and all through the ages he is building eternally many things, and on all planes of nature he is laying up treasures with which to adorn this wondrous altar piece, the living Shrine of his own soul.

In India there are many wonderful shrines of gold and jewels, brass and glorious lacquers, stone, and wood, carved by the hands of the faithful into ornaments and decorations to embellish and make grander the altars of the gods they worship. It is said that only the heathen build shrines, but we know that this is not true, for only the finest, the purest, the most noble of human beings can build a shrine, and not even the end of time as we know it shall bring to completion the shrine building of the soul.

Now, the world as we know it at the present time is the great rough block from which man must cut this beautiful shrine. With love, compassion, joy, and a deeper understanding of the mysteries of life, he must take the brutal, the cruel, the rough, and the unfinished, and with the vision of the true seer carve with loving thoughts, joyful hands, and a contrite spirit, this rough and broken mass into the glorious shrine of spirit.

Let man realize that he is building a strange and subtle thing, and a new power and zeal inspires his efforts. Its wonderful pillars he carves from the granite blocks of matter. With thought, word, and actions, he decorates it and glorifies it until it becomes a thing of beauty and grandeur. Into the settings he has fashioned, he places the stones of knowledge and love, each flower, each little figure, carved by loving hands for the glory of his God. As he works through the ages, he realizes that his own body, the world in which he lives, and the world of his friends and those around him are the materials from which this shrine must be built. It is from the dross of his own soul that he must cut the golden key, and his own being must become the glorious setting to contain the most precious of all jewels, the Pearl of Great Price, and the Philosopher's Stone.

Man is ever human and being human. He is impatient, thoughtless, and unsettled as to the reason for his own being. Therefore, he makes a great mistake, a sad and terrible mistake, yet who shall blame him for it? It is a mistake which seems almost godlike and which sometimes even the Masters make, and yet how can we judge them? When man builds this sacred shrine, he fails to realize there is but one thing worthy to fill that hallowed spot.

Some gods of earth he seeks to raise to heaven's height, enshrined beside the Infinite, a cherished thought, a loved one of this world, who has called to him or who has heard the whisper of his soul.

But how can a god of clay fill a shrine of gold? The answer lies in the broken heart at the foot of the shrine, when the one we sought to raise to the height of a god proves to be only a creature of earth. How many hours and years of sorrow man must experience when he allows the human to fill the shrine of the Divine! None can answer that problem save those who have seen the shrine shattered and the figure crumble, which they worshipped as a God. Therefore, the Shriner learns that the sacred place is the dwelling of the Most High and that there can be no other gods before Him.

As man labors through the ages to build the shrine, he must never seek to fill it with an idol of wood or stone which he glorifies as the divine, for soon the beloved lies at his feet a broken ruin, only less broken than the heart of the worshipper.

Close to his heart man must keep the ones he adores, deep in his soul should he etch the picture of those who are dear, but never let him place within this hallowed shrine any save the living God. Our world is filled with those who have known the pain of a broken heart because something of earth came too close to the things of God. Broken we lie at the feet of our idols, crushed and disconsolate, and for years we do not labor with the shrine because it seems that whatever we build into it, a glorious love or life, is shattered into a thousand places and nought have we in our hands but broken clay. The soul of the dreamer is broken with the idol at his feet. The heart of love is cold as it sees the creature of its adoration fall in a heap of broken dust before it.

But there is the mystery of the shrine. Through the ages, man is to build this glorious altar, but not to fill it. Man will never know, it seems, the glory of being able to fill that shrine with those adored. His is the work to build it, to finish it with all the beauty and grandeur that his soul may know, but forever the empty niche must face him, never to be filled. Forever he seems to be building a golden ring around an empty void, but from his hands there shall come a strange craftsmanship. The mercy seat shall be built into the shrine, and as the last touch is completed and the architect lays aside his plans, the shrine builder shall kneel in adoration before his works and know at last the mystery of the Shrine.

In the heart of the altar he has finished, in the niche of that sacred shrine, a great Light shall come and descend upon him. It is the Light he cannot build; it is the presence of the Lord, which nothing of earth can give him. Whatever else he may worship becomes as nothing before that mystic thing and whoever in this world he cherished no longer fills the shrine, for each loved thing has an altar, everything we cherish has its own little worshipping place in the heart. The shrine of the soul is for the spirit alone, and when man has finished his work and built his temple after the order of the Most High, then shall the spirit of the Lord inhabit it and the shrine shall be filled forever.

No longer will the idol crumble for now the ideal fills the shrine, no longer will man's heart be broken as those he trusts fail him in the moment of his extremity, for the presence in the shrine will never leave it but as a pillar of flame by night and a column of smoke by day the Shriner is ever protected by the Light of God.

So, in Masonry we have the privilege and duty of building this mystic shrine, the living temple of the living God, and the beauty of this wonderful Mohammedan degree is as sweet and as divine as any Christian concept. So, seekers of the Great Light, let us make our pilgrimage to Mecca and there pay our homage to the green banner of the prophet, and then wrapping the veil around our turbans or fez let us return to build more wonderful and more mystic shrines as we labor in the completion of the great one which is to be within us the dwelling place of the living God, for there is no God but Allah and Mohammed is his prophet.

Five times a day, the Moslem calls to prayer. Five times the son of Islam faces the Kabba and there offers up his prayer to the living God. Let us pray to the same God that the time may not be far off when we shall more truly build His shrine that He may dwell within it.

ADAM AND EVE AND THE FLAMING SWORD

I DO NOT SUPPOSE there is anyone who does not speculate, at least a little, over the story of the cherubim with the flaming sword that guarded the way to the gates of Eden to prevent the return of our primal ancestors to their heavenly home. The same little story is played out every day of our lives, if we will but see it.

First, Eden represents paradise or heaven, that particular form of earthly joy which is the direct result of man's living in accordance with the plan of his being. In other words, when man is in a harmonious state of consciousness, when his organism is properly balanced, etc., he then lives in a new world of his own creation or rather to which he has become attuned through his life, and this is in fact the garden of the Lord.

Man has been cast out of the garden of balance and peace by his perversions, and the flaming sword of Eden undoubtedly represents the descending spirit fire which drives the spiritual consciousness of man out of his peace and joy. The cherubim with the flaming sword that stood at the gates of Eden had four heads. These four heads symbolize the four bodies of man, while the flaming sword is the fire of passion. It is the emotion body of man, uncurbed and unregenerated, that stands as a flaming sword between him and the higher worlds. Nearly all the suffering in the world at the present time is the result of emotion in which individuals have lost control of themselves and have allowed the passion body to dominate their lives. So long as this is permitted, the cherubim with the flaming sword will stand between the spiritual consciousness of man and the realization of his ideals. It is only when this body is mastered that peace can return.

When man masters his lower being, the down-pointing sword is turned upward through spiritual regeneration and man is then able to enter again the garden of the Lord. But so long as we are a slave to our lower natures and to the animal fires, just so long does the flaming sword stand between us and our true spiritual home, and we are forced to wander the earth dressed in the skins of animals until as purified egos we pass through the fire of the flaming sword and the bodies which like the Sphinx of old guard the entrance to the higher worlds.

THE MYSTERY OF INITIATION

DURING THE LAST few years, a great wave of mysticism has swept over the world. The heart of mankind is hungry for greater knowledge. The soul yearning for fuller understanding has sought to tear away the veil which forever drapes the figure of Wisdom. Man has sought to learn those mystic truths so long lost to the world, and in his study and search he has found that there are strange and mysterious beings known to the world as Initiates. Among the ancient works and the mystery schools of those peoples now dead, strange ceremonies called initiations were given in some mysterious way and the popular mind has come to believe that there is a mystic rite, an initiative ceremonial, which makes man one with the immortals, and in the name of this wonderful and mystic concept terrible crimes have been committed against the spiritual and occult teachings. There is probably no word in the English language that has been so abused, so misused, so often used and so little understood, as the word "Initiation." Every dream, every phantom form, every unusual happening, has been called the initiation and all over the world temples have sprung up in the name of the mystery schools to initiate candidates into the Wisdom teachings, some of them without cost but in the majority of cases a heavy fee accompanies the initiation in which for, say, $25.00 the candidate is dubbed "Sir Somebody" or made a leading luminary in some mystic shrine.

The result of this perversion is that the sacredness, the beauty, and the true realization of the meaning of initiation has been lost to the world, for it is very true that there are none who can so damage a religion or an idea as those who claim to be its followers. How long it will take the world to learn that initiations are not ceremonials it is difficult to say, but sometime each individual must realize that swinging robes and incense burners and other trimmings do not constitute initiation, and that no one on the face of the earth could buy it for the fortune of Croesus nor in any way receive it until he himself by his life has become worthy of its mystic blessing.

There are few in this world who know what real initiation is, and there are fewer still who having discovered it really want to so live that this mystic rite may be unfolded within their souls. The true Initiate is a very wondrous and mysterious being and any words that we can say concerning such a one are very poor, in deed. Those who have not already walked the path can have but a feeble idea of what an Initiate really is, for such a one has unfolded within himself or herself, as the case may be, certain principles of which the average layman knows nothing. The powers of life and death, the powers of destruction and construction, the mystic principles of integration and disintegration, all these are in the hands of the Great Ones of God. The knowledge of life is the mystic power of the Initiate, for only those who have walked the ways of many can ever know what the laurels of initiation mean. Only when his heart is filled with love for humanity and with the great suffering and great peace of those who know, can he so express the powers within himself that he is of use in so great a plan?

The Initiate has the mindless mind of spirit which thinks only the thoughts of life, to the source of which he each day draws nearer; he is filled with the understanding of nature's plan for her children and only this knowledge holds in check a heart that would otherwise break with sorrow. He knows that strange, sweet melancholy, that mystic feeling few have ever realized, such as must have filled the soul of Jesus as He wept over Jerusalem. The true Initiate is initiated by God and not by man and he will give his life, his soul, his very being, to lift the suffering in the name of the Father.

It is only those who have a heart great enough to enfold all creation, a consciousness as great and broad as life itself, who are even on the road to initiation, those whose very being is a mirror of the Divine, whose every thought is to save, whose every power is expanded to raise, whose every action is a blessing, who reach out with hands ever stronger to aid suffering humanity. Those and those alone know the true meaning of initiation. Those whose eyes have never seen suffering, those whose hearts have never been broken, those who are tied by earthly ambitions, can never receive that celestial influx of life which comes to those who have prepared their vehicles in the way of the law and the great love.

The Initiate is slowly reaching out into the Great Unknown, lighting each corner of chaos with his own glory, bathing all life in the warmth of his own soul, limited only by his own unfoldment. On through the ages, he is dispelling ignorance and darkness by the ever-broadening sphere of his own light. It is those who have dedicated their lives and being to feed the flame of the Eternal One that its light may shine more brightly whom we call the Initiates and, oh, how few they are! How few have given up the kingdoms of the earth! How few are ready to give up earthly desires to walk the path that leads to Divinity, holding out the little alms-dish of the Buddha for the words of wisdom and love that are given to those who seek for help that they in turn may serve? To those who seek it in any other way than this, initiation is only a terrible demon. The student may gain growth, the wisdom or so-called power of the Adept may come to him, but still if selfishness is his motive he is cursed to suffer and to go without the things of this world as well as the other, for he is cursed with knowledge, and knowledge brings with it a weight that few shoulders are strong enough to bear.

It is only when that mystic thing comes, the strange, spiritual power of initiation, that to man is given the strength to carry knowledge in the way of light. There are only a few who are ready to take up the cross and follow in the footsteps of those who have consecrated their lives to their fellowmen. There are only a few with strength enough to see the veil of the future lifted and remain sane. There are few who could see the veil of their own destiny raised and still have strength enough to walk the way, and even to those who can stand this great light there comes the still greater test of standing alone in the high places of the world without even the staff of comradeship, for the Initiate is ever alone but when truly ordained of the spirit is never lonely.

For with this knowledge that no tongue can speak, no coin of man can buy, there comes something else, a still whisper, the word of eternal life that passes eternally through the soul of the saved. While the Initiate sees the bleeding hearts of his fellowman and the breaking and tearing of living things, he still sees the eternal justice of all things, to him there comes the realization that all is working for good. He sees the divine hand working through the apparent chaos of things and that behind the human discord, there is the divine reason.

Can we face this Great Unknown as the Great Ones have faced it? Can we pass through with the glorious vision of Nirvana forever before us? If we can, we are on the path upward that leads to the feet of the Great Ones, who look down on a man with never-changing eyes of love. Very few are there in the world today who are ready to make the great renunciation which the world knows as initiation.

There comes a time in every soul when there is a parting of the ways, and there are few who will take the stony path, give up the kingdoms of earth, and ascend the rocky crags to the feet of the Liberator. Those who take that path are the true essence of the life we live. Eventually, all will take the path as the light dawns upon them.

If we would take that silent way, we must renounce the selfishness of materiality and slowly and painfully meet bravely the buffets of the world and go on and on, the endless paths that lead into the Unknown. It is those who have done this, sacrificing all without a murmur, whom we know as the Initiates, and we owe them respect and love for they are in truth our Elder Brothers who have gone a little way before that they may come back and show us the path to tread.

A time comes when each soul, after having passed the first degrees of initiation, receives the greatest test of all. It is when he reaches the veil that divides him from the world. Nirvana, with all its blessings, shines before him while those wandering in the wilderness cry out for help from the darkness below. He stands at the parting of the way which path will he choose? The path of initiation is forever the path of sacrifice. No glory, no power, just a selfless willingness to serve the highest. In the robes of the mendicant, the Initiate returns to wander the earth and serve others. While they are apparently imperfect and torn and slandered by the world, yet the hosts of heaven look down and bless them. Those who give up all, even the paradise well-earned and the rest that is theirs and come back to walk in the muck and mire. They are the Initiates. It is at that moment the Star of Bethlehem shines out to tell that another Son of God is born among men.

There are many on earth who have made this great renunciation. They have given up peace to walk the streets in rags, to be laughed at and ridiculed, to teach the few who would listen. They have gained great knowledge and great intellect but still they live and speak of simple things. We only see them occasionally and we say that these great ones have been blessed but we do not know the price that they have paid, how they have bathed their souls in tears, how they have been garbed only in their own blood and crucified by their own disciples. This is the price of initiation and it is through these things great souls are born.

We have grown to think that there is only one Son of God but we are all his children, and when one really takes the path that leads to Light, the voice of the Father speaks spiritually within his soul, saying, "This is my Beloved Son in whom I am well pleased." It is only then that the candidate climbs the steps that lead to immortality.

It is sad to think how few who seek the powers of the masters are willing to pay for them with love and thought. With a few paltry dollars and a few fine robes, they honestly believe they can receive that for which Gods have died, which great souls have been crucified to attain and martyrs met their death in the arena. It is a pitiful thing, man's concept of the road to God. "It is sharper than a serpent's tooth to have a thankless child," and how many of them the gods have today!

What is the path that leads to the Initiates? It is the lifting of consciousness through this strange drama, which we call life. Along the great road, all beings are plodding slowly, old and young alike, all walking the same path, the road that leads to the feet of the Masters. There are many shrines along the way, many religions, many creeds, many little chapels where the seeker stops to pray and the weary to rest. But ever onward, all must go until they reach the temple on the top of the lofty crags. In daily life, we have our tests; the thought comes to our mind that we hate someone, but what have we to hate? Then thoughts of fear haunt us, and sorrow bows us down. Then through the ages comes the realization that all things lead to good. Slowly, we gain the great compassion, the great balance, the heart that is free of pain and pleasure. We have the vision of the great Truth and seek to enfold all living things within the cape of our love.

When thoughts like these come to the student, he is learning. It is that feeling of glory that brings with it the touch of pain. Everything we do carries with it a great responsibility. Those who wish to wear the robe of the Initiate must be willing to wear it over a broken heart.

With many people, their greatest desire is to escape responsibility or to gain the glory of a great reward but so long as these thoughts fill the soul initiation is impossible. Until the aspirant is living the ritual, he can never learn its mystery; until he can see in his own spiritual being the dying Christ on the cross, he can never truly learn of initiation. It is bought with the gold of spirit and service. When he has so lived as to be worthy of it, then comes the Light. In the darkness of his own closet, far from his brother man, in the silence of his own soul the great mystery unfolds.

Thousands of figures gather round him, and the Grand Master is there in his robe of Blue and Gold. The teachers of the ages gather round him; he is in the great hall of his own body through which he must pass to enter the inner room. There alone, he passes through things no mortal tongue can speak; there he sees the reason for his being; the things that he must do; the greater works he is privileged to accomplish. And having learned much, his new responsibility is likewise great; having seen the work to be done, he can no longer rest but must wander the world like a lost soul to labor in the endless cause. He lives for one brief moment with those things which are eternal and having glimpsed those wondrous beings, service means everything. He must help all living things to find the light that he has found. Just a silent soul alone, unfolding its wondrous mystery to its own being, that is Initiation.

Having gone through these tests and removed the love of materiality, he is given the privilege of knowing and realizing the true reason for at least part of the Plan. He goes on now, step by step, coming into the powers which were always his, not in heaven but in hell, for the place of the Initiate is not in the worlds above but in the worlds of darkness for he has consecrated his soul to the redemption of man.

We have among us today those who claim to have passed through great initiations, but do their lives show it? Are they willing to work unseen and unknown with the powers that never shine before the eyes of men? Do they work with the humility and simplicity which is the divine expression of the soul? All true Initiates point out the way by their own beings that others may follow the path to which they have dedicated their lives.

Everyone wants to be an Initiate but if they were, the sun would soon go out forever from their lives. Like children, man is always wanting something and weeping for it like a child. The soul filled with uncertainty, selfishness, and materiality can never have the strength of purpose and the unity of balance, to carry the burdens of Initiation. It is a blessing, then, that many are not what they want to be. If it were not so, hearts would be broken that have not the strength to mend. If we could be initiated now, it would do us no good, for each true, upward step must be hewn out of the solid rock of experience that each may take the path by removing from his life the personal things that stand between him and that which he seeks. We must take each cruel word and change it into a dove before we send it on its way.

When we go hence to enter into our Father's house, the greatest reward that can come to us is the privilege of laboring there. Not our will, but the Master's should regulate the expression of our life.

If those who seek Initiation today could only know what it really means, they would realize how false their concepts have been. What have we done that we have the right to join that little throng of God's chosen ones? If we would labor with them, we must take upon our shoulders their burdens and be one of those who are responsible for the lives of men, and when we have raised our consciousness, our lives, our actions and our thoughts to this point, then we are Initiates in spirit and in truth, for the light of God's plan for man shines forth and envelopes us in its glory and its first gleam shining upon our souls show us the end to which all Initiation leads, a lonely cross upon a hill.

ASTROLOGY

Key words under Airies

OR THE BENEFIT of those who wish a brief, comprehensive series of keywords, the general trend of which can be easily memorized, to assist them in judging the rising signs of individuals, we have arranged and compiled the following series which will answer practically all the needs of the elementary astrologer. The following sources have been drawn from in the preparation of this series of articles, which will appear each month until the twelve signs have been analyzed:

Astrology, by William Lilly, London, 1647.
Ptolemy's Tetrabiblos, edited by J. M.
Ashmand, London, 1822.
The Complete Dictionary of Astrology,
James Wilson, Esq., London, 1819.
The Astrological Judgment of Disease,
by Nicholas Culpeper, London, 1671.
The Celestial Science of Astrology, Ebenezer Sibly, London, 1785.

We will take the signs of the Zodiac in the order in which they come, listing under them a general compendium of known facts concerning them.

Aries, the First Sign of the Zodiac
Aries is a cardinal sign,
Fiery, Masculine, Dry, Hot, Vernal, Equinoctial, Movable, Eastern, Diurnal, Short ascension, Bitter sign, Exaltation of the sun, Detriment of Venus, Day house of Mars, Fall of Saturn.

General Characteristics:
Choleric, Luxuriant, Violent, Fortunate, Hoarse, Commanding, Tempestuous, Militant, Self-assertive, Pioneering, A ruler, Scientific, Explorative, Amative, Versatile, Energetic, Powerful will, Sharp, Hasty, Domineering, Combative

Physical Appearance:
Usually slender, Strong and spare, Body rather dry, Piercing eyes, Long face,

High cheekbones, Black eyebrows, Rather long neck, Thick shoulders, Swarthy complexion, Red or dark brown hair, Disposition violent and intemperate, Loose-jointed and strong-boned, Aries governs the head and face, Subject to accidents.

Health:
Aries is subject to many forms of sudden ailments, also all things which have to do with impediments in the dynamic system.

Listed below are the ones most commonly met with:
Smallpox, Eruptions on the face and body, Measles, Sunburn, Ringworm, Headaches, Shingles, Vertigo, Epilepsy, Frenzy, Temper fits, Apoplexy, Lethargy, Fevers, Forgetfulness, Convulsions, Catalepsy, Palsy, Megrims, Coma, Falling sickness, Baldness, Diseases caused by heat, Cramps through various parts of the body, Melancholia, Trembling, Toothache, Hair-lip.

Aries is also susceptible to ailments as the result of early indiscretions, and it also burns up too much energy and often lives for many years on plain will power. Aries is also susceptible to ailments in the liver and kidney trouble and poor digestion on account of excitement and Aries energy which tries to do too many things at once.

Domestic Problems:
Aries is not a home-loving sign and, in the majority of cases, is too strongly organized and energized to remain quiet about anything. Aries' homes are usually more or less unhappy.

Countries Under the Influence of Aries:
Great Britain, France, Germany, Switzerland, Denmark, Lesser Poland, Syria, Palestine, Naples, Capua, Ancona, Verona, Florence, Ferrara, Padua, Saragossa, Marseilles, Silesia, Burgundy, Utrecht, Cracow,

According to Ptolemy, the fixed stars in the sign of Aries have the following qualities:
Stars in the head of Aries produce influences similar to Mars and Saturn; Those in the mouth have the qualities of Mercury and, to some degree Saturn; Those in the hinder foot of the Ram have the qualities of Mars; While those in the tail of Aries take the qualities of Venus; Aries, according to the ancients, is a constellation consisting of twelve stars; modern astronomy says otherwise.

Colors:
Red and white.

According to Henri Cornelius Agrippa and, later, Francis Barrett, F.R.C., the following list is found under the head of Aries: Of the twelve orders of blessed spirits, Aries rules the Seraphim; of the twelve angels over the twelve signs, Malchidial is ruled by Aries; of the twelve tribes, Dan; of the twelve prophets, Malachi; of the twelve Apostles, Matthias; of the twelve months, March 20th to April 20th; of the twelve plants, the Sang; of the twelve stones, the sardonius; of the twelve principal parts of the body, the head; of the twelve degrees of the damned, the false gods.

BROKEN DOLLS

AS YOU WATCH life through the eyes of one who has walked the path, you see spreading out before you not only a graveyard of broken hopes and shattered ideals but also a wondrous kindergarten where men, gods in the making, pass through the hours of their childhood until the Eternal Hand calls them to greater things.

Here we see the little ones, often old in years but young ever in spirit, laughing and playing each in his own freeway, few of the worries and responsibilities of real life in its true sense realized or understood for man knows little of living but with carefree spirit he goes on in this way and in that, playing through the years of his youth and his manhood and passing into the Great Beyond still clasping a toy in his arms.

Off to one side, away from the laughing, playing children, there sits a little one alone for whom the world has come to an end. The little chubby cheeks are streaked with tears, a little heart is broken, and from one little life the light of the sun has gone out forever. With its face clasped between its hands it sobs its little soul away, while upon the ground before it lies a broken doll with its funny little face seamed and cracked and its sawdust body broken and twisted by the ruthless cruelty of an older child.

This is the endless story of the broken doll. It may seem at this age of the world that man does not play with toys like these but still in his heart he is ever a child; to the very day when ends his work here he is just a little one laughing with the children, playing with them, and then creeping away to weep alone over a broken toy.

The world is not filled with sinners, but with thoughtless people. It is filled with those who do not realize the agony greater far than mortal mind can ever understand, the soul anguish which gnaws to the very being of a child when its with the children, playing with them, and then creeping away to weep alone over a broken toy.

The world is not filled with sinners, but with thoughtless people. It is filled with those who do not realize the agony greater far than mortal mind can ever understand, the soul anguish which gnaws to the very being of a child when its toy is broken. If man could only understand how the little things we love, the little castles we build in the air, the little shrines we make and in which we place gods and goddesses of clay if the world could only realize the soul each of the other it would not with the ruthless hand of hate and the heartless touch of selfishness tear down these little dream castles of the air; it would not leave us crying by the empty shrines made desolate by their thoughtlessness; it would not leave us heart-broken before the toy that. It has shattered, the ideal it has forever slain.

Our toys are very fragile things, just one harsh word, a few unhappy seconds, and the dream of the child is shattered, and its life is bent askew. All the children of men are dreamers, dreaming wondrous dreams and building in the heaven's castles of rainbow colors. To many these dreams are just toys, just make-believes, and too often our quick word shatters them, and while to us they meant nothing they seemed all to some little soul who must walk the lonely way in darkness because we have torn down the fairy world which made its life sweeter.

So let us be careful of their playthings for the heart of the world bleeds too often and little souls pine away beside the toy that is shattered, which in its broken little pieces often symbolizes the shattered soul of the dreamer. Let us realize more fully that man is ever a child, living ever in the world of make-believe, and that the things which he cherishes and the ones whom he loves become gods and goddesses in truth.

His life to the very grave is filled with fairy stories and forever to the soul of the mystic child the prince comes riding, forever in our souls we build little toys, and when all others go away and leave us, we bring them out from their sacred closet and sitting alone with our own souls plays with the dolls of the years gone by. Again, the little tin soldier comes out of his box, the fluffy little dog is there, and the old rag doll in whose simple, homely being our hearts are often hidden. Only these are no longer physical toys, they are the playthings of the mind and the soul. Instead of being of wood and painted lead the little toy soldiers who fight so true are our friends and those we love, and when friendship is broken, when man betrays his trust one to another, the soul sits alone in its closet and cries heart-broken over a shattered toy.

Let us realize that each of us in enshrined in the soul of another somewhere in the world and that when we betray our trust someone must cry over a broken doll, a soul not strong enough to stand the weight of a thing to us so trivial will know the pains and anguish of a broken heart over the toy which we have shattered. If we could only realize in our homes how love builds toys in the soul, we would not tear down these gods from their shrines, we would not break the hearts of those we love by our thoughtless words and heartless deeds which to us mean so little and still fill the world of another with sorrow and sadness.

The soul of a man must stay young. He must forever be a dreamer, building from subtle, unseen things toys to fill the loneliness of life. Let him build them, let him dress them as he will, let him play as he will, and deny him not his toys, for when you destroy them you leave behind a mark deep in the soul of things, a scar which the years cannot heal, which only the Masters understand who have wept for ages over broken dolls.

Man must worship something. Someone must seem to him divine, someone in whose ear he may whisper the thoughts, the emotions, and the ideals which surge through his soul. Something either of this world drawn by bonds unknown or a little cherished toy hidden in the heart, something he must worship in the name of God.

Wherever this thing is not, life is cold. So let us always help our brothers in the world to play more beautiful games in more beautiful ways with their toys. Let our words and actions make the rag doll more divine and, in the true spirit of compassion, let us play with the child so that its castles may be fairer. Never, in the name of God, tear the toy from the child's arms and leave it sitting on the curbstone which borders the road of life with broken heart and shattered ideals, weeping in an anguish that our hearts can never know for a broken doll.

SHIPS THAT PASS IN THE NIGHT

THERE ARE FEW who realize the power that they themselves as individuals have in molding the destinies of peoples, worlds, and gods. No man lives by himself alone, neither do our thoughts or actions affect us alone. They go on and on in a world of many mysteries and these little birds of clay which we mold fly on eternally ever closer and closer to the circling orbs of light.

The world is a great sea and the eternal, never ceasing sway of living things can be likened to the soft swishing of the ocean waves, and in too many lives, this world in which we live is a stormy sea where the waves of broken hopes dash themselves to pieces upon the rocky shores of discouragement. Too many times in life we hear the moaning and sighing as of mighty winds and the night cries in the wilderness when the snowy crests of breaking waves beat against the encircling arms of the shore.

Through this stormy sea of oblivion, this endless battle and turmoil of life there silently pass thousands of little ships, the souls of living things seeking to cross this endless sea, hoping to find a peaceful harbor and there to rest in safety protected from the buffets of the storm. Too many times, this world is filled with darkness. The thunderclouds fill our lives, and all seem bleak and desolate. Too many times we sense the great oppression, the indescribable sense of loneliness, and the utter chill of the world. We do not see beneath this surging water the softer, sweeter and more beautiful, but lonely barks upon an endless sea with the rudder lashed and sails set, driven by every wind that blows and manned only by a crew of ghastly specters, our ship passes silently and hopelessly through the night of cosmic oblivion.

Let us, for a moment, float like some mystic specter from another world over the darkness of the seas and watch the ships that pass silently in the night. Through the darkness they come, lonely, bleak, and desolate derelicts on the ceaseless waves of night, and they pass, looking neither to the right nor to the left. We shudder, a chill comes over us, we feel the oppression of that ghostly crew of broken hopes and shattered ideals.

Many a living ship is manned only by the ghastly crews of death, set faces that cannot smile peer out from broken portholes and eyes that stare with a glassy fixedness of despair gaze out from these silent ships that pass in the night. They do not know where they are going. Long ago, the compass of courage and ideal has been swept overboard, long before the captain has fallen a victim to the mutiny of his crew. The soft, sweet human touch, the cheery voices of the sailors as they draw on the ropes, and the song of the willing workmen. All these are silent. Many a human bark, battered and tossed by the sea of life, waits longingly for the waves to break forever over its broken craft, there are souls crying out to their Creator to end their suffering in blissful dissolution.

These are the ships that pass in the night, these are the grim skeletons of dead hopes, these are the vessels that have for ages wandered in the darkness of the storm. One by one, the noble aspirations have died, one by one the fiery desires have been chilled forever, and the hearts that once beat as other men's now dream only of lost hopes. The world is filled with these ships that must wander it seems until Judgment Day when through the darkness of the night a light shines out, there is the cheery ringing of a bell, or the starlike gleam of a lighthouse, which brings peace to these broken wanderers, rest to their shattered lives.

Far out in the darkness a tiny pillar of stone rises upward in the night on a broken crag of rock where the endless beating of the waves alone is heard, and the white crests reach upward to envelop this frail thing of man but as the lonely lighthouse stands so great souls have gone out forever from the peace and security of the shore to be broken as battered ships in order that they may keep alight the lamp for the world. The lighthouse keeper at sea is serving ships that pass in the night as the world is served by the lighthouse keepers on the rocks of life. Their gleam shines out no longer from the revolving lenses of the tower above, for in this world the lighthouse is our own being and its light shines out through the eyes, through the soft words, the generous ideals, and the great compassion which marks the lighthouse keepers on the broken seas of the world.

Still the waves break and toss and battle with each other through the eternal night of human ignorance, still the lonely vessel rocked and torn by the storm wanders o'er the sea of life, awaiting the day of liberation and the haven of peace.

A LITTLE EPISODE FROM LIFE - II
(Continued)

business man with a bowler hat over his eyes and a full cut spring overcoat draped over his portly frame. He is one of the leading lights of high finance and is considered a Rockefellow in the making. He is headed for the cafeteria for the bells within and without have summoned him to lunch. He passed with a springy step, his head set straight forward on a copious neck, his nose turned slightly askew to allow the smoke of his cigar to go upwards without passing back into his nose. He passes the little figure, the notes of the accordion strike his ear, but he has no time to waste, he knows but one master, the call of the inner man, and the only music that can touch his soul is the gentle cadence of sizzling bacon, and the gentle purr of a knife across a beefsteak.

As he passes from the field of vision there comes up the street from the other direction a tall, slender youth, the most conspicuous part of his attire being his light violet, striped socks and a roll-down jersey. He has a Lucky Strike under one ear and his cap is tilted well over his nose and threatens to slide off from his polished hair, glistening brightly with a generous dose of brilliantine. He is whistling "Clementine" with sundry original variations, including the "Stars and Stripes Forever," and with his hands in his pockets and his chest slumped in he is headed God alone knows where, but the graveyard is undoubtedly the end of the trip. Upon his ears, also, fall the strains of the accordion but he is not interested, he has just had a break with his "steady" who'd seen him out with his "once-in-a-while."

Just then from across the corner there hove in sight one of our leading society dowagers, the heavily constructed Mrs. Gotrox, accompanied by her daughter, this season's prize for the highest bidder, who has been acclaimed the most eligible and desirable debutante in the west district. Mr. Gotrox has just made millions in his seedless pickle project.

"M'dear," says mother, "what is this peculiar squeaky noise I hear?" "It must be that old lady over there playing the accordion," gurgled the blossoming member of the younger set. "Oh, dear!" exclaimed the mother, who had been Cylenthe McGillicutty before her marriage, "I wish they'd pass a law against allowing beggars on the street, I'll bet she has more money than I have, every one of these old women is rolling in cash, but I'll tell you right now she'll get none of mine!" And with quite a gust of personality they sailed off, a streaming duo of ostrich plumes and real mink, headed for a well-known beauty parlor where Madame was taking out wrinkles for mama and trying to add an indestructible kink to daughter's hair.

Several seconds passed and the corner seemed nearly deserted when another figure appeared, a promising young clerk from one of the downtown stores in the neighborhood. This young lady was one of those liquid types which threatened to collapse at every step. She was built on the lines of a weeping willow and, from the head downward, every muscular articulation expressed itself as a drizzle. As this figure came galloping by it extracted with a hairpin a small wad of gum affixed to the third molar and with a semi-hysterical gesture animated by a general disintegration of the trapezoid muscle, threatening a general collapse, she lazily tossed the gum over one shoulder, said gum landing on the head of the old lady playing the accordion.

Happening to follow its course, this promising member of our younger generation twisted her mouth under one ear and bellowed forth. In this fashion: "Well, grandma, if ye hadn't been there it wouldn't 'a hit yuh! Whatever you think you're doing, parking yourself on the sidewalk, this ain't no bone orchard?" and with this elegant excerpt from the classics our flapper careened off with as much grace and dignity as four and a half inches of French heels and weak ankles would permit.

The old lady still sat playing the accordion. She had brushed away the gum and was perhaps recalling the days when she had been as young and foolish as the girl who had passed and possibly wondering if that girl's fate would be the same as hers. One by one, the people passed, the highest, the richest, and the most educated in the fair city. Here and there, one would drop a nickel or dime into the cup, but the majority went by. Then, through the crowd, another little figure appeared.

It was an old lady dressed in black. She wore a little bonnet with the ribbons tied under her chin, an old-fashioned cashmere shawl hung around her shoulders, and her plain clothes, while neat, showed the thrift which is the result of none too sufficient funds. She was the mother of a large family very likely but one after another they had gone away to their separate lives and as is usually the case none wanted her. She was alone and though the black she wore showed that her own partner had been laid away in the grave, no doubt his picture rested ever in her heart. She was one of the few of an age of simple things, fast disappearing from the things we know. For her it was a problem to make both ends meet but with frugal life and simple tastes she seemed like one of those who live on some little pension away from the eyes of the world.

As this old lady reached the huddled figure in the doorway playing on the squeaky accordion, she stopped and her sweet, old face grew sad and with a little, black-bordered handkerchief she wiped away a tear from under her glasses. "You, poor, dear soul!" she exclaimed, taking out her little pocketbook which contained only a few small coins, "I know how hard things must be for you, for the world has not been kind to me, either. Here, this is all I have to give, but, oh, how I wish that it were a hundred times more!"

The figure huddled in the doorway tried to smile, but tears came into her eyes, too, for she had learned the tragedy of life. The little old lady in black went happily along, smiling through her tears at the pleasure her gift had given her, and no doubt went without the things she needed as a sacrifice for the little offering she had made. It was not the first time this had happened; the lonely woman in the doorway had witnessed it many times.

This is one of the little tragedies that is played out so many times in life. The rich and the thoughtless go their way, each living for himself, while only the poor it seems have learned to help the poor, only the suffering ones have reached the point where they know how to share one with the other.

In those darkened places where the down and outer huddle together, we find more brotherhood by far than in the homes of riches. Some broken figure, aged and gray, itself standing on the brink of dissolution, will gladly share its crust with another, some life broken with sorrow will enfold another suffering one within its arms and try to bring peace to another breaking heart when its own has long since died.

Is not this in truth a tragedy, yet a divinely sweet symbol of the soul of man? Only those who have walked the silent ways know the joy of sharing, and so as we watch the beggars on the street, we find that it is nearly always the poor who give to them of the little which they have which often leaves them poorer than the one they serve. Here we see again the Master's face as it shines forth from the souls of those who have but little.

If the Master came today into this world and stood on the street corner begging for the soul of men, it would be the poor and the suffering alone who would feel the depth of His message. It would only be those who have not who would long to give while those who have plenty only wish to receive.

So, the little old lady still plays the old accordion in the open doorway. She knows something that it takes many years to discover, and yet life is much sweeter and more beautiful when we realize how sorrow softens the heart, how poverty broadens the soul, and how true brotherhood rises among those who are down and out.

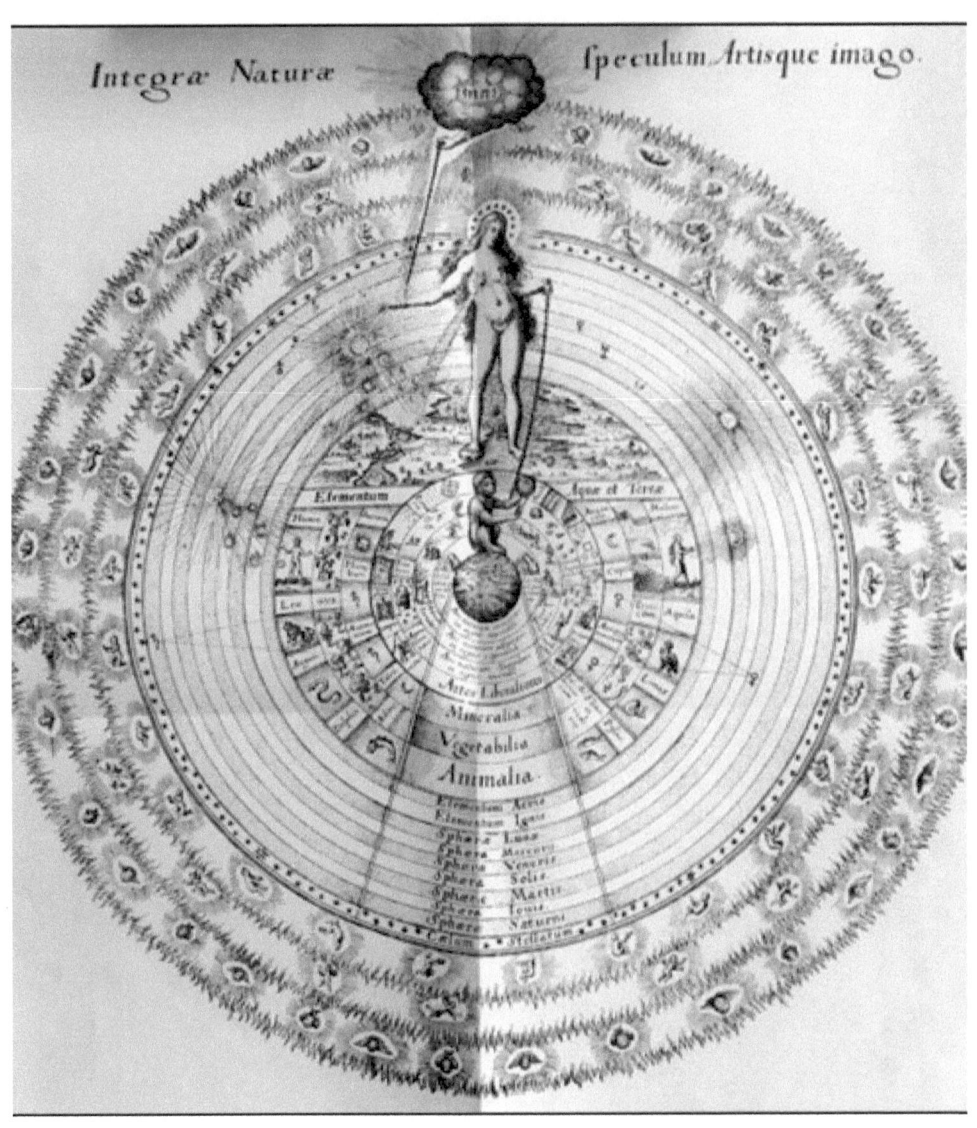

JULY 1923

MID NATURE'S CHARMS

By an Inmate of Folsom Prison

As down the open road I go
A thousand things are dear;
A boon companionship I know
In all I see and hear.
My love is as the buxom wind,
I taste the breath of flowers,
To me the whispering leaves are kind
And sweet the swaying flowers.
Contented kind turn friendly eyes
That know me as I pass,
I find a welcome in the skies,
A calling in the grass.
A kinship deeper than of blood
Holds me to ties of earth,
As now their source is understood
The rankest weeds have worth.
The tendrils growing by the spring
Tempt me to share their drink,
And 'mid the forests shadowy
Birds tell me what they think.
I have not glimpsed the wide world over
To scorn one thing as mean,
For beauty charms me all the more
The deeper I have seen.
And I rejoice in everything
that stirs my throbbing heart,
By myriad rampant whispering
To lofty thoughts impart.
On mountain-tops, 'mid prairies sweep,
And o'er the rolling sea,
These friendly comrades vigil keep
And guide me tenderly.

EDITORIAL

MENTAL HAZARDS VS. HEREDITARY FAILURES

SINCE the beginning of time man has leaned. It seems part of his nature to drape himself upon something or someone. In the beginning he leaned on the Lord, then he leaned on his relatives, and after many ages of evolution he finally learned to balance himself gracefully against his own spinal column.

The world is so large that it would seem man could live in his own little plot without implicating others in the various phases of his growth. But this he is not able to do and all through the ages he lives not either for himself, by himself, or with himself, but is eternally involving others in the complexities of his expression. He creates a very personal God to look after him and an even more personal Devil to blame for all the misfortunes of his life. In other words, he surrounds himself with a series of self-created and mental hazards and scares himself to death with bugaboos of his own making. These bugaboos are many-fold in their expression, differing with the stages of development reached by the temperament creating them, and the more highly evolved the individual, the more spiritual and wonderful, complex and intricate, seemingly, is the bugaboo that he creates, until finally when he becomes proficient it is very difficult to differentiate between nature herself and man-made hazards which sometimes are so perfect that they will deceive the elect.

Of all the mental hazards which people serve, that strange, weird figure known as the Past is probably the greatest. Somewhere concealed in the family closet is this grinning skeleton which is the dowry bestowed by ancestry upon ensuing generations. A person without a past nowadays is like a servant without a reference, and little by little man is making ever worse pasts out of promising presents and unawaken futures. This grinning and rattling skeleton is now pedigreed and distinguished by being termed the Family Tree, and azure shields on gold backgrounds, et cetera, or a fistful of watercress, form the family coat of arms. Very few people will admit that they haven't got one of these peculiar creatures snuggled away in the family vault where every few minutes it points bony fingers at the next generation and whispers that not living creatures, but mental concoctions of diseased intellects are to rule each generation of the world.

In spite of the fact that we are living in a democratic age, most of our families are nourishing somewhere in their conservatories a family tree with the same love and sincerity that one of our tenement inhabitants might guard the solitary rubber plant on the windowsill. In the majority of cases, this family tree is a weird and wonderful piece of horticulture and like many of the Burbank varieties carries more than one kind of fruit on a single stem. Often, we find lemons and prunes growing side by side with some luscious, rosy-cheeked apple, all nourished upon the single trunk of that family tree. Only in the human variety the luscious apple was Uncle Joshua who made five million out of shoe-eyelets while the lemon was Aunt Samanthy who married below her social position when she eloped with the gardener.

So, the family tree grows on and on until at the very peak of this rather eccentric plant with its exotic fragrance, John Doe is born as a glorious orchid bringing with him into the world of affairs a strange combination of mysticheterogeneties. According to proud and doting parents, he is something as follows: He was born bald just like his great grandfather who was scalped by the Cherokee Indians; his bleared eyes came from his mother's side of the house where his great grandmother's sister-in-law went blind at the tender age of 103; he has a peculiar shaped face, has John Doe-his jaw is a little on one side-he inherited that peculiarity from his uncle who had his own jaw smashed while fighting Moorish pirates. His big mouth he inherited from his grandmother, who talked a great deal, while his high cheek bones came from his great granduncle's brother, who married an Indian squaw. From the very start in life John was heavy, the same as his father's cousin, while he learned profanity at a tender age, the same as his great-granduncle's nephew who fought in the Civil War. He inherited the color of his hair from his mother, the shape of his teeth from his godfather; the size of his ears from the minister who baptized him and his blurred complexion from his eleventh cousin. In other words when we gaze upon John Doe, we behold Joseph's coat of many colors and a grand composite coadunation of hectic botany. And there he nestles amid the branches of the family tree, predestined and foreordained since the beginning of the world to be bowlegged because his grandfather rode horseback.

After he has been raised in this environment for a few years, his own little mind starts working, and he soon joins that great line of mystic shadow-shapes that bow with humble reverence before the molding scarecrow of antiquity. And in a short time, he really believes that his grandsires have measured the possibilities of his worth and that he will never be anything because an unkind fate placed him in a generation of failures and because his family crest boasts only ne'er-do wells. He soon believes that the mean traits of his temperament are perfectly natural and desirable because that temperament belongs to the heraldry of his house and soon, he is listed as just another little nut hanging on the family tree.

We very often hear this as we go through life: "No, I can't help it. I realize I have a mean disposition, but I inherited it from my mother. You should have seen the way she used to bend rolling pins and lead pipes around papa's fourth cervical. It's an inherited trait and there's not much use in trying to do anything with it." This mental frame is the incubator which hatches forth one after another the mental hazards and pedigreed non-entities which rule our lives after we once abdicate in their favor.

It is for no other reason than this: At the present time there are many people wandering through life on reputations or who are considered great, strong, and noble because their aunt's sister had a husband who wore epaulets. Then, of course, we must not forget the titles which come down with the family tree. Anyone who has had that experience socially knows what it means to be acquainted with a count or a duke or a lord somebody and with what zealous care these titles are re-silvered and nickeled for the express benefit of each new generation, when in many cases the inheritance consists of a title, scrofula, and bad bills.

Take the average individual and show him his weak points and he will lead you into the conservatory and there protected by a wonderful glass domicile stands the hereditary elm, and he will in a perfectly serious tone and an earnestness excruciating explain to you exactly which branch was cracked when he came along. You tell him he is a liar; he will admit it freely but will explain with perfect gravity that he can't help it, and he will point out a raisin dangling on the family tree that was a Har also and who wished his failing upon him about three hundred years before the death of Cromwell. If you tell him he is dissipated, he will immediately reach into the foliage of said tree and pull you out of a wild cherry that came over in the Mayflower from whom he inherited his rakish temperament. If you tell him he is sour, he will point to the glorious yellow lemon on the family crest and explain to you that there was someone in his heredity responsible for it. If he is a failure, he will point out certain qualities in the prune that grows amid the shadows of the self-perpetuating elm whose mental qualities were productive of failure in the nth generation.

Slowly, there dawns upon our minds the realization of a fundamental truth. The family tree is the greatest of all excuses for humanity's faults and people who are too weak, too silly, and too hopelessly lacking in backbone to do anything themselves are continually blaming their ancestry for their own inherent weaknesses. It is very often the case that people who do not have family trees, or rather who do not know about them, are often far more successful than the offspring of generations, or shall we say degenerations, of admirals, marshals, and Lord Whatnots. The fact slowly impresses itself upon our consciousness that failures are individual, self-sustained combinations of intricate mechanisms that would never have been successes under any other conditions.

The only cause of failure in a family tree is the mental hazard of this lonely elm upon which hangs suspended anywhere from one to a hundred generations of deceased ancestors who have gone to their happy rest and are not in any way worried over the work of implanting their qualities in their already suffering descendants. There is nothing in the family tree, but fossilized concepts given power by those who believe in them. If these past generations were alive, they might cause success or failure but as dead they can only affect dead ones and those who allow the dead to run their lives, are themselves listed with the deceased.

Any living creature may be, if he so acts and lives, the first success in his family regardless of the wizened appearance of the family crest or the drooping attributes of miscellaneous progenitors. It is also true that those who do not strive to live up to their best can, in a few short hours disgrace the noblest heraldry that the world has ever known. Successes in this world are the ones who do things, who labor to master environments if they are evil or to be worthy of them if they are good, realizing that all great things rise out of effort. Therefore, the worse the family tree, the greater the opportunity for the individual to shine out as an illustrious denial of his inherited debits.

Then we have another type. They are the ones who while unhampered by ancestry and unpolluted by blue blood have gradually become failures through inherent qualities and mental reactions during their own lives. This type we generally list under the style of "Type B". Their slogan is, "If you'd been through what I've been through, you wouldn't be anything either, or with variations something like this. "If I hadn't married so and so, I wouldn't be what I am now," or else, "I never had a chance." There are several sub-varieties of this type as follows: "I always have had tough luck." Also, "If your family treated you the way mine treated me and cheated you out of everything you had you wouldn't talk either." And then the grand closing hymn, "It's my hard life, dearie, that's done it!" These are sour apples grown and developed upon their own tree without the overshadowing presence of heredity, for such examples as these need no ancestry to produce failure, they are self-containing.

There are a large number of people who do not seem to realize that the harder you are thrown down the higher you bounce, but they spend the last sixty-five years of life in a spiritual wheelchair because they slipped on a banana-peel when they were young. Once having made a mistake and having had a beware label hung on the heredity elm alongside of them, they feel that they are ruined forever and ever, amen, and believe it is their God-appointed duty to spend the remaining scores of their lives putting the capping-stone on the general ruin.

People who live in the past and like Lot's wife look back eternally upon the things they did in '64 or the scrape they got mixed up in '83 will never get anywhere mentally, physically, or spiritually. The thing for these people to do is to remember the lesson, forget the incident and keep plugging in, realizing that if they had never made a mistake, they could never enjoy the privilege of doing better.

Then there is another type, "Grade C," who believe that they have been elected by the Most High and chosen by the Divine One to be the eternal brunt of His ill humor. There are thousands who honestly express themselves as believing that the Lord had a grouchy fit on when He made them and that He has been down on them ever since. They go through life manifesting the incarnated essence of concentrated gloom, dissolution, and despair, for no other reason on earth than that they firmly believe God has it in for them, therefore what's the use in trying, anyhow, It is difficult to imagine what an awful feeling it must be to have God down on you and to know that the All-loving, all-wise, and kind Father has sent seventy-seven deputations of demons with matrimonial problems, financial worries, kidney trouble, sour stomach, gloomy religion, and general indisposition to prod you continually with pitchforks of incessant catastrophe for no other reason at all than that you happen to be a blonde when the Lord likes brunettes. Yes, this exhibit is quite common and those people who believe that stomach trouble is the vengeance of the Lord for missing church and that falling arches have been sent to man to teach him contrition of spirit or simplicity of soul are in a class all by themselves.

In other words, a large percentage of our population are failures, but lamentably, few of them believe that they have personally done anything to deserve it. They are all suffering from hereditary ailments, counting either their family tree or their God as the source. There are few who are strong enough to stand up before the world and honestly say that they are the one and only cause of their shortcomings, that regardless of heredity or environment they can be successful when they will live in such a way that it is possible for them to secure balance. A family tree is a pedigreed non-entity which only affects those who believe in it. Past mistakes are only the seed grounds of future successes and the idea of God's wrath which He showers upon us as brimstone and sackcloth is the greatest, most honored, and revered bunkum that the human race lists in its category of superstitions.

Man is not a failure until he makes himself one, as no granduncle can do it for him. So long as he goes through life with a prickly disposition because his grandfather owned a cactus farm, he will be listed with the world's genuine failures, self-ordained and self-perpetuating. Great souls rise over adversity and use it as a steppingstone to heights above, while weak backbones bend beneath the load, blaming the Lord for the weight of the material which He has given them to build their temple.

So let us go out with Paris Green and a sprayer and set to work on the family tree, effectively destroying the insects, bugs, grubs, et cetera, that are nestling in its branches and used by mortals as excuses for bug like tendencies and wormlike consciousness in their daily lives.

If there is any person, creed, or religion that in your haste or thoughtlessness you look down upon or dislike, it is there that you must look for the help and development that you need. It is the plan of the Great Ones to show those on our plane of existence the great doctrine of universal brotherhood, they often teach this by sending the truths and knowledge that we need to us through those whom we dislike, and this great thought may be safely kept in mind in all stages of human development.

A doctrine that is based upon a personality dies with that personality, while a teaching based upon principle is eternal.

The veil of form that conceals the face of God can only be cut by the sword of enlightened spirit.

Truth cannot be bought or sold but it is the birthright of all who will live in harmony with it.

The emanation body functions by means of air while the physical body develops through food. The more one eats, the less one breathes; the less air, the more waste there is in the body. Science states that the average individual breathes one-third as much air as he should and eats about three times as much as he should. The result is disintegration and crystallization and general shortening of life.

Evil is misplaced energy; it is the right thing in the wrong place. Whenever energy is misdirected, it tears down something, be this misdirection mental, spiritual, or physical. Laziness and ignorance are the causes of misapplication of energy, and we know that misdirected energy is the cause of all our misfortunes.

The secret of youth is oxygenation, and the secret of death is carbonization. Misdirected and wasted energy destroys all things.

THE LAST OF THE SHAMEN
Dedicated to the Memory of a Dying People

THE majority of people know little if anything of the American Indian, of his ideals, his hopes, and his fears, for there are few indeed who can pierce the stoic attitude of these people who while they are fast dying still preserve in the majority of cases the dignity and self-control which mark the ancient races.

I was raised in an Indian country and from early childhood mingled more or less with these strange, broken people, now scattered remnants of what was once been the most powerful of all races. There is something very wonderful and fascinating in the study of the Indian and I must say that I have always liked them. An invisible cord, a mystic bond, drew me even in my childhood to these wandering nomads, and I spent many years in the study of them. I lived not far from one of the greatest of the American Indian reservations and have been with them many times, and maybe I am just a little liked by them too. I have seen young braves dashing madly on half broken bronchos and Indian ponies down the main street of the town, covered from head to foot with yellow ochre or green and blue aniline dye, shouting and screaming their war cries in truly terrible yet wonderfully fascinating ways. I have stood beside tall, blanketed figures in the years that are past as in the drugstores they spent the money gained from horse selling and cattle raising for various colored pigments with which to smear their being. I have stood on the street corner where the squaws sat, surrounded by pottery and bead work fashioned by their skillful fingers, crying out the value of their wares or cooing cradle songs to the little papooses fastened by thongs to their beds of wood.

They are now but a broken people, these red men of the plains, and few there are who care much about them, few there are who concern themselves as to the fate of the Indian. Nor can you blame them, for everyone does not know the beauty, the sweetness, and the deep mysticism of their ancient but now broken ideals. Every race, like every individual, plays its part in the great plan and its work done vanishes from the light of men. In his soul the Indian knows that the path of his race is run, and while his heart is sad still the voice within whispers and the old brave knows that the Great Spirit is calling his children home from the corners of creation, and calmly and serenely the aged warrior, philosopher, or stateman gathers the folds of his blanket around him and walks along that apparently endless way that leads to Manitou the Mighty.

Of course, I did not always feel as I do now, for I did not always understand the Red Man as I did after I met Uncle Joe. It was in a small town in the western states, where the main event of the day was the passing of the Southern Pacific, that I met probably the strangest Indian in America, yes, in the world. He always reminded me of that wonderful character created by Eugene Sue in "The Wandering Jew," for it honestly seemed that this Indian had lived forever. Nobody knew where Uncle Joe came from, but some of the old-timers remarked that they guessed God made him with the country, nor did they realize how true those words were. Everybody agreed that he was over a hundred, but nobody seemed to know just how much over, and he never answered personal questions, and when you asked him, he would only grunt and wrap his blanket more closely about his face.

There were very few people who were friendly with Uncle Joe, for he was a strange, lonely wanderer who belonged hundreds of years back when the Red Man was in his glory. He still wore the picturesque garb of his people, but he was very different from the Indian, and although his face was wrinkled and copper colored, his heart was of pure gold.

He was no fool either, was Uncle Joe, nor was he lacking in education, for he spoke better English than the white men who scorned him. It seemed he had traveled widely, also, for he could tell you of distant countries and he spoke a dozen or more foreign languages. A polished gentleman in temperament and nature, he seemed a strange misfit among a rabble of half breeds. Some said he was a great chief, others that he was the medicine man for a once mighty people, while the eternally suspicious ones whispered that he was a secret agent for the government. But when it came right down to it, they all admitted that they did not know anything about Uncle Joe.

Every few weeks he would mount his little Indian pony and head out all alone into the broken and rocky desert filled with broken mesas and shapeless crags which lay to the south of the town. Everyone used to wonder where he went and try to follow him. They would get just so far, however, each time and then he would vanish as though the earth had swallowed him up and no one ever found the secret which Uncle Joe guarded somewhere out among the painted rocks.

I lived in the little town many months studying Indians and listening to the dinner bell when the trains pulled in, and my love and admiration for the strange wandering Red Man must have been felt by Uncle Joe for he became very friendly with me and we had many talks on the future of the Red Man, his history, his government, and his philosophy. Uncle Joe was no ordinary Indian, as I have said before, but a real scientist and philosopher whose knowledge and shrewdness of mind won my admiration from our first meeting.

I became, in the course of about three years, his closest companion, for I was with him nearly all the time except when he would go out into the desert, then he would say, "I go now into the hills. Someday I shall take you with me, but not now." In a short time, he would return and then, for many weeks, we would be together again. So, the time passed, and I learned much of the history of the Red Man, his secret customs, his religion, and his great ideals. Uncle Joe would sigh as he told me of the dead ambitions of his people and now and then a tear would steal softly down his cheek, as he spoke of the way of the Great Spirit and of the gods who had come to care for and instruct his people.

One day as the third year of our acquaintance was drawing to a close, Uncle Joe laid his hand on my shoulder and his great black eyes seemed to look into my very soul, "I am going out into the desert", he said, "and I shall never come back again, for my gods have called me and my father's fathers have whispered to me in the night". In all the years that have passed I have never taken anyone with me on this trip, but today my gods have spoken and said that one at least of the coming race should know the secret of my dying people. So, if you will go with me out into the desert, you may, and there you will know the reason why Uncle Joe has been here all these years and why no man has ever followed him."

I jumped at the opportunity for I knew that there was some great secret that the old Indian had been guarding all these lonely years, and so the next morning we started out together on two little pinto ponies in the direction of the broken ground which lay to the South.

As we rode along, Uncle Joe told me some wonderful things about the Indians. Some of them I am not allowed to tell, but others! May relate. He told me that among the Red Men was a mystic body who, for thousands of years, had kept the records of these wandering people. Little was known concerning them, they were hidden from even the Indians themselves, for they were a small body appointed by the Great Spirit to labor with his people. This little band of Sacred Ones had come out from the silent East where the rising sun rose, they came from a wondrous city of shining lights that had vanished forever beneath the waters of the mighty ocean. They were the priests of Malkedek, the priest kings of the ancient Red Men, Arrayea in robes of birds' feathers and shining gold, possessors of the wealth of emperors and the wisdom of gods. These strange masters had brought out of the silent East the knowledge of the Great Spirit and had formed the Red Man into seven great nations like the planets in the heavens. For thousands of years these wise men had labored with the Indian who before that time had been a straying, savage race, dwelling on the outskirts of a more ancient civilization. They had brought with them along the path of the sunbeam the great serpent of wisdom and had guarded the Red Man's destiny all through the years of his development. But now the Red Man's work was done, the Manu was calling his people, and the Great Spirit had given to his sons the work of gathering in his broken tribes like the harvester gathers in his wheat.

I listened while the old man spoke. It was all very wonderful to me to hear such words as these from the mouth of one whom the world called a savage, yet I realized, alas, more plainly than ever that the world has little power to judge who its philosophers are.

We had been riding for some time and slowly the broken stones rose up about us, bearing the marks of water on their roughhewn sides, showing that once a mighty ocean had carved them by its ebb and flow. But now all was dry and dead and here and there the whitened bones of some animal showed that, alas, water was but a memory of the past. We were on a tiny trail that wound in and out among the reddish rocks and shifting sands.

Suddenly before us rose a mighty pinnacle of sandstone and the twisting trail seemed to end at its base. The aged Indian stopped, raised his hand, and muttered a few words in his strange, guttural language, at the same time making the mark of the cross upon his forehead. As he did so the rocks dissolved and a gateway appeared in the mighty sandstone mountain, and motioning me to enter the mystic arch Uncle Joe followed me and darkness surrounded us, for as we entered the rocky door closed behind us leaving no mark upon the outer wall.

"For many hundreds of years," whispered my companion, "this rocky cavern has remained unknown to the white man, and it always will for in it is buried the lost people, and there are few who know the mysteries of the Red Man. Even the young brave growing up has forgotten and will never think again of the power of his sires."

I remained spellbound at the strange miracle for I had never believed in supernatural things up to that time, but as we rode slowly along in the gloom a strange feeling of awe and reverence came over me for my companion.

"Who are you" I asked, "who have these strange powers and know so much of these ancient people?" My guide gave no answer, but we continued on through the gloom until we finally came out into the light on a beautiful little plateau way up on the side or a mighty mesa.

Here the Indian dismounted and I followed suit, and we stood together overlooking a grand expanse of rolling and broken country which stretched out to the distant mountains a mass of brown and yellow sand in strange relief against the glorious blue of the summer sky.

The old Indian waved his hand, "Behold the land of the Red Men, now a broken desert. Water alone made this a fertile land, and the waters of life pouring out from the heart of the Great Spirit alone made the Red Men a great race. No longer the waters come forth, for the work of the Red Man is done and soon he will be as dead and broken as the desert which stretches before you. But come, my son, child of another person, you are the first white man who has ever lived to enter the presence of the Red Man's god."

Taking me by the hand, Uncle Joe led me to a small opening in the side of the cliff, just a narrow slit which led into unknown depths. I passed in and the Indian followed me, and after going some hundred feet into the mountain the crevice broadened out and became a great room dimly lighted by a blazing fire of mighty logs. Of living inmates, there was no sign, but the whole room was filled with ghastly figures. In a great circle sat a row of mummies robed from head to foot in the grandeur of the Red Man, preserved against decay in that subtle atmosphere by some force unknown. Twelve of them sat cross-legged upon the floor and in the center of this ghastly circle was a great throne before which burned the fire of never consuming grandeur. The great throne was empty and seemed of solid gold with a glorious sun globe and the thunder bird carved upon its back.

The aged man pointed around the ghastly circle. "These, my son, are the Chiefs of the Red Men. They were the last of the line of priest kings who dwelt here and who came out of the land of the sky-blue waters. One by one, they have passed beyond to the land of their ancestors. Each time one of these Great Ones died the hand of Manitou was cut off from a race of the Red Men. One after another they have been carried here and in the heart of this mountain of red sandstone they lay, mute testimony of faithfulness to the end. They were the Order of Malkedek, the Priest Sachems of the roving nomads of the world. Here you see all that is left of them, my son. Their spirits have returned to the Great Father for their work is done. Their children cry in the wilderness for the Manu has called them and one by one they join that silent throng, passing over to the Blessed Isle. No longer can the hand of the gods guide them, for their work is done; one by one they are gathered in and taken over to another shore where some day they will come forth again a mighty people."

The old Indian leaned heavily on my arm as he was talking and slowly, we went out again into the sunshine of the day. The Red Man sat down upon the ground on the edge of the cliff and there we talked for many hours, and he told me the glories of his dying people and begged that someday I would tell the world of the wonderful labors of his race. Slowly the shades of evening fell and the short purple twilight that divides the day from the desert night hung over the plains and prairies and the broken desert which stretched out before us. The Evening Star rose a glorious light in the heavens and the whole world seemed to rest safe where here and there. The howl of a coyote broke the eternal silence.

The old Indian pointed unto the gathering clouds, whispering, "Look!" As I did so a great procession seemed to form out of the mist and crossing the sky in an endless train they vanished where the last dull gleams marked the setting sun.

"They are the dying race," whispered my companion, and I am one of them. Each night as I sit alone or wander in the desert, I can see my people passing slowly by, one after the other. Long since I have buried my race and they're out in the desert, a few broken sticks alone mark their resting place. No longer does the smoke rise from their peaceful tents, no longer do the white wigwams dot the plain, never again shall the Red Man hunt the bison, no more shall he rise at sunrise on the mountain peak to worship the Great Spirit. See them, my son, see them? Chief and priest, brave and squaw, are passing on in an endless file to the home of the gods. Just a few short years and they will be no more. The hand of the gods feeds them no longer, their work is done. Why should they stay?

Remember, my son, they go not like slinking coyotes in the night, like cowards crawling away from the field of battle, they go like kings and emperors, for they know that their work is done. They go not as failures to the chastisement of their gods, but as those who have finished claiming their rewards. The white man will never know the Red Man, for the white race has made him a stranger in the land of his birth, a nameless vagabond in the beautiful world created for him. But it is well. For as today the Red Man sinks away into the eternal night, so shall the white man, when his day is done, drop silently to rest."

All the while he was speaking, the endless procession swept across the sky. Mighty chieftains in robes of wampum and war bonnets of eagle feathers, braves on desert ponies, squaws and children, medicine men with the heads of buffalos, and priests with their feathered staffs, -a ghostly file of specters passed on in triumphant march, all with heads up, eyes to the front, and with a dignity and regal grandeur which bespoke a strange pathos, yet a sweet and masterly understanding.

The old Indian beside me gazed longingly at the passing throng and pointed upward to the stars, "Look, my son, my peoples' campfires are burning in the heavens!"

I followed his finger with my eyes and there unrolled to me in the sky millions of little campfires stretched out as far as the eye could see, millions of little tepees flowing in the ethers, and the dull murmur as of reverent prayer. "That, my son," whispered the old Indian, "is the bivouac of the dead. I can see them every night and as the shades of evening fall the braves dash across the sky hunting the buffalo or float in their beautiful canoes down the rivers of stars. Still again through the night there comes to me the plaintive wail of the moonlight as the Indian youth plays his love tunes, the smoke of the signals on the hills, and the sound of the ancient war drum. Once again, the great braves gather from all their peoples to listen to the words of their Chieftains. It is all gone, now, my son, but still, it lives in the world of spirit, and there it is eternal. And I am old for I have lived since the Red Man was born, I was with him in the days of his youth, I was with him in the years of his glory, and one by one I have laid their wise to rest. From the mighty land of the Sioux, from the tribes of the Algonquians, from the Muskhogean and the wandering Iroquois, even to the distant Shoshoneans, I am known. Each time that one of the Great Ones has died, it is I who in the silence of the night have walked from mountain top to mountain top with his body in my arms. I have brought him here to the cave of the sandstone mountain in whose darkness my secret shall be locked forever, and never until the time when Manitou the Mighty shall roll away these mountains shall the twelve priests of Malkedek be found, for no white man shall desecrate them, no curious eyes shall pierce this darkness, no heathen laugh shall awaken their slumbers, no vandalizing grave-robbers shall in the name of science disturb their resting-place. They may search through the seven stars, but they will never find the secret of the Red Man for as he passes silently into the Great Beyond, he carries with him the truths of his creation.

"The years draw nigh when the end is at hand. I know, for I am the Spirit of the Red Man. None know where I came from, for I came not-I am. None know where I shall go for, I go not-I am. Each of my red brothers who is laid to rest knows me. I feel his going, and a drop of my own soul joins with him, a cloudy phantom of the night. One by one they pahimaway, their young braves live other lives, and the Red Man is forgotten. At last, the twelve have come, for in the silence of the night I brought the last. My people shall wander for a little while with man but their spirit is gone, gone back across the great waters to the Father, to wait until the appointed day when they shall come forth again on other wheels and in another race. The spirit of the white man rules the Red Man now and we bow before another god. It is well, for all things work for the Great Spirit and the Father of Fathers whose home is by the Great Waters where He watches the tiny grains of sand that dash upon the seashore. But the Order of Malkedek is no more. A few scattered seekers there are among my people, but they wander among strange gods, for in this day is sealed forever the Order of the Kings."

The tears were rolling down my cheeks as he told his pathetic story and yet it is a grand story, the story which is written in the soul of every Red Man unless his lonely heart has found rest under the banner of the white king. At last, I spoke: "You say you have lived through all the ages of the Red Man?"

The old warrior nodded his head: "I have lived with them and, my son, I die with them, for they are my chosen people. I came to them with the glory of the rising sun, as it rises a ball of fire from the silent waters. I rode across the heavens with them as their great orb of day brought with it peace and power; I fought with them through the storms of winter and loved with them through the calm of summer; and now that the sun of the Red Man is sinking and the last of the vanishing race is being led silently to rest, I go with them. For the sun will rise some day in a distant land and there I shall be once more the Spirit of the Sunrise as now I am the over-brooding Angel of the Night. This, my son, is the message of the Red Man, a wondrous people who in the years that are past and now covered with the sands ruled the world, whose libraries and universities were the glory of creation, whose scientists were the marvels of the world, whose domed temples and mystic arches rose to the skies in every land of earth.

"Listen-a voice calls from within. It is the voice of the ages, for the pyramid builder speaks through me this night, the Pharaohs of Egypt are still alive in my blood, the phantom of the Manu, he, too, is with me, and in my soul is the heart of the dying Montezuma. Amid the Andes, through the mystic caverns of the Sierra Madres, among the broken everglades that border the shores of Okechobee, along the silent Nile where the great stone faces gaze peacefully through the night, I wander, and I am one with them. Yes, I am the Spirit of the Red Man. You ask who I am, that has been asked before.

Once I answered, "I am the Morning Star," later I answered, "I am the Star that shines with the glory of the Sun, still later as my people sank to rest, I was the Evening Star who whispered of an eternal peace. But now it is all different, for now I am the Spirit of the Night, and you may call me Silent Tongue for I speak and there are none who hear my words. I am the last of the Shamen, the last of the priest kings who came out of the lost Atlantis, I am the last who was ordained in the Temple of the Rising Sun, I am the last to bear the mark of the serpent."

As he spoke, he dropped his blanket and tore away the shirt which he wore and there upon his heart and twined upward across his chest was a strange serpent tattooed in vivid pigments upon his breast. The upturned head of the serpent coiled around his neck while its little beady eyes and forked tongue seemed to end where the upper cervical vertebrae join the skull.

"That is the mark of Malkedek," he whispered, "a mark no living man knows from one end of the world to the other. It is the mark of Quetzalcoatl, the mark of the feathered serpent who is dead forever. I am the last living thing to bear that mark which was placed there four million years ago."

I looked at the Indian for several seconds as if doubting his words, but one look into those terrible eyes of living fire and I realized I was not gazing at a man but a god.

"Wait a few minutes," he whispered, rising, "then come back into the cave, for there are other things that I would that you should know."

And he left me gazing out at that endless procession of figures that still crossed the skies silently as the stars in their course. I waited for several seconds and then a voice whispered to me to rise and enter the cave.

As I did so, I gave a startled cry. In the great throne surrounded by the twelve dead sat the aged Indian we knew as Uncle Joe! He was robed from head to foot in the garb of the Red Man, covered with jeweled ornaments and the finest wampum, his bronze body shone in the flickering light of an endless fire, and his war bonnet of eagle feathers reached nearly to the floor even from the height of the throne-chair. On his forehead was a cross of living gold and from his breast the snake gleamed forth in many colored lights while the feathered staff he carried as a scepter swayed slightly as his arms moved.

"My son, the last of the Red Men, the last of the priests, has been called to rest. They were my kingdom, and now I am an emperor of the dead. You shall see me no more, for I go to the Land of the Setting Sun, the Manitou has called me, and I obey. But remember, my son, there is no death. I go on to other works, to other lands, for I am the Spirit of the Red Man, and I can never die but will live on forever to guard the destinies of my people, who while their race is broken still live and will continue their endless procession until the day when the All-Father shall call home even Manitou the Mighty. Somewhere in the bonds of the infinite we shall meet again, you and I, for you, too, are chosen of your gods. When your race is drawn silently into the unknown, I shall ask the Manitou the privilege of being there that I may greet another person coming home. Behold the Order of Malkedek, the sacred brotherhood of the Red Men, the priest-kings of Atlantis, for they are now in session for the last time! The fire that has burned for ages will soon go out and with it vanishes the last of the Red Men. No more the world shall see me, for on this throne I sit awaiting the last of my people. Though years may pass before they gather, I shall be sitting here, surrounded by the dead, the emperor of a dying race."

"So, as you go out into the world and people ask you what has happened to Uncle Joe, just tell them he is waiting, waiting through the hours of the night, waiting with the jury of the dead, waiting for the last log to burn and his people to come home. In the ages that are past, I said that I would become strong and worthy to be given charge of the Red Man. In many worlds and for many ages, I have filled that trust, even until today. So here I shall wait in the cave for it is not long, already my spirit is calling me from somewhere over the distant hills, and even as I speak another Red Man's soul passes me on the way to rest. I wait as sometimes you must wait for the last whisper of the dying, and here I remain until the last one goes when I shall seal the book of my works and return to my Maker. Goodbye, you have heard my words. Never seek me again, for no man shall know where I have gone. But remember that my spirit waits in the darkness of this cave for the last of my people in the Mountain of Red Sandstone. And when they come I shall gather them lovingly to rest, and then with the spirit of the twelve priests of Malkedek I shall go before my Creator with the glory of a million emperors, the power of kings, and the light of the Rising Sun and the Serpent of Wisdom, whom the world knows only as Uncle Joe, the last of a dying race, the last of the Red Men."

THE BROTHERS OF THE SHINING ROB - II
CHAPTER TWO-Continued
The Mirror of Eternity

As I gazed at the light of the star which seemed a great way off in the deep haze of the magic mirror it twisted and turned and twinkled and there arose from the broken, confused mass of swirling clouds twelve mighty mountain tops that seemed to rival in height the lofty Himalayas in the heart of whose hills I now stood gazing into the deathless mirror of eternity.

As I watched, I saw the spark divide itself like a wondrous, bursting rocket and one tiny gleam rested on the top of each of the twelve lofty mountains where it glowed and shone like a ruby. Again, the question flashed into my mind and once more it seemed that the Hindu read my thoughts, for he answered in his soft, musical voice strangely stilled and quieted: "Those are the mountains of the twelve Fates. Far up on the crags and crests of their lofty heights in the sacred caves of the holy men live the twelve Compassionate Brothers of humanity, and to each of them is drawn part of that tiny spark which now you see. Hark! My son, for they are calling you in the soundless depths of your soul. They bid you follow them and climb those same rocky crags as it has been written by the hand of Brahma. Of all the world you have been chosen for, the gods know, and man must obey."

Again, I turned my eyes to the mirror and as I looked closely into its deep blue ether; I saw lonely figures standing amid the glaciers that crowned like silver locks at the peaks of the hills, twelve lonely forms from whose hearts gleamed forth the tiny stars like promises of the gods to all mankind. In strange contrast were these little lights of purest gold from the dull glow which rose upward from the base to break the darkness of eternal night that concealed forever the foot of these lofty hills. Far below were the flames of hate and that weird, broken world which my guide had told me was the land of the Lonely Ones.

A strange hush came over my being and I realized for the first time in a dull sort of way that there were things in life that before I had never known or understood, and in the depthless haze of that mystic frame, held between the golden fingers of the gods, a new world had been unfolded to me a world invisible to mortal men, the mystic world of the soul. Still, I am ashamed to say that I understood but little of that scene, and it was more with curiosity than reverence that I passed through that night which I shall remember to the last moment of eternity. But then the Compassionate One within myself was still unawakened, and it was only in the years that followed that my soul, mellowed and deepened by experience, fully realized the privilege that was mine that night when I stood in the Temple of the Caves with the ancient Hindu Master.

Slowly the scene in the great void changed and there unfolded before my eyes a broken, rock-strewn coast where dashing waves broke with a mournful sound along the winding seashore. Somewhere in my dreams I had heard that sighing, and the broken crashes of the surf had sounded out from the depths of my own heart. But now I was seeing for the first time the wilderness and the desolation that I often had felt. The dashing waves broke along a shoreline, high strewn with the wreckage of scattered ships. As far as the eye could see, the dashing and never-ceasing waters cast broken crafts upon the rocky shore where they were ground to pieces by the endless tide.

As I looked in the mirror, a file of lonely figures, their white robes blown by the gale, came like phantoms from the darkness and walked silently along the shore. They picked up the wreckage and seeming to whisper soft words to the broken timbers; they held them above their heads where the water-soaked and shattered wrecks were turned, it seemed, into wondrous birds that flew away with sweet songs or hovered around the heads of the lonely figures. There were twelve of these silent forms who passed like specters through the night, and finally walking out on the surface of the waves, which were stilled as they passed over them, followed by the shadowy file of birds created from the broken wreckage, they vanished in the gloom of a limitless horizon.

The mirror cleared again. All that remained was the deep blue haze, as boundless as eternity itself. I turned eagerly to my companion for a more complete explanation of the strange phenomena. In the gloom of the temple, he seemed to gleam and glow with a strange light and his robe appeared to be of shimmery gold and opal.

"What does this all mean?" I asked in amazement, staring at the great eyes of the Initiate.

"My son," answered the old man in the same sweet voice, "this rock-strewn shore is life, these broken crafts of wreckage are the souls of men, while the white-robed figures represent the tiny band of servers who have dedicated themselves and their lives to the salvation and redemption of their fellowmen, and with the love and power which is theirs they turn the broken wreckage into birds that with the life and truth which they have given may fly upward to the sun. Although you realize it not, you are one of this band. As they have sworn, so have you dedicated yourself to the salvation and regeneration of your brothers. You must be one who is to salvage the wreckage of despair and redeem the broken crafts of life. Although you know not your destiny, soon you will understand."

"You say that I have sworn and dedicated my life to some mystic end of which

I know nothing?" I asked in amazement.

"Yes, my son," answered the white-robed Brahman, "and yet, is this not true of all? Are not all living things working to an ultimate they can never comprehend? Yes, indeed, for none but Brahma knows the ways of Brahma, yet all must serve Him and walk the path that leads to Him. And only when beyond the shades of Nirvana man is one with Brahma will he know the end for which he came into being or the works for which his Master and Creator has ordained him. From childhood to youth, from youth to manhood, from manhood to old age, from old age to dissolution-this is the path of those who know not Brahma. But for those who have seen the light of His shining face the path is from life immortal to life immortal, with only this shell of not-being for a moment and then eternity forever. My son, mysterious are the ways of Brahma and yet those there are who have seen His face, who have listened to the words that dropped like pearls from the lips of the Creator, to rest like beads of dew on the lotus blossoms of the soul."

The old Hindu's eyes seemed to pierce the wall into the endless eternity of not-being and he whispered to me, "My son, may it be that you shall see the face of Brahma, that the shining light of His eyes shall rest upon you, that the lips of compassion shall speak to you. For when you have seen as I have seen, nought else is there to see, for what can human eyes reveal to man after he has beheld his Creator? For Brahma is all in all, to all, for all. If you hunger and have seen the eyes of Brahma, you are fed; if you are cold and his face has been unveiled you are warmed; if you are unclothed but have been enfolded in His light, you are garbed as the prince of men; if you are weary and have slept in His arms you have had rest; if you are lonely yet have felt His presence, then indeed are the multitudes with you; if you are ignorant and have been within His power, then is wisdom yours; if you are sad and have seen Him, then are you glad with the sadness of the divine. My son, seek ye for nothing but Brahma for all else is maya, illusion. When you have found Him, you have found all; when you have not found Him, you have nothing. Behold! All the love in the world is from the heart of Brahma; all the peace in the world is from the rest of Brahma; all truth is the word of Brahma; all light is the glory of His smile.

My son, for many long years, have I lived in the darkness of this cave and yet I am ever in the light, for I have seen Brahma. Though I am weak and old, I am young eternally, for the life of Brahma brings back the youth that is gone. The world knows me as the mouthpiece of the gods, a master of men; but I ask no glory for it cannot come to me from the plaudits of the world. All that I ask is to be one with my Creator. Walk you the way that I have walked until you too shall reach the footstool of Brahma, for behold, His ways are good, and His compassion is everlasting. He alone can open the eyes that are blind and the hearts that are cold. Serve Brahma and live, serve men and die. Labor for Brahma and have peace, labor for man, and have misery. Treasure up the things of the world and lose them, treasure up the pearls of Brahma and they are yours forever. In the days when these hills were not, Brahma was; in the days when these mountains shall be no more, still Brahma is. For all that is, is Brahma, all that can be poured from His lotus lips. When you are one with Brahma, you are one with eternity; when you are one with men, you are measured by time. If you will live as Brahma would then alone shall you be free from the wheel of birth and death and rest in Nirvana as one with that which is, yet is not, yet ever shall be. My son, I speak the words of Brahma, in the name of Brahma, for the glory of Brahma, for there is no other Father, no other God. Be glad to serve Him, for He is just; be glad to glorify Him, for He will ornament you with the jewels of immortality. Oh, that man might know Brahma and live! But come, look again, and I will show you how you have dedicated your being to Brahma and how again you are to anoint yourself upon His altar in the name of the living God, Om the Unknowable!"

Again, I gazed into the mystic mirror and this time, a new scene appeared there. It seemed like a great pin-wheel of light, which twisting and unrolling slowly became a great spiral. The spiral took shape and a great scroll appeared and on its mystic pages I saw a history unroll and a voice within whispered that it was mine.

My guide spoke again. "This is the memory of the Eternal One. That golden star who now knows himself as William Edmundson."

Slowly, the scroll ceased to spin, and a scene unfolded itself in the mystic haze of eternity. It was an ancient plane which stretched out to be lost in the blue sky. Far in the distance there rose great twisting towers of snake-like spirals which gleamed and glowed amid mighty domes and minarets that marked a city of the plains. It was a glorious sight, a shimmering city of many-colored lights, like some mirage of the desert.

"Behold the City of the Golden Gates!" murmured the Oriental as he laid one hand on my shoulder.

It seemed that I was passing across the mighty plains until at last with the rapidity of lightning I floated through its gilded gates and entered a strange, many-sided room, lighted by lamps of virgin oil in niches on the wall. But I was no longer myself as I know myself today. I was an old, gray-haired, bent man robed in blue and gold carrying in my hand a cross which I raised upward to shadowy forms that gazed down from above, great specters that whispered of the days when gods walked with men.

The Oriental spoke again. "Here in the sacred temple of the Lost Island you took your vows to the Compassionate Ones. You took your oath that your being was dedicated to the realization of a great ideal. Today you are fulfilling your vows and in the name of the gods I warn you, -stay not the wheels of the Infinite."

The scene grew dark and blinding flashes of lightning and thunder broke upon the air and a hideous roar swept over my senses. "The sinking of the Lost Island," murmured the voice beside my ear.

(To be continued)

There are two forms of clairvoyance: positive in the brain, negative in the solar plexus. Concentration upon the solar plexus is a step backward in evolution for the white races. The priests of Chaldea are said to have lived a thousand years in one body, but there is no doubt that they had learned how to make better use of their time, for the average individual wouldn't do any more in a thousand years than he does now if he had the chance of living.

The man who cannot see God in his brother will never find him anywhere else.

The prayer most acceptable unto the Lord is the daily life in accordance with the plan of being.

A quick temper is one of the greatest curses from which a student can suffer. If an occultist carries a chip on his shoulder, the laws of nature will knock it off.

JUST LONELY

FEW people realize the absolute loneliness which fills the heart of a large percentage of children. The little ones who come into the world are indeed strangers in a strange land, and the vehicles which they are seeking to build have not yet the power and consciousness that come in later life or should come. Indeed, in many cases we go through life without ever breaking down the wall of loneliness.

There is a great obligation confronting parents for most of them forget their own childhood, and interested in other things, absorbed in their own lives, they seem to be unaware of the soul agony which so often fills the heart of a child that is eternally seeking for love and protection.

While we hear the little one playing with the children, it seems to be happy, and yet often with the laughter and the smile the discerning eye sees a pathetic little look that tells of a lonely soul. As the years go by there is often built around the child a wall which not even the parent can pierce, for in many homes the parents know less about their children than the stranger on the street, for the comradeship, the understanding, the mutual love is lost, because the lonely child has forgotten how to make a confidant of them.

This generation is producing millions of lonely little souls to whom home means nothing but shelter for the body because self-centered and thoughtless parents have come to believe that because the child is young, it does not feel. How many lives are broken, how many romances fall to pieces, because the child has been so lonely that it sought just someone to talk to, someone to make a confidant of, when at home a stone wall seemed built around it.

A large number of children instead of loving and confiding in their parents either despise them or merely treat them with respect and regard in accordance with social obligations, and in the majority of cases it is because the parent has failed to plant the seeds of love and trust in the heart of the child.

This condition is becoming more acute every day, for the world is filled with young people who are divided from the bonds of home by lack of mutual understanding. This is often the result of the fact that during the years of childhood and youth when things were needed the parents were not there, when there was work to do that the child might be what it should be they shirked their duties and the child lost confidence.

There is nothing sadder in all the world than to find a little child who has lost confidence in its parents, and yet at the present time there are few homes where a child can have real confidence, for a sweet temperament cannot be raised on forgetfulness and the average child feels that it is in the way at home, so It goes out and one of two things is the result. Either its little heart is chilled forever, and it becomes self-centered, secretive, and often dishonest, or in its hunger for love, it suffers all its life.

At this day and age of the world, there are no more unhappy creatures in all the universe than children. Instead of being welcomed and their years of youth watched and guided, they are regarded from the very beginning as a nuisance and as something which stands between the parents and the gay pleasures of life. So slowly the child drifts into other company, mentally if not physically, and oftentimes it picks very poor associates, not because of criminal instinct or of malicious intent, but it went astray just because it was lonely.

This condition faces us as a problem far greater than we generally understand. Many youths go into the business world or leave home because there was no companionship there for them. Many young girls have married at immature ages to escape the loneliness of home and to find someone whom they thought would be a friend. Too often this choice is unwise, but in nearly every case it is the result of the fact that there is no love and compassion and brotherhood in the home.

The answer to the problem is this. The father and mother should not be the boss of the children. Children are not servants or slaves and when treated as such and ordered around like puppets, they either sulk away, determined someday to make a break or else their spirits are crushed, and they become useless chips of driftwood on the sea of life. No one likes a boss, children no more than the rest, and children who fear parents will never love them. Brotherhood must be born in the home where parents and children are tied together by the bond of mutual sympathy and understanding. Kindly and wisely, like brothers, parents must love and labor with their children. For many, a little one has gone away to weep alone when a scar has been made in the soul that will last to the end of time over the thoughtless cruelty of the parent or an unjust accusation.

It is harshness and fear which make dishonest children and promote lying, stealing, and even worse habits. It is the lack of the feeling of brotherhood between parent and child that makes young children keep secrets which may injure them all their lives, whereas if confidence has been built the wiser and more mature thoughts of the parent will save years of suffering. But the privilege of the parent to help the child is lost when that privilege is abused.

So we find thousands of children who are just lonely, who, while they are properly fed and clothed, are merely strangers boarding at home. This condition is the basis of a generation of lonely souls, broken and misunderstood, who crawl away to melancholia or else sell their souls for the sake of a kind word. There are few who realize the power that a parent has and there are still fewer who realize how that power is abused today, when there is coming into the world a generation of lonely children, great souls who will never be understood and always blamed for the lack of those very virtues which the parents should have stimulated.

As you read this article, there are many of you who will recognize how your own lives have been twisted and changed by loneliness in childhood and the fact that you never were understood, and this should be a divine incentive within the soul of every parent that when young hearts come to them, they shall be understood and not be just little strangers in a strange land -lonely and forgotten.

EXPLANATION OF LAST MONTH'S PLATE

THE folder plate which appeared in last month's issue of "The All-Seeing Eye" was reproduced from the rare work on "Occult Cosmogony" published in 1619 by Robert Fludd, the English mystic and alchemist. It represents a speculative explanation of the phenomena of nature and of life, and while space makes it impossible for us to give a complete interpretation of it, the student who will study and analyze it in the light of the principles of mysticism and occultism will find it an endless source of information, and through the study of it may gain tremendous analogical powers.

Briefly considered, the plate is threefold: spiritual, intellectual, and physical, as can be seen by the three grand divisions into which the globe is divided. The cloud at the top represents the Spirit of God, and, as the word or name Jehovah signifies, it represents the form-building power of God or that part which manifests in matter. The cloud represents the body of the Celestial Being whose vehicle is a globe and who materializes necessary organs from that globe, as is shown in the hand which appears on the plate.

In the center of the plate is the Earth which is connected to the superior creature floating in the cloud by means of the female figure which represents the Spirit of Nature, the Divine Mother of created things. The stars represent the celestial hierarchies in the brain of nature, while the lunar crescents symbolize the spirit of fecundity. The figure is standing with one foot upon the water and the other upon the land, for she represents the two lower elements of earth and water. She is chained 'twixt heaven and earth, dominion wielding, while the little monkey sitting on the globe represents the Adamic man in his coat of skins and the compass with which he is measuring symbolizes material limitations.

All the kingdoms of nature are symbolized with their respective elements, qualities, powers, arts, sciences, et cetera, in the inner of the three worlds, while in the central sphere we have the solar system with its suns and powers. This is symbolic of the solar and macrocosmic man of our solar system, while outside of this sphere, consisting of the planetary orbits, we find the stellar worlds which are the symbols of the other created universes of our chain. At this point the second sphere ends, and we find the three rings of fire flames, which are symbolical of the three grand creative principles and the powers of the three worlds of nature. The inner circle of flames represents the form-building powers; the second row, the mind-building powers; the third or outer row, the spirit-unfolding powers.

Examination will show that the little figures in these rings of flames differ. In the inner ring, they have no wings and are material; in the second row, they have bodies and wings and are therefore partly human, partly divine; in the outer circle they have wings but no bodies, symbolizing the fact that they are no longer connected with material things.

The whole plate is symbolical of the human body, the creation of a germ plasm, and the unfoldment of a universe, and each student will gain from the study of it just exactly what he has within himself. The only way in which a student can judge his own advancement is by taking such a plate as this and opening it before him, sit down and say, "What does this mean to me, and how will it help me to live better, think better, and more completely carry on the duties and responsibilities of life?" If the student will then apply his own knowledge to the various parts which he can comprehend, he will find explanations of things which before he never understood. That is the reason for symbolism; it forces the student to express himself. For that reason, we are not going into detail as to the full meaning of the plate, but the basic principles set down will enable the individual, if he will study it, meditate upon it, and apply the knowledge gained from daily experience, to use these ancient pictures as concentrating points by means of which he may measure his own limitations and breadth of knowledge.

Practically, the entire scheme of human evolution is shown in the picture as the Divine Life passed through the many-fold expressions of Nature, however, will be able to read the mystery it contains.

In this magazine, you will find another rare plate taken from the same source, which shows the creation of the universe and the coming of the elements. In next month's magazine we shall have a few words to say concerning it, but the purpose of placing these illustrations before you are not to explain them but to enable you to explain them yourselves.

OCCULT EUGENICS
Reprinted and Re-edited with notes and corrections from our classes of 1922

OCCULTISM is a very unusual study. Many people enter into it in the hope of being transported into mystic worlds where hooded figures and strange lights flit through somber ruins. They believe that they will gain strange powers and great riches and find a world of happiness overnight. This is very far from the truth, and the student will find as he goes along that occultism is not a doctrine of miracles but of Cause and Effect, not of shortcuts but of slow, ever-increasing development, not of romance and glamour, but of serious study and self-improvement; it means not only to delve into forgotten lore, but to consider with uncommon common-sense life and its many problems.

To the brave student, it offers the great incentive of justice and a sure reward. To the coward and those who seek to shirk the duties of life it stands a looming mystery, a great giant between them and the easy road to happiness and success for which they seek. Good or evil, depending upon the eyes that see it and the hands that apply it, but standing in spite of all, the Mystery School remains unmoved from the first great dawn of creation to the last falling shadows of a dissolving universe. It offers no incentive other than truth, no reward other than a greater power to help your fellowmen.

The occultist must take his occultism into his life, his works, and his ideals. One place alone is the source of the joys and sorrows of the world, and from the half-closed lips of that looming mystery which man knows as the Occult Wisdom there comes forth these words, "The Strength of a people depends upon the harmony, unity, and virtue of its homes."

The great problem of Eugenics faces the world at the present time as it never has before, because under it is listed the study of causes and the improvement of causes, and the world is slowly coming to the realization that everything we know as an effect is the result of unknown and unstudied causes. Man with his ever-higher ideals now realizes that the day has come when it is in his power to mold the world into what he wishes it to be, greater and more glorious than ever before, if he will mold causations and develop them as he should. Man is beginning to realize that he cannot grow roses on a thistle plant, neither can wisdom thrive on ignorance, but that by the natural law of attraction each plant that we know bears fruit according to its kind, and under the head of Eugenics man is studying to build only those conditions and causes which will produce constructive, elevating effects. Eugenics not only holds good in the building of physical forms but also in political, scientific, social, and religious body and soul building.

We are in every case the causes that will produce the effects, mental and physical, which shall mold the great Tomorrows as Yesterday is molding us, and it is our duty to our God, our brother, and ourselves to study and live by the knowledge we have gained more in harmony with the divine plan for man.

There are listed below twenty-five condensed statements for the consideration of students of Eugenics in its various forms. The proof of these statements can easily be found by anyone who will spend even a short time in the consideration of living problems. It is suggested that the student take them one at a time and see just to what extent they are true in the surroundings of his life. If he wishes to be an occultist, a mystic or even a healthy heathen, he should not only consider them but if he agrees with them practice them in his own life and among those with whom he comes in contact.

First. The intellectual, spiritual, and evolutionary progress of a race depends upon the ability of higher evolved egos to find proper vehicles of physical expression among the homes and parents of that race. At the present time, they are needed in the world as never before, but they can only come where they will find harmony and purity, knowledge and love. When these conditions express themselves as causes in our race, the effect will be power, growth, and balanced genius.

Second. In this world, like attracts like and the same is true of the ego seeking incarnation. It will come where it can receive the growth needed for its own spiritual extension. Therefore, ignorance draws ignorance, wisdom draws wisdom, squabbling draws squabbling, and the little ones drawn to the home of man today will sometime rule our world with the same powers which attracted them and with which we are surrounding their young lives.

Third. Inharmony in a home where a highly developed ego is striving to gather its new body for manifestation here invariably results in one of two things. Either the ego, the spirit, will withdraw from that family because it cannot stand the vibratory rates or else it will have the finer side of its nature and its usefulness here impeded or dwarfed. In both cases, the thoughtless parents are guilty in the eyes of the spiritual law of murder in the first degree.

Fourth. There is a very mistaken idea in the minds of many parents concerning the faculties of a child, mental and spiritual. During its younger life and approximately up to the age of majority, it is completely under the mental and spiritual supervision of the parent who is responsible to God and man nor the qualities which are implanted in the offspring.

Fifth. A child is born clairvoyant and remains so varying lengths of time under different conditions, usually until the soft spot in the crown of the head closes. This makes it possible for the child to feel things and see things which the parent does not realize. Children know what their parents are thinking and doing, even when they are apart. Therefore, it does no good to kiss the child goodnight very sweetly, tell it to love everybody and be good, and then go downstairs and have squabbles and disagreements such as occur in many homes, and believe that the child does not know and will not be affected by it.

Sixth. By example as well as by precept, children must be trained. If you tell a child to do a thing and you do something different, you must not be amazed that the child follows your example. We cannot lie to children and then expect them to be truthful. It is often a wonder how children have as much respect for their parents as they do, and it shows that the little one has in many cases a higher sense of justice than the parent. No parent has a right to blame a child and punish it for a fault the parent has himself until first of all he has sought to correct it in his own being.

Seventh. Not ignorance but a thorough understanding of nature's plan is the basis of all virtue, and the parent who has not given its child an understanding of life's problems has failed in its most sacred duty and lost its greatest opportunity for self-development.

Eighth. In the Orient there is a rule followed that should teach the western world a wonderful lesson. Life there is divided into three great divisions. In the first third of life, the ego is guarded and taught by its parents the duties of life; in the second third of the grown person raises his family and takes care of his parents, he also earns the funds to take care of his life and those who depend upon him; and in the last third he in his turn is taken care of by his children and allowed to study and meditate. This system cannot be applied in full in this country, it seems, but it has many good points to be considered.

Ninth. A parent should remember that children don't "just grow" but require attention all the way through childhood. In America at the present time no attention at all is paid to the average child, and it runs wild until it disconcerts the entire neighborhood, and then the father and mother finding that the child is impossible to try to spank good manners into it with failure as the usual result. At least seventy-five percent of parents use this system at the present time, then these same people wonder why no one likes their children and why the landlords prefer lap dogs in their apartments to the young hopefuls, or rather hopeless generation of today.

Tenth. While on the study of Eugenics, which means to be better born, or to have a more harmonious beginning, there are other children which we should consider as well as our visible families. Many millions of lives are evolving and depending upon us, about which the average individual knows absolutely nothing.

It has been estimated that inside the physical body of man alone there are living, developing, and evolving seven hundred and eighty-nine quintillion monads, each one of them n complete being made up of millions, yes billions, of still smaller beings. These depend upon the superior development of the human ego for wise and humane care. When we through thoughtlessness, indolence, or ignorance fail to properly supply and intelligently preserve these parts of ourselves we break one of the most important laws of natural Eugenics.

Eleventh. When we read the story in the Bible of the Last Supper, do we ever stop to think how it is being repeated every day and minute of our lives? Do you remember how the Master gave his disciples the bread and said, "This is my body broken for you?" Let us remember that the Christ Spirit, the principle of life, is in all these cells and that thousands, millions, of living things die daily that man may live. In the running down of the body, many tiny forms must give up their vehicles of expression. The food that we eat is the tiny shell that our younger brothers have taken hours, weeks, and years to build. We owe these little lives a great debt of gratitude and we have no right to abuse their confidence in us and Injure them by misapplying the principles of nature.

Twelfth. The smallest of lives has a God given right to a chance of development and greater expression in the world of forms. Those who aid in the giving of these opportunities help each in his own way the development of the Plan, and as we help others to express themselves, we gain greater ability to manifest our own latent qualities.

Thirteenth. One of the greatest mistakes that a parent can make is to overlook the health of a child or exert an undue influence over its growth on account of their own ideas concerning sickness and spirituality. While it is often possible through the power of will for the parent to master inharmony within, and while many believe that sickness is only a concept of the mind, this idea cannot be safely applied in dealing with children. Parents are directly or indirectly responsible for ninety percent of sickness among children, and large doses of common sense should be administered to the mother and father instead of drugging the child.

Fourteenth. A large percentage of the aches and pains of the human race come through the stomach and that which goes into it-sometimes through that which cannot get out of it. The adult must learn to take care of himself, but with the child, the parents must use a different course and teach their children how to live in a clean, practical way.

Fifteenth. It is the duty of every adult in the United States and in all other parts of the world to spend enough time in the study of self to learn how to prevent the causes of disease which later wreck his body, if he does not learn in younger life how to use common sense in taking care of himself. Moreover, people who do not know these things can never hope to bring them into the world or to raise healthy children.

Sixteenth. No one has the right to call himself a student of any line of higher philosophy, science, or religion, who does not understand the fundamental construction of his own being, mental; physical, and spiritual, and any teaching that promises spirituality, growth, or broadened consciousness that does not include these principles is not listed among the Wisdom Religions.

Seventeenth. It is said by those in a position to know that a large percentage of adults in the so-called civilized countries have the brain development of fifteen-year-old children. In many, it is much lower. This is undoubtedly the result of the fact that the ego coming into this world is forced to build its physical vehicles, including the brain, from the quality of material furnished by the parents. Therefore, it is up to the parents to build better bodies that the next generation may be greater mentally, spiritually and physically than the present one, for the children of today are the law-makers, teachers, and citizens of tomorrow. In this way, each generation is largely responsible for the next and many people at the present time are laying up terrible Karmic debts.

Eighteenth. It would seem that the world should know these simple principles of life and many people consider that work of this kind is too elementary for "spiritual students," yet the very persons who say this, and in fact nearly all of the occult students, while standing apparently on the tops of the mountains, are daily breaking practically every law in nature, and as they break them they tell the world, they have become so great that they no longer need them.

Nineteenth. If you read the daily papers, you will find that during the summer months, great numbers of children die. Few people realize how many babies pass out before they reach their first birthday. People pray to God to spare their children and say the Lord took the little ones from them, when in reality they kill them through ignorance, indolence, or indifference, and this at an age of the world when all the needed information is within the reach of everyone. There is no need for such ignorance, save that people do not care enough about life to learn how to live, and it is necessary for them to keep on dying to find out.

Twentieth. It is very important that we understand that the ego coming into life is not born full-fledged, but through a gradual process in which one by one the vehicles of consciousness take hold, until youth reach the age of majority when it comes into control of its vehicles. The danger points in the life of a child gather around the fourteenth year when the fire or emotion body begins to be felt. It is then that uncurbed by thought; the child is most subject to those mistakes which have ruined the lives of millions. It is during these periods that the greatest responsibility rests upon the parents, and it seems that at this time there are few willing to take the responsibility of giving the incoming egos the proper start in life.

Twenty-first. It is well for us to understand that occult Eugenics not only teaches that man must produce better bodies, but that he must give birth to better thoughts, emotions, and actions. These are children of our own being for which we are just as responsible as for physical, visible children. With his evil thoughts, man is breeding demons that will later pave his way with hardships and his world with suffering. In truth the children of his consciousness must be better born.

Twenty-second. Education is a very important consideration, and this must take a great place in the mind of the parent, for in order to educate children in the practical things of life the parents themselves must first have knowledge of them. When we come to consider that less than one in ten of American children receives a complete education, we are confronted with another very important matter that rests in the hands, directly and indirectly, of every adult in this country.

Twenty-third. It is also of importance to remember that education consists of drawing out the latent qualities within the child rather than in cramming the mind, which in later life will be forced to forget many of the things it has learned in order to be practical.

Twenty-fourth. Parents should remember that they both have responsibilities in the rearing of their children. In the majority of cases at the present time, each is trying to shift the responsibility onto the other. Another curse is now springing into families at a deadly rate of speed, and this is the old story of the favorite child. In almost every home, you will find children who are tolerated as necessary evils while another child is pushed forward, and all attention heaped upon it. A condition of this kind shows that the moral and spiritual development of such parents is far below the average scale for animals, and they are a disgrace to the human race. The unbalanced and, in many cases criminal actions of parents, if continued, will bring the destruction of our civilization.

Twenty-fifth. Young children are like parrots, they are the greatest mimics in the world. They only understand that which they can see, and somewhere either in their home or among their acquaintances will be found all the mean traits which they demonstrate. They act and live and talk the way they see the old folks do, so when little Johnny comes out in the yard and swears like a trooper, loses his temper, stamps around, and throws tin cans at the cat, it is merely a reflection of what he has seen someone else do. In other words, the baby and the youngster are the thermometer showing the temperature, mental, physical, and spiritual, of the parents, and the most powerful way of teaching a child is by example.

This may sound as though it were a terrible rehash of antiquated precepts. It is. The entire civilization of the world for millions of years has depended upon the understanding of these principles. Our farmers have spent years in developing extra fine hogs and in learning how to produce the greatest amount of corn to an acre.

In every line of business and enterprise, man is being taught efficiency except in the line, which gives him the right to live. The work must be done over again and again because ninety-nine out of a hundred people, if they know these things, show no symptoms of their knowledge. God must judge us by results. Read the daily newspapers and see if the world has passed the need of studying the practical problem of natural Eugenics.

Occultism does not tell man what to study or to what creed he should subscribe, but it takes him out and showing him things as they are tells him that his duty is to improve himself and his world in the best way that presents itself to him. "By their works shall ye know them." unfolding consciousness of man which becomes his guide in the distant places and makes possible his ascent into the dome-shaped skull which is indeed the temple of the gods.

A LETTER FROM THE BROTHERS
OF THE ROSE CROSS - II
The Magical Mountain of the Moon
(Continued)

In the May and June numbers of this magazine, we considered in part the symbolism of this remarkable letter said to come from the secret order of the Rosicrucians. It is a well-known fact that these Adepts and Initiates were modern adaptations of the ancient Hermetic mystics who flourished during the 16th, 17th, and 18th centuries in Central Europe as alchemists and philosophers by fire.

If you turn again to the plate in the May magazine, we shall briefly consider a further study of its symbolism. In the upper corners of the picture, we find the Sun and the Moon. These have been used for many ages, in fact hundreds of thousands of years, as symbols of spirit and matter or God and nature. The Sun represents the fiery Father while the Moon represents the earthy and liquid Mother of all things, and as all products are the result of the combination of two or more elements, it was said that the Philosopher's Stone, the divine achievement of alchemy, was formed out of the Sun and the Moon by blending their elements in the philosopher's Mercury. We may call this the union of spirit and matter through the link of the mind or the focusing point.

There is a mountain that rises out of the darkness of ignorance. This mountain is built out of regenerated life substances raised out of the muck and wire of cosmic oblivion. The black circle shown here represents the elemental and chaotic worlds which are inhabited by the lower, destructive passions and desires, or, in other words, this is the land called by the ancients Egypt, the land of darkness, or the oblivion into which the spirit flees in order to escape destruction at the hands of degeneracy. Darkness is not necessarily malignant, it is merely a shroud or a garment which conceals and protects light, but in it and through it are the evil and destructive passion centers, thought creations, and astral larvae, so well described by Paracelsus and other followers of the alchemical schools. It is out of this valley of death that the Magical Mountain rises as the supreme accomplishment of the alchemist. This black circle at its base is called the region of fantasy because it is the world of ever-changing things, of grotesque ideals, and spiritual unrealities. It is the world of deception that surrounds and conceals forever the mountain of truth. Only one power known to man is capable of piercing the veil of Maya, and that is the faculty of discrimination. One of the most important steps in the unfolding of an Adept is the development of the faculty of discriminative thought. Anyone can think fantastic thoughts which are not logical and reasonable. We can dream fantastic dreams created out of the filaments of diseased imagination, we can live fantastic lives surrounded by the fantasies of the unreal, and the test of the student is his ability to discriminate between unreal possibilities and actual realities. Therefore, the path to light leads through the veil of darkness where the student faces the problem of discriminating between the powers of life and the false lights of passion creation.

The dragons, serpents, and beasts that people this world of darkness represent the animal qualities, beastial passions, and perverted energies which live and thrive only in darkness but are scattered forever with the coming of the true light. Every thought and action of man creates astral entities and powers, which, if destructive in nature, take strange and horrible forms and people the region of oblivion with hosts of demoniacal shapes which are nothing more or less than the perverted activities of ignorant people.

Within this circle is a circle of light illuminated by the light of nature. This represents the area of activities illuminated out of darkness by the light or candle of human consciousness, nourished by the tallow or oil in the spinal canal, which when raised out of the cube of matter radiates the illuminating qualities which bring cosmos out of chaos and keep the demons forever away from the germ of life and light concealed within the sacred box or chest of form.

All the mysteries of nature are solved by the light of nature, but those mysteries, which are not of nature but are of God can be solved only by the light of God.

The figure of the man blindfolded groping in darkness while within the circle of light represents the consciousness of individuals who believe themselves to be in the area of darkness when in reality darkness is only light to which their organs of vision, mental, spiritual and physical, do not respond. Therefore, the ignorant wander in darkness while surrounded by light because of the blindfold of conscious limitation which surrounds them. In searching for the light, they grope out into the darkness, failing to realize that the light is in the center and not outside. But this they do not know until they have sought for it in the ring of darkness. This represents the power of reason searching for the answer to the riddle of being.

On the other side stands the Angel of the Flaming Sword, who faces the light of nature and, with the flaming brand in her hand, points to the Magical Mountain. This flaming sword is, of course, the upturned spiritual consciousness of man which alone can show him as his guide and instructor the path that leads through the dangers to the foot of the lofty mountain. The cord she carries in her hand is the spinal cord up which he will climb in search of those wondrous grapes that grow in the land of Canaan. The figure with wings represents. (editor's note: para ended here and new para begins.)

At the base of the picture is the dragon with its tail in its mouth, the divine symbol of alchemical mastery. This symbol shows that all the broken threads of life have been gathered and their ends tied together in the endless band of never-broken consciousness. It means that the spirit spinal serpent has raised itself upward and fastened its tail and head together, completing the vital currents of the body and mastering the previous waste of vital energy by closing the circuit of its expression.

Inside of this ring is the seated figure of the philosopher counting and enjoying his great treasures which are the pearls of truth and of spirit and not material jewels. He represents the one who seated in the center of a purified, diamond-like organism, is surrounded by the jewels of unfolded centers of consciousness which are beyond the price of kings and are the inheritance of gods.

The entire plate represents the human body. The mountain represents the head, the lighted candles on the chest are symbolical of the heart, while the dragon represents the generative system which is the keynote to the regeneration of its forces and the purification of its centers.

Thus, the whole picture is an alchemical essay on human, mental, physical, and spiritual redemption which if studied and understood by students of the spiritual sciences will give them a great key to the Rosicrucian alchemical school. All of the Brothers of the Rose Cross were symbolists and their truths have been perpetuated only in symbolism. Each one of us takes the part of Christian Rosenkreuz, wandering in search of the answer to the riddle of being. Like him we are buried, that is our spiritual consciousness is buried, and finally raised from the dead, when the two phases of our being, the red lion and the white eagle, fire, and water, unite, and from their mystic blending is born the Philosopher's Stone which is hidden away in a mystic cave at the very top of the Magical Mountain of the Moon.

The end

WHAT WILL THE HARVEST BE?

AS we gaze out at the seeds, (mostly wild oats), which the present generation is sewing so thoughtlessly we cannot help but think of those immortal words which have sounded down through many generations, "What will the harvest be?" As we look out into the world it seems that we are producing a generation of anemics, hardly able to drag one foot after the other, who when they reach such a mature age as, say, eighteen, are broken-down wrecks of dissipation who wander aimlessly in ever smaller circles around untimely graves.

Let us classify a few of the specimens of modern manhood and womanhood that are to be the law-makers, the parents, the scientists of the next generation, and ask ourselves again, "What will the harvest be?"

As we gaze out in search of true timber for the building of worlds, it seems that we are gazing on the valley of dried bones referred to by the Bible prophet, for there is little material for the building of minds and bodies. Children with old and sunken faces and haggard eyes alone confront us, who while they have not lived long have ruined their opportunity for usefulness in the world of affairs. There is little in common between the humanity of today and the ideals of the human race. A large percentage of our population are morons and over fifty percent seem close to savage ignorance; the finer qualities are fast vanishing from our midst, and it seems that real thinking is becoming an impossibility. Responsibility and the realization of life's duties seem unknown, and those who pass through years of learning forget before they pass out of the portals of the schoolroom whatever useful things they may have learned. Five years after graduation, or even less, about all that the average boy or girl can remember is the football yell and the school dance. Everything else is merely a muddy blur stored away somewhere in an emaciated and under-nourished comprehension.

To speak in words of eloquence and refinement, we are producing as fine a generation of hollow-headed idiots as the world has known in many a day, and the few thinkers that do storm the tide of human indolence are getting ashamed of themselves and crawl away alone to escape the laughter and the jeering of those who know nothing. It disqualifies a man or woman at this day and age of the world to be a philosopher, while those who disqualify them can find no earthly reason for their own being. The thoughts of man are so far from heaven at the present time and his spiritual ego is so divided from its own true position that to find the centers of consciousness in the world today it is necessary to dress in asbestos.

Now let us analyze this year's crop of dashing anemics, which to tell the truth have been badly frosted and rather worm-eaten. Of course, there are a few exceptions which prove every rule, but generally speaking, we can diagnose the young man of this generation something as follows:

He is tall, or if not tall, at least slender in frame, finance, and brains. Taking a possible hundred percent as perfect, we shall find the general averages listed as follows: In health, he is about forty percent human; his lung capacity is about twenty-five percent of what it ought to be; his stomach is in convulsions sixty percent of the time; his eligibility to think sensible thoughts is about ten percent out of a possible hundred; his ability to smoke bum tobacco is ninety-nine percent perfect or better; in dancing he is very efficient, but in arithmetic not so good; he knows every burlesque show in town but couldn't possibly find the public library: his ability to make money, one percent of his ability to make dates the other ninety-nine percent. He is beloved by everyone who doesn't ask him to do something for them and if all goes well and in accordance with harmony and the plan of his being he should have, say, nine love affairs a year and be out of work about eighty percent of the time. He is usually slightly round-shouldered, possibly knock-needed, he is very important to himself, but absolutely useless furniture to everybody else. He usually gets married before he gets a job and then has a job trying to stay married, as he doesn't know anything and thinks less, he does nothing but wonder why his romance won't last and his best girl goes off with a handsomer man.

In other words, if we plant this type and wait for the harvest, we are not even likely to find a weed when the gathering time draws near, for there is not enough within the average gallant of our generation to cause even a commotion, much less a harvest. Leaving this angle of the problem to bury itself, if it has the strength, we will pass on and consider "Exhibit B," or, as Kipling would call it, "the female of the species," and diagnose the case from that angle.

Taking the general score of one hundred percent, as before, to represent the perfect, let us briefly consider, list, and label the attributes, accomplishments, and eccentricities of the species "feminalis." General physical health considered first may generally be termed zero; spinal curvature common; weak lungs common; anemia common; general lassitude prevailing. Each one of these ailments will be found in from fifty to sixty out of every hundred; in other words, if put to a hard day's work said rare specimens would last until they get started and then would call a halt for lunch. Intellectuality, doubtful in ninety-nine percent of cases; have never heard of Nathanial Hawthorne nor Samuel Coleridge, but will look in next month's "Snappy Stories" and see if they have written for it. Memory is good but varied, and usually turned into certain channels, most of them useless. Geography, mathematics, and history, one hundred percent imperfect. Occasionally an eccentric education in art and music, especially in landscape gardening, exterior stucco working, and general external decorations where some proficiency is shown occasionally. Memory of dates, scandals, and vacations, perfect; exceptionally fine in remembering names of motion picture stars. Chewing gum is one hundred percent perfect, never sounds a flat note. Cooking is a lost art except for cooking up trouble; domestic sciences, nil; mending, darning, etc., ditto. Usually proficient in dancing except when feet hurt; can wear five-inch heels without staggering; good appetite, especially for shrimps, sardines, and Granada olives. Common sense, nil; ambition, zero (movie ambitions excepted); average length of life, thirty; number of marriages averaging from three to twenty; strongest asset, pugnacious temperament of her own; plenty of energy to hold up one end of a scrap. Sometimes both ends, said scrap usually of a domestic nature, but not sufficient energy to do anything useful.

These form the leading features and hopeful prospects of our human race. Politeness, courtesy, simplicity, all of these sweeter and finer sentiments have been discarded for lack of time. Fineness of quality, love of study, art, and science, and all these things which tend to elevate are forgotten. Elevators do not seem to be needed, for most of the pool rooms are downstairs and the dance halls are on the main floor.

So, with a cigarette snuggled under one ear, a squashed Fedora hat over one eye, his nose squinted to one side, and his eyes half-closed with a drooping expression which is enhanced by a gracefully receding chin, we find him embellished with a high white collar and blare tie, big feet, and a small consciousness, perambulating towards the nearest dance hall or nth class movie with his steady swinging on his arm. So far as she is concerned, in this day and age of the world, we are not surprised at anything. She may be smoking a meerschaum or a Virginia cheroot or chewing tobacco. No one knows. But with a swing like a tar and a general makeup resembling an ex-prize fighter, she swaggers along. And these two are about to unite for the general betterment of creation to go through life together, sans brains, sans sense, sans everything, sans end. (With apologies to Omar).

And if these are to be planted in the great half-acre of the world's works, we ask you again to figure out on the pure principles of mathematics- "What will the harvest be?"

There are three things which, if considered and lived, will make the day of mastery closer for the individual who discovers their mystic truth. First, we must use the powers that we have in the best and most constructive way possible, for it is only those who show ability who will be given greater responsibilities. Second, we must look for greater opportunities to be given the power to fill them. Third, you must improve yourself every day so that when the appointed time comes, you will be a credit to your work and to your God.

THE DIVINE MASQUERADER

THERE are many people in the world at the present time who are not what they seem to be. There are those who appear to be poor but who conceal under the veil of poverty, riches unnumbered. There are others who seem to be well supplied with the things of this world, but who, in reality, when the last great moment comes, have little either in this world or the worlds to come. There are those who seem to be honest but who have evolved the subtle spirit of dishonesty. There are some who claim to be spiritual, but whose lives tell only of sordid things. Then there are others who claim nothing and who are listed with the saviors of mankind. In truth, the world is not always as it looks to be, but it is always what it makes itself.

Now, in the universe, there is a power which we can accurately describe as the great Unknown. This power is the sublime and supreme mystery, and for the sake of clearness we have named it the Divine Masquerader, for in truth that is just what it is, a strange and mystic one who masks Himself under a thousand disguises, is known in a million different ways, yet is ever the same.

One of the great incentives in life is man's eternal search for something, a strange and unknown power, which he realizes is valued beyond the gains of the earth. He only knows this power as the Masquerader, that mystic spirit of uncertainty, for none knows where He will come next or how he will appear when he does come, but consciously or unconsciously all growth depends upon Him. For thousands of years, this divine trickster has been masking under the guise of simple things. He is always with us, yet remains unknown because he loses his personality and is unseen behind the part He plays.

Shakespeare was right when he said that the world is a stage, for the Divine Masquerader is the greatest actor of all; He lives and is the very part that He plays. The old symbols of comedy and tragedy were the smiling face and the downcast face, and these faces are the masks of life.

Behind the mask of an ever-changing personality, there is hidden a soul which is ever the same. The great centers of spiritual consciousness expressed through this endless kaleidoscope of ever-changing manifestation are animated by the powers of a single mind. Life is always the same, but the mask is ever-changing.

There is a certain Mr. Raffles, a mysterious individual, and he has a price upon his head, for he becomes the servant of all who discover him. The alchemists symbolized him as the gold in the heart of the dross surrounding its precious center with a disguise of worthless stone. Just so with the Masquerader, for he conceals the greatest prize beneath the homeliest mask and every minute he is before your eyes donning a disguise which will bring him into your environment.

The Divine Masquerader cannot live without a form, but he changes this form perpetually. He is eternally whispering to you, but his disguise is too subtle for you to penetrate. What is the motive behind the actions of this strange being? Why does He hide His light eternally from the eyes of man. He is not trying to conceal himself, but in reality, uses His disguise that He may mingle with you and labor for you in ways that you can understand? This is the motive of the disguise that coming down from the great Divine, He may reveal himself in simple things and labor where you can understand and know Him.

He disguises Himself in a way that will bring Him close to the heart of everyone, but as the average seeker after the light looks for the great, the weird, and the unusual rather than the simple and the practical, we seldom recognize the Masquerader who is as one of us in our daily walks of life. We should realize, however, that in the circle of our daily happenings there are many things that are not what they seem to be, for behind appearances is this jaunty spirit of concealment who has put on a domino to appear to you as something that you know. If your daily labor is with a pick and shovel, somewhere among those working with you, the Masquerader will be hiding. If you are of the houses of riches and the homes of plenty, somewhere among them, He will be concealed. His disguise is always perfect, but man overlooks the simple and the direct and seeks the great and the spectacular. If the Master Jesus should come to the world today, who would recognize Him? We would receive Him if He descended in a cloud of glory surrounded by a host of angels, but who would know Him if He walked the earth in rags?

Everyone has seen the Masquerader today, but few have known him and fewer still have claimed the reward. This mysterious individual is the keyhole that leads to an understanding of how the door of life should be opened. Everyone has met and shaken hands with this Divine One who is not what he seems. Tomorrow, you will meet Him again and He will seem to be different, but ever He is the same. All the way through life there is never a moment when He will leave you, but with only the Masquerader as a companion, most people feel alone.

While we judge things only by what they appear to be, the Masquerader will never be found, but when man learns to judge things for what they are and what is within them, then this mystic stranger will be unveiled by the one who has become master of personalities. No one knows through whom this Masquerader will work next. It may be you. Every one of you may tomorrow become unconsciously the dwelling place of this Divine One traveling incognito.

The Initiates of our world are never known, for they go through the world living like the people they seek to serve, shrouding the divine powers in robes of clay.

The spirit of the Masquerader is always close to the hearts of men. It is the unknown quantity, the missing power, but in truth it is all there is to live for. The problem that confronts man is to know this stranger when he sees Him, to realize that opportunity comes masquerading every day, that truth and light and knowledge and greater understanding come to us in strange disguises every hour and moment of our lives.

When those come up to us who need our aid, we think little of them, for they are poor and have nothing to give. We do not see the Masquerader concealed there, the unknown One behind the mask, but at that moment there comes to us an opportunity to do something worthy, and opportunity is the Divine Masquerader who will serve all who discover Him.

The Masquerader plays as our enemies; He shines out from those we dislike, for He is the opportunity for reconciliation. He shines out to us from all with whom we come in contact, and we must wander the earth in rags until we find Opportunity. He is so subtle in his workings and so perplexing that we are often in doubt whether to accept Him or reject Him. One minute he inhabits us and a second later, the soul of another.

Growth is the divine result of opportunity and is hidden behind every hard knock of life. The spirit of growth is disguised as a problem or a disappointment which wrecks and tears our soul. He is like the spirit of temptation that seeks to lead us astray and still prays that He may fail. For growth is the divine good which man gains from trouble; disappointment and failure are the gloom masks behind which the true actor is concealed. When we tear these masks from the spirits of negation, there is nothing behind but Opportunity; when we tear away the mask of the devil, we find God underneath, for the devil is just another disguise of the Masquerader. When someone robs us, cheats us out of everything we have, it seems a terrible injustice, but tear away the mask and Opportunity is all that is really there, for tests like these are opportunities to do something great and to rise above our grief. When we lie on the bed of sickness, tear away the mask from disease and we find just Opportunity, for the Divine Masquerader gazes down upon all these things. When someone tears us down and leaves us broken at the feet of our life work, tear away the mask and we find again the same smiling face of opportunity.

The Masquerader hides Himself under the discouraging, disheartening experiences of life. They are the masks and shams with which He is trying to help us to greater works. He is giving us the opportunity to master Him and every time we win a battle with Him, we unmask the spirit of perversion and find the face of God smiling up from every disappointment. Over the battlefield with its shot and shell floats the spirit of opportunity. Even Death itself, when unmasked, is the spirit of infinite growth. As the last sail of the ship vanishes beneath the waves, nothing seems to remain but destruction, but even there is Opportunity.

All life conceals behind its strange and mystic workings, just one great principle-the opportunity for growth. We are here to learn, and our knowledge is of greater value than happiness unless we can be happy with the knowledge of work well done. Every disappointment, every problem, every hard knock of life, is given to man that he may grow, and in truth each one of them is Opportunity in disguise. Most people cannot agree with this concept. Few can see in those who injure them the face of Opportunity. There is in every life a place where there seems to be no redeeming feature; we know that failure must dwell there, for Opportunity could not so disillusion us. Yet unveil the problem and you will find the same sweet spirit there. Every enmity is an opportunity for friendship, every sorrow is an opportunity to rise to greater heights. We call Him failure, but he is, in truth the maker of success; we call Him discouragement, but without Him, the great achievement is impossible. Always found where you do not want Him, always pointing out the difficult things, confronting us with problems which seem more than we can handle, He is neither popular nor desired, and yet He is the creator of gods.

There is but one spirit, the spirit of good, the spirit of God. Everything is an opportunity to lift or be lifted. No two people can meet, but what opportunity is with them? In every life, there are three or four great opportunities, and most lives are not successful because people have not learned to recognize them. People cry out to God, saying, "Oh, Lord, give me this or give me that and please, Lord, give me something!"

But those who are wise know that the only thing they have a right to ask is the thing they have so often refused-opportunity. People want the fruits without the work necessary to produce them; they do not want a chance to work; they wish the rewards first; they want success upon a silver platter. They do not realize that God's greatest gifts to man are the powers of negation and opposition, which stimulate the soul to greater effort.

If opportunity came and gently tapped us on the shoulder and said "Kind sir, I am Opportunity, and I am going to give you a chance to be great," he could not even wake us up, we would merely roll over on the other side and sleep calmly until fate gave us a rap. But the Lord of Creation, with His divine wisdom, has decreed that man must go out and look for opportunity as the farmer looks for woodchucks. You may have to smoke him out or choke him out, set a trap for him, or maybe crawl into the hole and drag him out by the tail. The world is failing, not because it does not gain results, but because it does not recognize opportunity and seek to make use of it. The loss of an opportunity is a damning failure-the only failure in all the universe. Fools can follow where wise men lead. Many can make good when someone else has shown them the opportunity, but the only success is when we discover it ourselves.

The world finds what it looks for and there are many looking for Opportunity, but it is usually an opportunity to evade work, and to find a soft snap is too often considered the acme of wisdom. The world is a genius when it comes to digging up skeletons and a wonder in analyzing reputations, and there are experts of all kinds on unnecessary lines. But if people would only take out their high-powered magnifying glasses, put on their checkered suits and turn Sherlock Holmes to detect Opportunity they would find a new world opening before them, Remember, when you are laboring to unfold and bring opportunity to others, that you are then the Masquerader yourself and your duty is to remain unknown, to become the Spirit of Good forever concealed behind the mask of the Masquerader. Therefore, if you are working with friends whose profession is that of digging ditches do not go down in a tall silk hat and spats and deliver a doxology for you will only lose all opportunity to be of service. You must disguise yourself and your concepts as the Masquerader, you must have your mask and become a master of makeup, and be able to help people where they are and not where you are.

When people lose themselves in the parts they are playing, they are no longer acting, but are living many lives in one. As surely as every living thing is to you an Opportunity so you are the Masquerader to all other things. Our duty is to learn to play many parts. The Divine Masquerader knows all parts and just steps from one to another, that He may serve people where they are by disguising Himself as one of them.

Let us realize that the great Master is the one who can do the most good to others without himself being seen. So let each of us play this wonderful game of the Masquerader, slipping into other lives unknown, so far as personality is concerned, just to help someone along the way and then to vanish again as the Spirit of Opportunity, to receive and to give in the Name of the Divine Masquerader.

ASTROLOGICAL KEYWORDS

ON last month's edition we considered a few of the outstanding characteristics of the sign of Aries and we shall now consider Taurus, the second sign of the Zodiac, known to the ancients as Aphis of the celestial Bull. Students of Astrology should remember that these signs were named after animals or symbols which demonstrated the characteristics of the sign, and that by studying the creature or the symbol they may secure a very good understanding of the general temperament of the sign.

Briefly considered, we may analyze the keywords as follows:

Taurus, the second sign of the Zodiac:
Vernal, Cold, Dry, Earthy, Melancholy, Domestic, Nocturnal, Southern, Fixed, Succedent, Unfortunate, Four footed, Commanding, Hoarse, Short Ascension, Night House of Venus, Exaltation of the Moon, Fruitful sign, Detriment of Mars.

General Characteristics:
Taurus is a very peculiar sign in general characteristics. We find certain phases of it slow, unsympathetic, and cold, while if well placed, it is artistic, emotional, vital, sympathetic, and excitable. If provoked becomes malicious.
Strong Will Power, Tremendous Determination, Hard to rule, Can be coaxed but never forced, Usually rather material.

Physical Appearance:
Broad forehead, Rather curly hair, Square face, Usually dark, Handsome, Fairly short, well-set stature, Large eyes, Full mouth, Governs neck and throat,

Prominent face, Strong shouldered, Often short fingers.

If Venus is well posited in Taurus, it adds great beauty and balance to the figure and harmonious, symmetrical development to the form. If a malefic afflicts, Taurus is often deformed around the head and shoulders.

Health:

Taurus is often afflicted with poor health, both in her own region of the throat and in the opposing sign Scorpio, which governs the animal energy centers. Nervousness, muscular ailments, and often trouble in the liver and kidneys is noted, sometimes stomach trouble. Anemia is sometimes present, and Taurus is subject to sprains, strains, and twists of the body.

The following are the most prevalent diseases:

Consumption, Scrofula, Croup, Melancholia, Quinsey, Sore throat, Nervousness, Emotional ailments, Troubles in basilar processes of the spine, and through Scorpio regions.

Domestic Problems:

Taurus, under proper conditions and unless afflicted, is an earthy, home-loving sign and usually settles down after a certain time of youthful wandering. Astrologers agree that Taurus is usually successful in domestic problems.

Countries Under Influence of Taurus:

Ireland, Great Poland, White Russia, Holland, Lesser Asia, Archipelagoes, Cypress, Lorraine, Switzerland, The Campania.

Cities Under Its Domain:

Mantua, Leipzig, Parma, Nantz, Franconia, Sens, Blythynia,

Colors:

Green, Citrin, Red.

According to Ptolemy, the stars in the abscission of the sign of Taurus resemble in their temperament the influence of Venus and, to some degree, that of Saturn. The Pleiades are like the Moon and Mars; Aldebaran, the eye of the Bull, takes the quality of Mars; the other stars resemble Saturn and partly Mercury. Those at the top of the horns take the qualities of Mars.

According to Henry Cornelius Agrippa, Taurus governs the Cherubim; is ruled by the angel Asmodel; of the twelve tribes of Israel, Ruben; of the twelve prophets, Haggai; of the twelve apostles, Thaddeus; of the twelve plants, upright and vervain; of the twelve stones, the cornelian; of the twelve degrees of the damned, it is said to rule the lying spirit.

THE INDIAN SNAKE CHARM

FEW travelers have ever been to India who have not been fascinated by the street-jugglers and snake charmers of the East. You will see these old dilapidated-looking individuals, covered with very little clothing and a great deal of dirt, sitting cross-legged on the ground, while before them is a little native basket containing an Indian cobra.

The fakir plays upon a three-note flute or reed and as the strange sounds come from it, the snake sticks its head out of the basket and slowly rises upward lifting nearly one-half of its body off the ground. There it sits coiled up, its puffed head swaying back and forth to the tune of the snake-charmer and it seems hypnotized by the notes that he plays until he can handle it or do anything he desires with it.

There is a great secret of interest to the occultist and the mystic concealed under the story of the snake-charmer, for all of these ancient rituals and ideas have sacred origins and in the light of the Ancient Wisdom let us analyze the occult meaning of snake-charming. In India, the spinal spirit fire is called Kundalini and is symbolized as a serpent. According to the ancients, in the undeveloped man, this snake lies coiled in the basket of the solar plexus. It is from this point that it is raised up the spinal canal through the spinal nerves by means of the development of the neophyte. This spinal spirit fire is the force which carries with it the power of spiritual sight and illumination. The three-pipe flute or the reed with three openings symbolizes the three keynotes of spiritual growth, namely thought, emotion, and action. When man plays proper harmonies upon his three bodies, the flute of Krishna, then Kundalini, the sleeping serpent, rises out of its basket and ascends through the blossoms on the spinal column awakening them with its power. In India today this is called snake-charming, and its mystic message is perpetuated by the fakirs on the street who themselves know nothing of its inner significance.

AUGUST 1923

FAITH

As the sun rose over the gray parapet,
And the mosque with its dome of gold,
A figure alone on the tall minaret
Called the wandering sheep to the fold.
While out in the rolling desert sand
The prayer rug is spread each morn,
And there each roving Bedouin band
Offers prayer to the spirit of dawn.
To Allah, the Greatest, they sing their song,
And I a Christian beside them pray
That my God and their God all day long
May keep us in the perfect way.
Be it Christ or Mohammed whose praise they sing
It matters but little to me,
For a wonderful peace the faithful bring
To those who have eyes to see.
Though race and religion divide us,
Together we kneel and together we pray
That the hand of Allah may guide us
Through the night to the dawn of day.

EDITORIAL

THERE are now over one hundred and fifty organizations in the United States alone which have brotherhood as their motto. Nearly all of the religious concepts of our day are based upon the rock of spiritual fellowship, unity, and truth, and in nearly every case we find their members sneaking down dark alleys late at night with sandbags and lead pipes lying in wait like beasts of prey with thoughts far from loving fellowship for all members of other than their own groups. Over their front door is a glorious, gilded motto with such inspiring words as "Love ye one another" or "Fellowship in spiritual conclave" while under the back stoop there are other sentiments expressed, such as "Do one another and do 'em good," "Each good soak deserves another," and other similar epigrammatic concepts of sweet charity and loving service.

It is the same with individuals as with organizations. Our leading exponents of divine brotherhood spend half their time knocking chips off other people's shoulders or hoisting young oaks on their own. Where there is no brotherhood, there is no growth, no spirituality, and no power. Man has a very analytical mind, and it seems that he loves to argue, to pick flaws in, to dislike and to find fault with individuals, when it is just as easy to seek the divine spirit of good and truth within themselves and those with whom they come in contact.

It is a very sad thing to see how much brotherhood is preached and how little it is lived in the daily life of our people. Among those who claim to be spiritual there is a wonderful opportunity to combine forces, to fight with the sword of truth and light side by side, unselfishly and unreservedly laboring for the furtherance and expression of that noble spiritual teaching which the world recognizes as the Ancient Wisdom.

Brotherhood is the key to the new age. It is shouted from the pulpit and rostrum and its noble ideals are portrayed in every expression of life, and yet nowhere is there so little of it, it seems, as among those who claim to be fellow servers and brother workers in the name of the one God. The inevitable result of this competitive and combative expression of religion is the undermining of noble work, the tearing down of great ideals, and the ruination of ethical enterprises, for where the spirit of cooperative brotherhood, one-for-all, and all-for-one, is missing there can be no work done either for God or for man.

One of the great things that the exponents of Christianity and occult philosophy must learn to realize, is, that the desire for self-superiority is the greatest known cause of competitive ethics, and that when one man seeks to be greater, holier, or more exalted than his brother he loses entirely his usefulness in the plan of human evolution. Spiritual workers must cease to feel that they are better than anybody else; they must come down off their high horses; they must kick out their pomposity and "persnicketies" and annihilate forever the spirit of "conspishiation" which they manifest in every expression of their lives. Side by side, each helping the other, each working for the other, each sweet and kind to the other, they were born and must forever remain free and equal.

Simplicity and self-abnegation are the secret of spiritual power, for only those can have power who save it. Those who waste it can no longer have it. The exercise of power constructively without the taint of domineerance is the test of the soul, and the one who masters and passes successfully this test is the one who has learned to possess power without exercising it. The exercise of power over others by those who have not reached a conscious unity with the divine initiators results only in competitive theologies and combative lives, and where such sentiments exist the spirit of God is not.

The Initiate is always marked and known among men by his sweet simplicity and nonirritating personality. He carries no chips, issues no commands, demands no obedience, and hampers the free expression of none, and as a result he is surrounded by those types of spiritual entities who will serve for the love of serving and will obey him unto death because he has never asked them to carry out a single command. With one hundred and fifty organizations preaching the principles of brotherhood in the United States through hundreds of thousands of branches, it would seem that we should see more of it but the end will never be gained while the spiritual consciousness of individuals is a slave to personality, for it is eternally personalities that open the way to misunderstandings. The spirit of man is never insulted by anything for it recognizes nothing but its God; the spirit of man is never tempestuous nor fussy nor does it have that terrible habit of straining at a gnat and swallowing a camel; neither is it on the lookout for opportunities to express power. These things are of no interest to the spiritual consciousness, but they do mold to a great degree the personalities of living creatures, and man is only subject to irritabilities and temperamental uncertainties when he is mastered by either his personal dignity, his conceit, or his emotional "persquisitiveness".

It is here that the spiritual student has a glorious opportunity of showing the beauty of his creeds but in the majority of cases he just becomes another swell-headed idiot who proves by his every thought and action that he hasn't nearly as much spirituality as the average guinea-pig.

Man cannot serve two masters and when he is a slave to his own feelings and is jealously guarding them, he cannot be a servant of his God. But, alas, at this day and age of the world, man is supremely jealous, supremely selfish, and divinely egotistic, not to mention heavenly impossible. He may fondly believe that he has mastered these things and is qualified to stand in the slippery places, but when he has really reached that state of simplicity and selflessness he has arrived at that stage of consciousness when he isn't sure of anything except the need of further effort.

Selfishness is the true cause of contention; it is the basis of religious and fraternal eruptions and individual brawls. When people claiming brotherhood are living like cats and dogs and organizations whose keynote is fellowship are at each other's throats half the time, we cannot blame people for wandering through the world faithless and apparently disillusioned.

The reason for these conditions is that selfish fellowship is based upon the "me first" platform. There is no fellowship where there is inequality of ideals or personalities or where people build walls around themselves. There is no fellowship where there are people who egotistically know that they know more than others, for fellowship consists in the bridging of gaps and the uniting of opposites and brotherhood stands for the cognition of the fundamental oneness of life and form. Too often this is forgotten and in order to produce the sham mask of apparent cooperation, many have to bow in unwilling servility at the feet of domineering overlords. Such a process in which people serve because they must and are restricted in their expression of individuality produces only eye-servants who do as we will when they are with us but hate us and belittle us behind our backs, in which case there is no one to blame but ourselves. Domineerance is not productive either of growth or spirituality but is the war-cry of personality, and that war-cry is the death-rattle of a dying civilization based upon the principles of individual omnipotence.

Brotherhood consists of overlooking unpleasant conditions and not altogether seeking to exterminate them. It demands the breaching of the aura of impregnable egotism which surrounds individuals and the uniting of the spiritual consciousness consciously, for unconsciously it has been one since the beginning of the world. People must learn to be elastic, never rigid, and taut in their lives, always ready to bend to the center, their motto being, "I'd rather be imposed upon a hundred times than to impose upon another once." The answer may come back that when we live in this world, we are the brunt of injustice, but that problem does not concern the spiritual seeker, for being absolutely selfless there is nothing to be hurt, offended, or angered by the world's returns. When man is subject to the actions of others and his happiness depends upon the subjugation of those about him, he is still living in those barbaric ages when physical brawn was the keynote of worth.

The sting must be taken out of life before brotherhood can be established, and brotherhood is the one and only base of spirituality. The brotherhood of body cells makes the individual, the brotherhood of organs perpetuates his form, the brotherhood of brain cells makes possible his thoughts, and the brotherhood of worlds makes possible his cosmic evolution. Wherever nature is expressing herself, in the higher and more divine sense, she is divinely cooperative, placing herself upon the level of all things and never standing above looking down.

Life is filled with petty jealousies and stings; it is filled with the love of revenge, the holding of grudges, satisfaction with others' discomfiture, and all those hellish little qualities which produce pandemonium on earth. There is always a certain satisfaction which we feel when we can discomfort a rival, there is a certain glory with which we gloat over unpleasant conditions into which we entangle people whom we do not like. All of these qualities belong to the lowest, most detestable and most hopelessly materialistic concepts of life, which are the result of the development and encouragement of organs and centers of consciousness, which are entirely personal and selfish in their sentiments.

These conditions are no more present anywhere than among our spiritual students who go around perpetually seeking for opportunities to pick scraps or else they are so covered with chips and sharp points that people cannot get close to them without friction of some kind being started. If you tell these very same people that they are mean, niggardly, and undesirable they will lose the wrath of the gods upon your head and leave you in a flutter of righteous wrath because you have failed to agree that hairsplitting, bacteria-amputating and dissecting and concept-pulling is not the height of spiritual and ethical professions.

There is a divine quality in the human soul which overlooks things. To this quality grudges, buffets, et cetera, do not attune themselves and there are those who are capable of transmuting every unkind thought, every harsh word of others into such a shower of blessings that they are ready to worship the person who has offended them or who sought to offend them. We must have more such people as this who sweetly and unselfishly go through life blessing those who despitefully use them and praying for those who injure them. It is safe to say that those who do not forgive and overlook injuries and mistakes will sometime wait a long while to have theirs forgiven.

It is within the spiritual range of everybody to pick a fuss. It can be done without half trying under any known human conditions and if you are looking for trouble, you will always be able to find it within the aura of your acquaintances, for it sticks its nose out of every conceivable place at every inconceivable moment. Anyone can catch and express irritation and can do so without any spiritual training although it usually takes considerable experience to become truly proficient in insolence and meanness, qualities for which many people have earned diplomas. It takes, however, a master to go through the world without picking a fight or having an argument or raising Ned with somebody under the glorious arch of some religious or fraternal order which has "Love ye one another" painted in gold letters over its door.

If you listen to some noble exponents of brotherly love and divine simplicity, spiritual fellowship, et cetera, when their acquaintances are not present you will hear such sweet sentiments as these pouring out from their souls when some unsuspecting creature steps on a pet corn: "You d-d little runt you! you blooey, smooey, bang woof! you insect! you rat! You microbe! you non-entite, know-nothing! You crook! thief! burglar! grafter! you d-dd-d- Blang! !&@"&'@"**(**" (Heard at one of our lectures).

Such sweet sentiments as these are not uncommon among occultists, especially when two combatting theorists get together. They take books, inkstands, hymnals and Bibles, open them to paragraphs on brotherly love and slam them in each other's faces, praying to the Lord to give them strength in their right arm. Or if they are not of a violent nature, they will sulk for three or four months over a stolen lollypop or because someone told them the earth was flat instead of round or that their favorite teacher looked like a zebra or an ape.

So it goes. And every night theoretical stretcher-bearers are carrying out the combatants from mystic and occult gatherings while astral entities and forms resembling daggers, bombs, and stilettos flit around the halos of our divine incarnations of spiritual wisdom. And so, the world wags! The brotherhood label is still on the bottle, but it is often filled with carbolic acid and H_2So_4. Brotherhood is a very elusive insect which can slip away in a very few moments and seldom survives a hard word or hasty action. We do not expect a great deal of it among prize-fighters and professional thugs, but we do expect a respectable amount of it from people claiming to be following in the way of Initiates. But as usual, blessed is he who expecteth nothing, for we seldom find it in a truly useable form.

Below, we list a recipe for the development of brotherhood within the soul of anyone who will forget his own likes and dislikes long enough to follow it. We might add at this point that there are no students too great, too advanced, or too close to initiation to be brothers for the greatest of all is the one who will give his all for his enemy every day of his life.

The recipe is as follows:

First: Forget yourself. You are not very much anyway, and nothing will be lost if you forget what you are. If by any chance you feel that you are made of a little better stock than your fellowmen, you are merely sick - go out and run around the pasture for a while. If by any chance you have within your soul that inherent feeling that you are close to God, remember that the one who is closest is the one who has come the closest to hammering down the wall of personality with its likes and dislikes which in the majority of cases is thicker than rhinoceros hide.

Second: Put padding on all your sore points. If you have certain traits of temperament which stick out and get in other people's way, chop them off and use for firewood, they don't mean anything, anyway. If you have any bunions, trim them. If you don't keep them short, don't blame anybody else for stepping on them. If there are any places where the skin if off, slivers under the nail, et cetera, get them out and forget them -never nurse them. If you have boils, carbuncles, or spiritual itches, keep them to yourself until cured, nobody else wants them.

And if you have a mean streak on, jump into the ocean from the highest building you can find and be sure there are plenty of rocks beneath. This will at least divide you from your personality in very short order. (Not to be done literally, however.)

Third: If there is anyone you do not like, try to figure out why you don't and you will find it much easier to like them than to find the reason for the dislike. It is impossible to find any real reason for ninety-nine percent of the grouches which fill the aura of our being. Most have had a case of stomach trouble and they started to hate someone because of the general discomfort that filled their being and once having started to dislike they do not want to admit their mistake by making up.

Fourth: If you happen to be jealous of somebody, forget about that too. Only small minds are jealous. Learn to do or to be the thing in which they excel, which is the cause of your jealousy, and if you must have consolation, look for it in the dictionary, you will find it listed under the C's.

Fifth: If you think for a moment that the Lord has placed you in charge of his workmen, forget it. (There are many things to forget, and most people would be much better off if they entirely forgot themselves.) Cooperate with everyone but never try to be the big cheese, for it is full of holes and doesn't mean much. Many people who think they are holy are merely holey or filled with a masterful combination of bubbles and general disintegration which lends that heart enthralling aroma to rockefort and limburger.

Sixth: When looking for a mean disposition or when we find it necessary to expend animal exuberance on something, let us look in the mirror and behold the greatest fool that ever lived, bar none, and realize that in the average case the only point wherein we excel is in the ignorance that our laurels are uncoveted.

In other words, man is a compendium of foolishness and sore spots, and he howls in five different colors when anyone hurts him, leans roughly on some soft little corn or steps on his tail. Consequently, he jumps for the other fellow's face and starts something which makes it impossible for his neighbors to sleep or his world to be at rest. In other words, dissension, stewing, fussing, jealousy and deceit, not to forget sore-heads, are nothing more or less than the teething process of human consciousness which, while not serious, keeps the individual in a fever for years. It doesn't mean anything but only shows how awfully small we are to people whom we are trying to impress with our size.

So let us call it off, forget it, have a new sign painted and hung up to cover the old one which was smashed in a peace fight, and still claim fraternity and brotherhood as our slogan and try to do better, realizing that any fool can start a fuss but it sometimes takes the Lord himself to stop it when once started. Therefore, let us follow in the footsteps of the truly wise man who takes the sign of brotherhood away from the door and hangs it in his own heart, there to shine forth as an illuminating light through his daily actions, his thoughts, and his ideals.

THE DOPE PROBLEM

IT IS safe to say that there has never been a time in the history of the world when the dope problem was more acute than it is now, when in spite of ever stricter laws and the increasing vigilance of city and state officials, co-operating with the national powers, the menace still flourishes, eating to the very heart of our homes and extending from the humblest of our people to the very highest places in the land.

In our days of prosaic and unsophisticated thought, when superstitions are limited to horse-shoes, bent pins, ladders, and four-leaf clovers, we have very little time for anything that is not tangible to our physical senses or capable of analysis in the scientific laboratory, but the greatest of philosophers and thinkers, whose books are now in our public schools and whose names are listed with the benefactors of humanity, have realized that behind each visible, tangible effect there is an invisible, intangible cause. In spite of all that may be said to the contrary, we must realize that there is something deeper and more subtle than the physical drug behind the dope problem.

Man is learning more and more rapidly that there is an unseen, unknown element which may be called the third party in the transaction of being. For ages we have heard of the spirits of the plagues and how the messengers of death have walked with men, and we know from literal statistics how disease and seismic cataclysms follow war and martial disorders as the result of subtle, intelligent, natural reaction.

Somewhere in nature there is a reservoir in which is stored the expressions of energy radiating from the actions of man. There is a little sorting room there such as can be seen in a postoffice where mail is being distributed. Among the other divisions there is a rendezvous where bad spirits congregate, these bad spirits being composed of human weaknesses and perversions. These gathering together from the many subjects to the same shortcomings produce vitalized forms capable of being felt in world affairs.

The ancients said that great vices such as dope, wars, crime, etc., built forms which they call demons and elemental beings who after a time nourished by the perversions of mankind and supplied with power by those addicted to their perversion become menacing creatures, which brooding over the world gather into their tentacles those who while not strong enough to withstand this concentrated force would otherwise never become addicted to crime, dope, or excesses. Each new addict joins the great throng who worship at the altars of death and bow before the shrine of self-destruction, and through the languor of morphine and heroin they feed the great demon spirit of dope with their own lifeblood, while cocaine with its frantic outbursts of uncontrollable passion not only wrecks the addict but the expression of his perverted energy perpetuated in the living substances of nature go forth on an endless round of destruction.

Not only must we fight the dope problem from the purely physical basis, with the two-edged sword of education as a precautionary and medical treatment as a reparative measure but we must also fight this invisible something, -the Spirit of Dope. This can only be done when the great bloodless boycott is laid upon every expression of nature and each individual mentally and physically combining for the good of all labors to stamp out this plague and blight against proper thinking and normal living.

Man is learning more and more rapidly that thoughts are things. Certain vibratory rays pour from him as the result of thought, action, and desire, and he himself may be responsible for suffering and pain thousands of miles from his own being as the result of the energies which he radiates through nature which are perpetuated like the little rings in the water when a stone is dropped. Our thoughts and emotions have much to do with the external things of nature which fact has been proven by our latest scientific investigations.

Auto-suggestion, as demonstrated by Dr. Coue, is a mental process which undoubtedly has an effect upon the organism of the patient and in a similar way the combined thoughts of individuals affect the entire human family. The demoralizing effect of dope upon the manhood and womanhood of America results not only from the habit-forming qualities of cocaine, heroin, and morphine but also depends upon a certain, subtle something, unformed and intangible, which takes hold of the victim when he first makes himself receptive to its influences by building the dope into his physical organism which action ties him by the law of attraction to the Spirit of Dope.

The power of thought and its effect upon the physical organism has been proven, and as the human race in the last analysis is but a single organism so the thought power of the race is brought to bear for good or ill by thoughtless individuals upon the ailments and dissensions of the race. All mental, physical, and emotional excesses of individuals help to perpetuate the crimes of their peoples. Weak-kneed and destructive thinking is a curse to humanity. The "I-told-you-so's", the "I-knew-it-all-the-time's", the "Well, he-deserves-it", and those people who are ever feeding nature with destructive thoughts and criticizing eternally their brothers are helping to nourish and feed the spirits of crime and are the mainstay of diet for demons such as dope, while each constructive thought of helpfulness, cheerfulness, and the innate desire of individuals to assist the suffering and to cleanse the stables of the world with clean, constructive thoughts, busy hands, and soft hearts will help to stamp out this Demon Dope in a way which will never be possible through the powers of law alone.

THE SPIRIT OF THE SNOWS

"YES SIR, I have been through more'n most of them in this here country, but I don't mind tellin' ye, pardner. I'm down on my luck. If ye'll stake me, I'll give it back to you some of these days when I strike mine, honest I will." The figure leaned over the little table, a strange, pathetic expression in his big, gray eyes. He was a sourdough from the creeks, was honest Jim Harley, as straight and honest a man as ever, came over the trail. He was a typical Alaskan, as the country was in the days of its glory; for though he was rough and unkempt with grisly beard and matted hair, Jim Harley was a gentleman from the boots up.

It was whispered around that Jim was a man who had been something in the old country but that he had got into a scrape at home and had fled unknown in the early days to the new Bonanza, not so much for gold, though he had planned of it plenty, but just to be away where no one could see him and where none would talk to him about things which filled his heart with sadness and despondency. Those were the days when Jim Harley had the biggest poke in the country and wherever he went, he was loaded for bear; they were the days when the sourdoughs shelled out the gold just to pan the sawdust on the barroom floor, for gold flowed like whiskey when Jim Harley was in his prime.

Jim had married up in the country, but I guess you know that already. He married Rosy, one of the dance-hall girls, and built a little cabin where a small creek ran into the Yukon. If you talk with Jim a little while he'll tell you the story and he'll tell you another, too, of how the romance ended, and he'd never known anything about it, he says, if it hadn't been for the Jap, he met on the riverboat coming up the inside passage.

He made friends with the little fellow from the island of the Pacific and he says that the Jap was a wonder, Hairukoo he called him and I guess that was his name, but he sure was a queer character, for he brought with him the legends of his own country and through the long winter nights he and Jim Harley would sit by the hour while the Oriental told the strange stories and legends of his people.

Jim Harley was always fond of that kind of stuff, people used to say he was queer, and after a certain night when the Northern lights came down like wondrous arches of coral from the sky, and strange temples of gleaming fire shone forth and wavy lace curtains of light streamed across the heavens, everybody agreed that he was insane. They called him "poor Jim Harley" after that, but he went on his way. And if you get him a drink or stake him to a meal, he will tell you about what happened on a certain night in November when the alcohol was down sixty below and even the malamutes were shut up and no sound broke the night but the cracking of logs and an occasional "pung" when a nail flew out of the wood.

Jim and Hairukoo were sitting by the fire, and Jim's wife was in the other room for Jim had some cabin in those days-it had two rooms in it-when-but I suppose I'd better let Jim tell it himself, so I'll slip him a five and you shall hear it from his own lips. "Here y'are, Jim. Things are tough with me, too, but here's five. And by the way, I don't think you ever told me that story about you and the Jap."

"Didn't I?" exclaimed Jim, brightening up, "Now, pardner, I sure am obliged to you, 'cause as soon as summer comes, I'm goin' up in the country ag'in-back where the mountains are. But y'know I never go up while the snow is on. No, sir, it's twenty years since I been outdoors while it wuz snowin'. I don't suppose you know why, but that's the story. And if ye'll shove up a little closer, I'll tell ye what happened to me in the snowstorm of '99 when Hairukoo, the wife, and I wuz stakin' it in Nugget Creek.

"Well, sir, it wuz evenin' and I plumb fergit what the wife wuz doin', poor kid, when Hairukoo and I were sittin' close to the stove-close as we could git-for y' know that wuz the coldest snap of the year and the snow wuz heapin' up over the roof of our little shack. You should'a heard them logs crackin', pardner; why you could pretty nigh see 'em move she wuz gittin' that cold. But that ain't the story, I must tell you about Hairukoo.

"He wuz a strange fellow, that little Japanee. Yes, sir, as white a soul as I ever met and no fool neither. Y'know I ain't never been a religious man or anything like that, fact I couldn't tell you the names of the saints from sardine labels today-course I knew 'em then-but it seems as I've forgotten everything, pardner, everything but that night. But I can tell you I never felt in all my life so much like religion as when that little Japanee wuz around. He used to tell stories about Buddha and the ways of the holy men in Japan and the East, and y'know I got so I lived better and felt better every time Hairukoo was around me. "Well, we wuz sittin' there and he wuz a'tellin' me one of the most beautiful legend stories I ever heard in my life. Just then an awful heavy wind started to sigh and cry and above it all a strange tappin' sound came at the door of the cabin. I'll swear the little Japanee turned white, and I wuz powerful frightened myself 'cause we both knew that there wuz six feet of snow in front of that door.

"Gently the tappin' sounded agin'. "Yuki-Onna,'"whispered the Japanee, graspin' me by the arm, 'I've heard it before, and I know what it means.'

"What is it?" I asked in amazement. "It is the Lady of the Snows," he whispered. "she comes through the silence of the storm and Death comes with her. Silently she taps, you can barely hear the gentle rappin', but she will come in before the morni' and kiss one of us to everlasting sleep."

"I turned to my companion to see if he wuz in earnest but one look at his staring eyes and drawn face told me that he meant every word he said.

"'Have you never heard of the Lady of the Snows?' he whispered as the gentle tappin' continued, 'who steals softly with flutterin' garments and closes the eyes of those who die in the storm? She is Yuki-Onna, the Lady of White, and when she taps, one must go forth to join the spirits of the snow.'

"For some minutes we set in silence and slowly the head of the little Japanee sunk on his chest and I felt a strange drowsiness creepin' over me, too, which I couldn't understand. I tried to set up but couldn't and little by little my head too sunk on my breast, and I seemed to slumber. But though I could not move, my eyes wuz open and I could see what wuz happenin' around me.

The tappin' continued gently on the door and slowly I saw the wooden beam that closed it move from the old wooden socket and gently, oh, how gently, the door opened and in there poured an avalanche of snow, swirlin', twistin', and turnin', fanned by the wings of the storm!

"Then slowly out of the snow there formed a strange creature, a woman of shinin' white robed in glistenin', gleamin' snowflakes. Her skin wuz as white as her garments as wuz the glorious pearly curls of her hair. Yes, she wuz indeed a creature of snow, yet alive. She didn't have any feet, for her body trailed off in a swirl of snowflakes as she seemed to float and flutter in the cabin doorway.

"Without a sound she entered, and I felt a strange chill come over me as she leaned over Hairukoo and myself, a strange chill like that of the cold snow that marked her comin', and I remembered the time when I had been lost in the snowy waste with my dogs dead and the food gone for the same chill as of eternal night crept over me now as then. Slowly, the floatin' form passed on and stood before the door that led to the other room.

"A great fear gnawed at my soul and in terror I tried to move-wuz this white specter goin' to claim the one I loved? I could not move and wuz forced to watch in agony. The door slowly opened and the figure of blindin' snowflakes passed into the second room. Only a few minutes went by and then the portal opened agin but there wuz two shinin' figures instead of one. I gave a scream of mortal agony for my wife was the second figure of shinin' snowflakes that passed slowly out into the great unseen world of swirlin' death and gleamin' ice!

Then the door closed once more, and the room seemed just as it had been before. It wuz just about that time that somethin' snapped in me, and all went black. "When I came to, I found Hairukoo trying to bring me back to consciousness. The first words I asked him wuz of my wife and he sadly shook his head.

"'Yuki-Onna has taken her away,' he whispered softly, and true enough the girl I loved was dead, stolen away by that cursed spirit of the snow. An open shutter, a frozen form, a room filled with swirlin' snowflakes, was all that remained to tell of the tragedy of my life.

"Well, sir, I told Hairukoo how the second figure had gone with the first and he sadly shook his head.

"'Yes,' he answered, 'she has gone forever. She has become another spirit of the snow, for all who die in the frozen northlands become spirits of the snow and live forever in the soft and crystal whiteness of the snowflakes.'

"Well, sir, that's my story. Yes, sir, and it's true. I ain't never been the same since that night, sir, for my Rosy took my heart with her out there into the snow-out there into the wintry night-where she now lives forever as one of the spirits of the snow. So, I never go out in the snowstorm now, sir, cause I don't want to see her out there, livin', dancin', swayin' in her robes of shinin' colors and like Yuki-Onna kissin' the wanderers to sleep as they join her in a rendezvous with death. She's there, pardner, she's there, and somehow, I know that someday I'll be with her out there in that eternal whiteness.

"I know y'think I'm crazy, pardner. They all do. But I ain't. It's God's gospel truth. But thanks for the poke, pardner, I'm goin' out soon as the snow clears to stake a rich one in them mountains, because I know it's there and I want all kinds of money, sir, yes, just to pay up all my friends as has been kind to me. And when I find that big stake, it's gonna be worth millions and I'm gonna stake you to a quarter interest, pardner, for the five you loaned me tonight. Goo'bye, pardner, I must be goin'. It's quite snowin' and I'll have time to get to the company store 'fore it starts agin. God bless you, pardner, and whatever you do when you go out in the snow, remember Yuki-Onna who will come as sure as fate, and you'll hear her knockin' at your cabin door."

Jim Harley staggered to his feet and pulling his rough hat down over his matted hair lurched out of the little room where I had been sitting with him into the cold Alaskan night. And that is the last time that Jim Harley was ever seen alive-when he left my cabin door. He had only been gone a few minutes when the blizzard broke again, blinding sheets of snow and swirling hail, which lasted for many hours. When it stopped and the temperature rose, some fellows went out and there. They found Jim Harley lying dead in the snow less than a block from my cabin. He had a piece of paper in his hand and a broken pencil stub, and he had tried to write something, but no one ever knew what it was. His face had a happy look, and he seemed glad so I kinda reckon the Lady of the Snow must have found Jim, too, and as her white form bent over him and her cold lips rested upon his forehead, I kinda guess he must have looked up and seen the face of his Rosy who died in the cabin so many years before. I'm just sayin' that 'cause he looked so happy.

Well, about the Japanese Hairukoo — I don't know anything about him, I guess he went back to Japan. Maybe he's dead, too. Every time it snows around here, I can't help but think that maybe the spirits of Jim Harley and his Rosy are somewhere among the snowflakes. There ain't no tellin, pardner, maybe one of these days I'll wander out in the snow, get in a drift on the Great White Pass or lined up on the White Horse or maybe just naturally get mine in the freeze-up. If I do and you don't know what's happened to me-I don't know where I'll be -maybe it'll be in hell, 'cause I ain't done nothing good in my life-that is particularly good. Or maybe I'll be out there somewhere among the snowflakes-'cause

Hairukoo says that all who die in the snow live on forever in the snowflakes.

THE BROTHERS OF THE SHINING ROBE - II
CHAPTER TWO
The Mirror of Eternity
(Continued)

I gazed into the great abyss of the mystic mirror, fascinated by the terrific scene that unrolled itself before my eyes. Little can man understand the great cataclysm that burst over the Atlantean world, sweeping a mighty continent from end to end with flames and ashes and burying it forever beneath the ceaseless waves of a mighty ocean. I had never realized it myself until I gazed into that great frame of living glass in whose crystal depths the world's works were unfolded.

The Master beside me still had his hand upon my shoulder and I felt a strange thrill pass through me as though a power unseen was radiating from the tips of his fingers. My flesh grew warm beneath his touch and before I realized it, I was cringing, for it seemed that the hand upon me was a blazing coal that singed and seared the flesh. I seemed to live again in the days that were past and before my mind's eye unrolled the picture of my Atlantean life, and from that moment the doctrine of rebirth was a fact to me. I knew that land torn and broken by nature's wrath and the avenging hand of a mistreated God had been my land, and my heart ached as I saw its wondrous glory vanish in the darkness.

"O! that such glories as these should vanish from the light of men, " I whispered to my guide.

"It is the way of men," answered the Oriental. "All through the ages, man has fought for the great illusion; he has made a truth of that which could never be and has glorified the unreality. Remember the world we live in, the things we touch, the ones we love, they are the great illusion which never has been and never can be the answer to the problem of our souls. There is but one reality, the spirit of Truth. All else is Maya, the great illusion. Behold the City of Illusion! For here, man built his towers, his temples, and his minarets; here he measured and trued and labored among the things of earth and in a moment, they are gone. Just one brief second and the labors of a million years, the thoughts of sages, the problems of philosophers, all these are gone. The labor of a million hands, the prayers of a million hearts, all vanish in a single night. And how much like this mighty city of the shining gates is the life of man and the world of his desires?

For though he labors to build, though he dies that the works of his hands may live, the storm passes over and they are no more. The illusions return again to the dark treasure chest of the unknown. The works are gone forever. What remains?"

The old Hindu gazed long and meditatively into the depths of that mystic haze through whose somber shadows the last ruins of an empire dimly shone.

"What remains?" He turned to me. His eyes lit up with a fire that spoke of powers unknowable. "I remain. Forever my works go back to the formless clay from whence they came; the dust that I have molded with my fingers is scattered to the cloudless wastes of eternity, but I remain. Cities that are built fall, armies of men scatter the stones of their fortresses, and the ploughman with his oxen ofttimes ploughs fields where once mighty temples raised their domes. They are the great illusions, for there is no falseness as false as the reward of works. The works are the great eternal truth, their fruits the endless illusion. Labor not for rewards, neither build among the impermanent things, for they shall go and the place shall know them no more. Yet through the endless ages of oblivion there shines one light divine, I AM. My works are not, my thoughts are not, my bodies are not, I AM. That which is not I remaineth but a little while and is gone, for from the open mouth of Brahma pour out sparks unnumbered and one by one they shine out in the everlasting vistas of eternity. Brahma remains, unnamed and unknowable, before mountains and valleys were brought forth, before gods and worlds were ordained, before the stars were fixed upon their course, I AM. My works have vanished in an endless night and yet I have all that I have ever done. I am wealthy with riches that far exceed the heritage of kings, for the fruits of all my labors mean nought beside the power that has come to me through the works that I have done. Man labors for two in his life, the forms that surround him and the life which ensouls him. But the work that he does he performs to learn the way it should be done and those who are slaves to the things they do are worshippers at the shrine of illusion. When man serves the whims of man, he but builds lofty temples from the substances of not-being which some day must fall around him a broken ruin like the city whose fallen towers and crushed ideals loom in the shadows of this mystic frame. Serve not the impermanent, nor store up your treasures on earth, for the ever-changing globe soon swallows up forever the creations of man and the place where they were is broken and barren and the life that loved them is stricken with remorse. Serve rather the light, the permanent, the true. Not the passing day should we consider, but the Eternal Now, unlimited by time, unmeasured by comparison, that should we serve. In the ages past, in the dark vistas of the unknown, you laid the foundation of a great work which you vowed that you would achieve and having finished it allow it to slip through your fingers to be forgotten. For the joy of man is to forget, while the joy of God is to remember. Blessed are those who are untied by pains or pleasures, unfastened by remorse, unchained by the shadow-shapes of Maya. Out of the world you have been called to learn the way that leads to heights eternal, a chosen son of God ordained in the temple of the rising sun to serve without reward, to labor with the great unknown and never to see the works of your hand.

"Look! the mirror is clearing, the red blood of a people bathed in iniquity is giving place to the pale calm of cosmic night. The clouds of doubt and misgivings which surrounded these ancient people are gone. But it is not to see these things that you have been called out of the ranks of men to labor with the divine. It is because a great work must be done, a work without limitation, a work which you vowed you would accomplish before the stars took their present course. A great battle is to be fought, a bloodless war, a war of love, a war of compassion, a struggle concealing itself beneath the garb of peace. The world in which we live is facing a great crisis, far greater than the eyes of man can see or his heart can comprehend. In the silence of this cave, I hear voices, the chanting of the Shiddas and the low muttering of the Zin. A great day is dawning for the world stands as it stood in the days of the Lost Continent, the red walls of hate and lust are blotting out the light of heaven's sun, the hosts of evil have armed themselves for a conflict to the death. The battle which you have been called to fight is a battle of intellects, a battle of souls. The hosts of light are gathering at the sound of a call that is ringing through the seven worlds. Little does humanity dream of the silent powers which are molding the destiny of its world; little do the souls of living things understand how the sons of light, the flame born spirits of the eternal God, are gathering in endless train in the spheres. Little does man see the waving curtain of power which sway like streamers through the cosmic night, nor does he know or understand those secret powers of death, hate, crime, murder, and perversion which stalk like demons amid the depths of ignorance. The powers of Baphomet, Prince of Darkness, have gathered from the spheres of gloom and that great negation, the spirit of death, is loosened upon mankind. The same dark clouds gather that gathered o'er the temples of Atlantis, the same powers hover here today that once changed the destiny of worlds. And you have been called to fight with the powers of Light that the black-robed specters of evil may not master the lives of men. The Brothers of the Shining Robe are being called and though they know it, not the vows they took in the ages past they are now about to fulfill.

"The world is crying for light, yearning for truth, praying for help through the darkness of ignorance. And here in the Temple of the Caves, the silent conclave meets to carry on the sun-globe in its thunderous path. The powers of darkness shall not win, for the gods are fighting for souls and spirits and the life of man. You are one who has been called you may not know who the others are, your duty is to go out into the world of men and acclaim yourself as you are one of the helpers seeking with spirit and with truth to fight the battle of human growth. This you shall do in accordance with the plans laid out for your being and this night in the silence of this cave you shall be ordained anew as a Brother of the Shining Robe. Then shall you put on your garments of glory, you who did not know that you possessed them, and go out into the world of men to carry the message of the Great Light?

"Thus, it is written in the Infinite Hand, thus shall you obey."

Slowly the old priest moved away from the mirror and as I followed his stately figure in its robe of gleaming gray which now seemed iridescent like mother-of-pearl, shining with the colors of a thousand rainbows, I heard a strange voice within me speak as though from the depths of my soul. Its words were,

"Go thou, also."

I turned towards the aged Mahatma whose eyes rested upon mine with a wondrous compassion. As I neared him, I grew dizzy and was forced to stop. The walls of the temple seemed to fade and swim around me in a hopeless mass of lights; the carved elephants gleamed and glowed and finally vanished in a mystic haze until only the figure of the priest remained seemingly suspended in the midst of an endless oblivion. As I watched him, his body seemed to unfold in great streamers of light that poured forth in swelling radiances. Blue and yellow and the most glorious shades of violet and rose, the gold of the sun and the silver of the summer moon, seemed to shine out from his soul, a great, gleaming heart of living fire that blazed within the center of his being. For miles it seemed these strange streamers poured into a vast eternity until his body became but a tiny speck surrounded by a wondrous halo of a million-colored flame.

I was blinded and raised my hand to cover my eyes, and although they were closed, I could still see the shining figure. My body seemed thrilled with the rays of light which poured into it from the mystic form. As I watched in spite of myself a great globe of golden light detached itself from the center of the glowing form and passed out like a tiny sun of flame towards me through the radiance of the mystic aura. I knelt upon some unknown foundation that I could not see and as I did so, the globe of light struck my breast and was swallowed up in the darkness of my own being. But it was not hidden; from my hands and feet, my eyes, and even the pores of my skin, it poured out, and I too was surrounded by a shining light which dazzled me with its brilliancy.

A voice from the great halo which gleamed around the mystic, shadowy form of the Mahatma spoke:

"In the name of the living God, Brahma the Divine, go to thy works, my son, for from the beginning of time thy labors have been ordained. Go carry them out into the world of men, for thou art one of that mystic band, the Brothers of the Shining Robe."

It all faded as though it had not been, and I found myself kneeling on a broken pinnacle of rock on the side of those lofty mountains which reach up to touch the sky. Before me rose that mighty mountain in whose heart was the Temple of the Caves. But now it seemed my way was in another direction for the narrow path that led back to the home of men stretched out like a tiny silver thread against the darkness of the night.

(To be continued)

BALDER THE BEAUTIFUL

YOUR little story is laid among those romantic cliffs and fjords which make Norway and Sweden God's masterpieces in natural grandeur. It seems that each stone and hill have a mystic legend all its own and the whole land tells of strange heroes, wondrous gods and goddesses, who while now forgotten by many still claim the hearts of those who attune themselves to the mystic grandeur of the Northlands.

Mountains, valleys, picturesque waterfalls, and quaint villages dot this beautiful country while sturdy folk with simple ideals and hearts of gold dwell among the rocks and cliffs and valleys of this strange land. This is the country of the Norsemen and the Vikings of old, sturdy warriors of the seven seas who in their winged dragons sailed even to the coasts of Vineland when Eric the Red was their leader. This is a land of torn and warring things, but now the sturdy hearts are at rest and busy with the toils of the day. They have forgotten the glory of the past.

The Scandinavian Peninsula is a world unto itself, a land of romance and mystic glory. Still the bards seem to wander from hamlet to hamlet telling the story of gods who fought with men, of Odin the All-father, of Thor and his mighty hammer, and of Balder the Beautiful. Still in the shade of evening one may live again in those mystery schools where the drotters taught their disciples of the wonders of the soul, of the great temple of Upsala, of the world tree Yggdrasil, and of Asgard the temple of the gods, and Valhalla the home of the slain. Still in the silence of the night if you have the poetic ear of the seer, you may hear the cry of the Valkyrie and shadowy shapes will seem to pass through the shades of night as when the gods of old rode out on the Great Hunt.

Indeed, this is the land of mystic beings and oh that the soul of man might learn to live again in the mysteries of the past. But they are forgotten forever, it seems, for the younger generation that dwells in this wondrous country of romance and legends knows little of its divine allegories, its sublime myths, and legends, which conceal under rune and symbol the will of the gods.

In a little village surrounded by this mystic grandeur of a faith forgotten there lived two youths who had for many years been brothers in spirit until the rivalry of love had broken their bond of friendship and turned them into bitter enemies. These two were as different as the snow of winter and the heat of summer in the strange land that was their home. Olaf was a true son of ancient Norway, still in his soul was the heart of the Viking, the tempestuous spirit of barbaric, freedom. He had never embraced the Christian faith of his country but still a youth he lived in the ages of the dead and the ancient spirit of the Northland ran through his veins in streams of living fire. Wild, tempestuous, yet wonderfully loving and sweet, in his childlike simplicity he seemed a figure from ages past when the sailing dragons weathered the storms of many seas, and the crown of rulership was placed upon the head of an infant king in some mystic cave. Karl, on the other hand, lived in a world of modern things. He had been educated in Stockholm and his life was much the same as in this country. In line with his family, he was a Christian and honestly believed the concepts of the Master's faith. All he knew of the ancient faiths were the legends he had read in school. Peaceful and quiet, he lived on a little farm raising cattle and tilling the fertile ground. So, while Olaf wandered among the mountain crags and precipices, Karl tended the flocks that he had gathered and lived the uneventful life of a farmer.

It was these two who had sought to win favor in the eyes of Hilda, and she had chosen the better educated, prosperous Karl rather than the uncertain, wandering spirit of Olaf. It was then that rivalry took the place of friendship and as the hours drew close when Karl and Hilda were to be married in the little church in the valley, Olaf, brooding and grieving, wandered among the hills and cliffs crying out to his gods and nursing within his soul the spirit of vengeance. It was so unlike Olaf, too, for his spirit was as carefree as that of a child, but in some way this disappointment of the heart had turned him against the world. From rock to rock, he jumped until at last he stood at the very peak of a lofty precipice below which in the valley the little village snuggled in the encircling arms of the hills. As Olaf looked over toward the town, he seemed to see the little church with its spire and with bitterness and hate he felt that this strange God of the Christians had something to do with this separation from the one he loved. The youth sat down on a broken boulder, his head between his hands, devising some way to win back Hilda or discredit his rival. There through the hours of afternoon Olaf sat like a figure of stone and there within his soul was born the spirit of hate which glowed like a dark red coal, clouding his whole being with its angry gleam, his bright, boyish face shaded by its clouds that stole from him the beauty and sweetness which marked this son of the frozen North.

Slowly, the shades of evening drew around him and the little village vanished in the shadows of the hills. Tiny sparks of light shone forth as lamps were lit and their warm glow seemed to deepen the chill in the heart of Olaf. The fiery hate of the Norseman was in his soul, but his hands clenched only the empty air when he would that he could close them over the sword of a Viking.

Suddenly, a peal of silvery laughter sounded up from the winding road below that twisted in and out among the rocks. Olaf shrank back with a cry; he recognized the voice and also another which now spoke up and he knew that along the winding path below him Hilda and Karl were walking. The voices drew closer and closer until at last Olaf, looking over the edge of the rocks saw some ten feet below him the two who so strangely claimed dominion over the two sides of his nature, Hilda whom he loved and Karl of whom he was insanely jealous. On a little cleft of broken stones below him the two stopped and seating themselves, whispered of the plans which they had made for the future, little realizing the presence of the agonized listener above.

Olaf crept to the edge of the broken rocks and gazed over, then slowly there dawned upon his mind a plan. He was surrounded by broken boulders. What if one of them should fall and strike his rival? The fierce light of hate flashed again in his eye. No one could ever know. His hand closed over a stone and his fingers clenched its surface until the very bones ached as there surged through his being, a passion indescribable. Slowly he raised the rock with which he intended to shatter forever the romance below.

As he picked it up to cast down on the head of the unsuspecting youth, something seemed to say within his own soul, "Is that what your gods would decree?" He hesitated. "His god?" Olaf closed his eyes and thought of his father and the mystic lessons that his parents had given him in the forgotten religion of his people.

"What do the gods care for the works of men?" he laughed to himself. "Mayhap I shall suffer, but no agony could be like unto that I suffer now." And again, he lifted the stone and poised it over the head of his victim. A merry laugh sounded from below, which tore Olaf to the very soul and, with a hand steady with some power unnamable, he aimed the stone at the dim form of his rival.

"As the gods decree," he whispered and cast it with all his strength. As he did so a great arm appeared out of the night, a phantom form of shining light which carried a mighty shield from the surface of which gleamed forth a golden sun. The stone struck the buckler and vanished in a cloud of dust, never reaching the two seated upon the rocks below.

Olaf, with a cry of terror, leaped backwards and fell half senseless to the ground. As he did so, there appeared before him a shining figure such as the eyes of man have seldom looked upon. A glorious youth stood before him, robbed from head to foot in pale turquoise blue, trimmed with white fur and golden ornaments. His cape was thrown back, and his breastplate was a lion's head of solid gold. On his arm he carried the mighty shield which Olaf had seen but a moment before, while in the other hand, this phantom stranger carried a branch of mistletoe.

It was not his garb, however, which fascinated Olaf. It was the face of the mystic form. The figure that stood before him was a glorious blond-haired, blue-eyed youth whose flowing beard of golden yellow melted with the curls upon his forehead and the ringlets on his shoulders. His whole being spoke of light and warmth and peace.

"Who are you, sir?" cried Olaf as he gazed upward into the sad eyes of the stranger. "Who are you that come thus in my moment of agony?"

"I," answered the stranger in his wondrous, musical voice, "know you, not who I am? You who have lived so long and believed so truly the ancient faith, which is now forgotten, know you not the son of Odin, the All-Father?

"Yes! yes!" cried Olaf, "I know thee now, for many times hast my father spoken of thee. Do with me as thou wilt, Master, I am thy slave, for art thou not Balder, Balder the Beautiful?"

The figure nodded its head and spoke once more.

"I am he. Do you not love me, Olaf? I who am indeed the spirit of love and truth?"

"Yes! yes!" cried the terror-stricken youth at the feet of the god.

"Then," answered the stranger, "if you love me, do not slay me. Do you see this mistletoe branch? This was the rock you threw at Karl."

"I do not understand the words you speak, Master," answered the trembling youth.

"Then listen, in the name of the ancient faith, and I will tell you. I, Balder, am the spirit of love and truth, gladness, and sunshine, and those who love and are loved are under my protection and shall rest in safety beneath the shelter of my shield. For I have been given by my Father the work of guarding the joys of mankind. When I was a child, all nature swore to love me, all but this branch of mistletoe. Nothing can harm me but this, a parasite. Know you that this mistletoe which alone can kill the god of light is jealousy, the murderer of truth."

As he spoke Olaf gave a gasp, for there appeared in front of Balder, another figure, a giant of living flames who carried in his hands a bow of angry red.

"This," said Balder, "is Loki, the keeper of the fires."

The figure of fiery light wrenched the slip of mistletoe from the hand of the god and quickly formed of it an arrow which he drew to the head of the flaming bow that he carried and fired it straight at the breast of the light-god and then with a cry of exaltation Loki vanished in the night.

Balder the Beautiful swayed for a second, his eyes lit up with an agony divine, then the god fell at the feet of Olaf who sprang to the side of the figure which lay dying upon the ground. It was then that the dying god whispered in his ear in a voice faint and broken the mystic lesson of his life.

"Oh, Olaf, from your angry thoughts was born Loki, god of the flames, from that rock you cast the mistletoe. And here at your feet I die, murdered by your shaft, never to rise again until all things of earth are redeemed."

Olaf fell broken-hearted at the side of the god, who continued in his soft, sweet tone as the blood poured from the wound in his breast.

"Oh, son of earth, listen to your teacher, the spirit of God, and know that I am hidden in your soul and in the soul of all that lives. I am the spirit of love and harmony and peace. I rule supreme in the temple of the gods as the beloved of my Father until Loki, the spirit of hate, passion, and jealousy, is born in the soul of man. Then, with the mistletoe arrow of perversion, I am slain by my own children. So have you slain this night the god of love who has never done anything but love you and guide you and serve you, for from your own hate is born the demon who slays the god of harmony. Let me not die in vain who has died so often for the world."

Suddenly, as Olaf watched, the figure changed and was robed in a simple white garment and on his head was a wreath of thorns.

"Yes," continued the god, as Olaf gasped in amazement, "I am the same. I am the spirit who is slain eternally for the sins of the world. I am Balder the Beautiful in whose heart is the arrow of Loki. I am the Christ in whose side is buried the spear of the centurion. And, oh, if the children of men would only know that they slay me every day when I do nought but pray for them!"

Olaf said no more, for his heart was too full for words. With a cry, he fell upon the body of the god. A hand rested upon his head and a voice weak and dying spoke:

"Forgive him, Father, for he knows not what he does."

The god fell back and lay face upward, bathed in the light of the silver moon shining over the top of the hills. How long Olaf lay there he did not know, but it seemed like all eternity. When he came to himself again, he was lying on the plateau of rock stretched out across a broken heap of stones. Rising to his feet, he gazed in all directions, seeking for the dying god, but there was no one to be seen.

The sun was already peeping over the cleft in the mountains. Day was dawning. Olaf gazed down at where the lovers had been sitting, but of course, there was no one there. A strange, new life had come, however, to this spirit of the Vikings, a new world had opened to Olaf, and as he climbed slowly down the hills and returned to the little village a great glory shone from his being until he almost looked as radiant and wonderful as the god himself.

Three days later, in the little church, Karl and Hilda were married and Olaf, the restless spirit of the Northlands, was there. Yes, Olaf was the best man. And it seemed that through him a hand invisible united those two souls, and many of the old folks whispered that Olaf looked more like a god that day than a mortal man. Others said that in his eyes shone the fire of the immortals and one saintly soul whispered to another beside her that it almost seemed that Balder the Beautiful, the spirit of love and truth, was at the wedding.

DESCRIPTION OF PLATE IN LAST MONTH'S MAGAZINE

In the July issue of the All-Seeing Eye, we published another rare plate taken from the writings of Robert Fludd, the name of which is "The Principle of the Great Creation or the Creation of the Great Universe."

Some of our students have asked that we have the Latin translated, but it seems that greater good would be gained if the student will have that done himself and search and wait, if necessary, some time to find this information rather than have it given to him.

These plates are not issued just to amuse or entertain but rather to instruct and the student remembers best that which he has the greatest amount of trouble in securing and he prizes more highly the thing which he is forced to labor for himself. For that reason, the explanation accompanying the plates is very meagre, leaving it for the student himself to work out the problem.

The following points may be of help, however, in giving the student a basic principle with which to work:

First: The plate represents the creation of the universe out of the four elements of earth: fire, air and water, as you will see if you study the picture. These four elements represent the four fixed signs of the zodiac, which we commonly known as Taurus, Leo, Scorpio, and Aquarius. These four elements represent also the four ethers, and it is the nature spirits working through these elements who bring forth the material universe out of chaos. Each one of these elements is under control of one of the four great life waves which have already reached human consciousness or passed it.

Second: The four elements as shown in the plate also represent the four bodies of man and the spiritual principle which animates them. According to the ancients, the air represents the mind and as it surrounds all the other elements; it illustrates how the universe is protected by the encircling power of the Divine Mind. The flames represent the fire principle in nature, the base of motion, heat and emotion and the great urge behind action and the power of desire, and is particularly correlated with the human heart and the red blood. The third element, water, is located in the solar plexus of the human body and represents the ethers which play so great a part in the evolution of man.

These waters represent vitality and are the basis of growth; they are lunar in their power and are susceptible to the crystalizing influence of the moon. The fourth element represents the physical body, the earth, or, as occultists call it, the last creation. And these four added together contain the vital elements of the seed or the germical essence and protoplasm and are the basis of all expression, for each element creates the others out of itself and reacting upon each other they bring into existence all things in the lower world.

Third: These elements also represent the cross, for they are the essences in which is buried the spiritual germ life in man. The four elements represent bodies and have been symbolized by the ancients as a cube. These bodies limit expression, consequently, they are said to crucify their lord and master.

Fourth: The reaction of these elements one upon another is the basis of growth and the harmonization of their principles is the basis of initiation and mastership. They are the principles with which man is creating his own universe out of himself by the purification within himself of these four vital streams of life and power.

Further study will bring to the student's mind other wonderful facts in connection with this problem. But with this as a base, great things are possible for the thinking individual.

This month's edition of the magazine contains a very remarkable chart or table referring to the celestial powers, the superhuman hierarchies and the forces controlling creation. It is taken from the same work as the preceding two and we will have a few words to say about it next month.

THE VEIL OF KRISHNA
AND THE DOCTRINE OF RENUNCIATION

BEFORE we take up the subject of these individual incarnations of the light spirit, let us first analyze the foundation or the source from which all of the Christos legends arise. There are in nature three great powers: the power to create, the power to preserve or regenerate, and the power to disintegrate. Scientists and philosophers of all people have realized the power of these three invisibles but omni-active agents. Whoever studies nature and her works finds them. Wherever we seek for light and experience, we ultimately arrive at these fundamental phases of consciousness, birth, growth, and decay; the coming in, the perpetuating, and the going out; and, after all, the resurrection.

The ancients sought in nature for incarnated principles with which to correlate their gods and they all agree that there is one great life behind all things. This life is unseen, unformed, and unknown and they call it the All-father. They also knew that there was one of His eldest sons whose work was to illuminate, to give life, and to carry on the works of his Father, the Unseen. They looked through nature to find something that was eternally feeding, nourishing, and unfolding material things and all who looked found the same thing, the Sun. Wherever they looked for the symbol of light, the sun was the greatest of all lights; whenever they looked for that which gave energy, vitality, and heat, they found the sun; when they looked for the positive expression of energy, once more the radiating orb of day greeted them as the greatest of all symbols.

Consequently, among nearly every race of people, the sun has been worshipped as the savior of the universe. Light saves the world, and the ancients knew that when we are turned close to the sun, we have the summer months of growth when all dead things come to life and that when in winter the sun goes away, all things die. The sun is the light and life giver and has always been symbolical of the preserver of created things. The sun is a round globe, therefore it was called punctos and the dot in the circle of creation; it has been symbolized as the smiling face of God for when the sunbeams on the world all are happy; in the Bible, the sun is called Samson and when his hair was cut off by Delilah (Virgo, the first of the fall months) he lost his strength.

We find two kinds of theology, solar and lunar. God was, of course, a Great Man and naturally must have eyes like man and according to the ancients His eyes were the sun and moon, for one or the other of them was supposed to gaze on us all the time. Sometimes He would close one eye very slowly and that was when the moon changed its phases. The moon was small and not so strong or as luminous and was a reflector rather than a center of illumination and as man was then the ruling power of the world and woman was in subjugation the moon was called feminine and the sun masculine. There was, of course, also a deeper reason for this, which will be taken up at another time. The positive is the father ray, which is the greatest and strongest in nature, and the energy which makes people active and industrious and dynamic regardless of their sex is the influx from the father ray. The sun is the center of every world religion because it is the spirit of benevolence which guards and takes care of the earth in a paternal way. The unseen spirit shows his love for mankind through his sun, therefore the sun of God comes to bear witness unto his Father and to glorify the Father whose energy he uses, and in the words of an incarnated principle of the sun, It is not the sun but the unseen Father who doeth the works but whosoever hath seen the sun hath seen the Father for the Father is in the sun and the sun is in the Father. The sun, the principle of the Christ, the divine illuminator, is the celestial preserver of creation and is revered under the name of Christos or fire-oil in nearly every country of the world. The lesser luminary was called the Holy Ghost or the breath because he has charge of matter with its breath-like ebb and flow and working with the lowest expression of creation is referred to as the least of the three, although he is the bodybuilder.

In different nations, the ancients gave the sun different names. He was called the Great Illuminator; and as he works with nature and unfolds form, he was called the Great Architect; as his vital rays healed the sick, they called him the Great Physician, and so on. Rather than giving him a name, they designated him according to his attributes. To some he was one eyed, therefore they called him the All-Seeing Eye: In Egypt, India, Chaldea, Phoenicia, and Arabia he carried various names, but they were always the same in meaning. In Persia, he was Mazda, and we have called our electric light bulbs by the same name, for they are also givers of light. We talk about heathen gods, but we know not whereof we speak, for all nations are merely giving names in their own languages to the nameless principles of nature. Odin is the Father-god of Scandinavia; his name means "the one-eyed". The spiritual life of the universe is somewhere behind the sun, but it is manifesting through this single globe, which is its mystic eye. Sun and son mean the same thing; the Sun of God is the spiritual globe, while the Son of Man crucified is that phase of the same energy which sacrifices itself for the regeneration of matter. The sun of light is a reflector of God, the sun reflects the light which strikes against it and pours out to the other negative bodies in the solar system the unseen life of God; therefore, it comes in the name of the Father that all men and things may be saved.

Buddha means "an eye" and is a title given to those who have built a sun within their own souls, while Zoroaster also brought the mystic truth of the worship of light. Wherever we find fire, light, unfoldment, growth, and perpetuation, we find a son of man who is the incarnate, personified principle of the sun, the great savior of nature. In Egypt, the rising sun is called Ra, which means "a glorification and a rejoicing" and the Father-god was called Ammon the Great Unapproachable. We find the Egyptian kings called Rameses, or servants of Ra, the spirit of light.

Man fell from heaven that he might have light, for light is the basis of self-consciousness and those who are in the light are slaves of no man. Man has been chained to the rock like Prometheus because he brought the light down from heaven, for while it is the spirit of good, in the ignorant it is a destroying power. It must not only be present, but its value depends upon its proper use. Light is the universal symbol of the world's religions, the cry, "More light, Oh God, more light!" has sounded down through the ages since the unknown beginning.

In India, the Spirit of Light carries many names. He is generally known as Vishnu, the great preservative spirit of God, the second expression of divinity. He is said to have been incarnate ten times and each time he comes into the world to do a certain work, to overcome certain limitations, and to bring greater freedom to his people. Like the story of our Christ, he is connected with the fish and in one of his incarnations; he was thrown from a fish's mouth. In India there was born one who bore the name of Krishna, which means the same as our Christ, and the wise men of India heralded his coming as the wise men of the East heralded the coming of Jesus. In many instances the life of Christ and the life of Krishna are the same for they are both legends of the sun given in different ways to meet the needs of different peoples. Krishna is called the Blue Lotus and is probably the most revered of all the gods of the Brahman theology, for Shiva is violent, Brahma is over-powering, Kali is also violent and tempestuous, but Krishna is the ever lovable. Krishna is the god of love because he seeks with peace, compassion, harmony, and light to teach the world the secrets of salvation. God has two ways of doing things: one way is by force and the other way is by love. He always uses love first and seeks to help man in the way that he should go; when love fails, He uses force, but His force is always tempered with love. God is the creative fire which has two powers, one to warm and the other to burn. We have thus these two principles, the principle of light, knowledge, and truth through suffering and the principle of light, knowledge, and truth through love. And Krishna always comes in love and simplicity. The various gods of India speak often with an angry voice, even as Jesus came to man and showed the principles of love, faith, and justice, yet sometimes justice with a sting. But Krishna came to India with nothing but love. His cult has always taught brotherhood, love, and compassion. Of course, his followers do not entirely carry it out, but neither do any other people. If humanity followed the instructions of their initiated, it would be in heaven now. But regardless of their misapplications there is no doctrine in the world that teaches with greater love and beauty and compassion than that which marks the wisdom of Krishna, the Indian Christ, for his love was divinely just and compassionately stern and immovable.

Krishna was the incarnation of Vishnu, the divine sun principle. He came to India at a time when the country was torn with strife and contention. He was born of an immaculate conception as was Jesus and being different from all other things was called like Buddha a white elephant. Krishna is the Child of God and is seldom worshipped as a man but usually as a child from five to fifteen years of age and as such he is pictured. The reason for this is twofold; a child is not ruled by the mind but by the heart, for the cord that connects its mind has not yet united. Therefore, Christ and Krishna we prefer to consider as young, for they both taught the heart doctrine of childlike faith and simplicity.

Among the followers of Krishna, we find a very beautiful custom which has been preserved for many generations. The true devotee always carries with him a little package which he keeps spiritually close to his heart. It contains several little things, usually a little book of Sanskrit Mantram's and sayings of the Blessed One and also a little picture, hand-painted, sometimes on ivory or bone, but always a work of art. It is the picture of a little child standing on a lotus blossom or in the forest playing upon a flute. It is the beloved Krishna, the child god of India. The strange feature is that the body of the little figure is always painted blue.

And this little Blue Krishna, who represents the essence of love and simplicity, is the most sacred ideal of the East Indian. He is the god of harmony, for he is always at peace with all living things and his doctrine is compassion and love. In moments when his heart is torn by indecision and discord, the Hindu will take out this little picture, probably given to him by his mother or father, and think how pure, sweet, and beautiful Krishna was. It helps him to live and serve better through the memory of this beautiful child who came to teach the world love and simplicity. It means to him that he must be as a little child, too, with the same purity, faith, and simple unselfishness that characterize the beauty of early childhood. He honors him and tries to be like him and kneels as a child in prayer to his god in the same deep sincerity which marks the childlike faith in the all-guiding Father.

Krishna is said to have the sweetest love story that the world ever knew, for when he was just a child, he chose from among his people Radha, a beautiful young shepherd-girl. Radha was the spirit of nature and Krishna was the spirit of the sun, and he heaped upon her all the glory that was his. They used to swing together in a swing of flowers out in the forest among the birds and beasts. He would play beautiful melodies on his flute and all the animals and fowls of the air would come to sing with him and nestle at his feet for he was the god of love and truth who made life sweet for all of them. When he played all nature listened for, he represented the spirit in man who plays the divine harmonies and quiets the storms of passion in his own bodies.

In due course of time, Krishna was called heavens and float over the world in his great winged dragon boat. This ever-youthful spirit of good represents the immortal in man which knows no age and his spirit floating over the world personifies the sun which never grows old but inspires all living creatures to noble things.

When Krishna was alive it was said that always between him and the world was a strange haze which was called the veil of the gods for it was said that Krishna was not of earth but of heaven, and while the gods gave him power to come to earth and teach man they forever protected him and nothing in nature could harm the spirit of Krishna, the god of love, and while he might suffer and die for humanity, he was forever surrounded by the blue veil of the Initiated. And this is the reason why he was called the blue god.

The blue veil of the gods is the blue of the sky, and the sun always floats in the deep blue haze, as did Krishna in his veil of immortality. He is also said to be the progenitor of the blue peoples, the next world race whose bodies will be made of ether, which is blue, and as Krishna was superior to all living things, they said he belonged to the mystic race of the gods whose bodies were formed of the deep blue spiritual ethers of the heavens.

The ancients said that there is ever a veil between the mortal and the immortal and while the immortals walk with man; they are not one with man nor are they of man, for between them and the lower worlds is the blue veil of the gods. In this world, we cannot see the color, but we can feel it, for it is a wall that divides us from others. There are people who are different from all others, they are behind the veil. Some are buried deep beneath the red veil of materiality and others are behind the shining veil of spirit. There are those to whom you feel drawn in spite of yourself and others you feel do not belong near you, for they are millions of miles away in a spiritual temperament.

There are those you would not slap on the back although they are your best friends, a power you cannot understand holds you back and surrounds them with a wall you cannot break. There is no apparent reason except that in some way they are different. There are people who serve all, labor with all, yet notwithstanding their brotherliness and love you can never become familiar with them, a mystic something divides you from them. They are not of the world and the world knows it. Between the Initiate and all others is a veil which cannot be pierced, it is a wall which divides the false from the true, and none may cross that awful gap save those who in simplicity and renunciation pass through that veil to return no more.

Those who go behind that spiritual wall may believe that heaven is going to open up to them, but they find that this is not so, they only discover that they are strangers in a strange land and their joy, or their sorrow depends upon the motive which brought them behind the veil. If they came seeking peace, rest, and personal comfort, only suffering and agony await them; but if they came with service as the keynote of their being, then indeed they are in heaven.

But he who would become one with the gods must renounce forever the things which are of man, for when the blue veil surrounds him the candidate is no longer of earth but of things celestial, and forever there is a wall between him and the things he has left behind. That wall seems as limitless as consciousness itself and to the uninitiated does not exist at all, but those who have passed behind it know that it is more solid than the thickest granite, more resistless than steel, and thousands have battered themselves against the wall of the gods whose fortress is impregnable.

Students studying out of the body often strike this wall and are thrown back into the body again; in spite of all their power, they cannot pass the invisible barrier against which they strike to be thrown back time after time. But if the student is ready for the thing concealed behind that wall, it vanishes as he passes. There are walls of vibration which divide all grades of consciousness.

The Master is of a different grade from man and is separated by his own works and his own ideals from the world of men. Once, having seen a great truth, man cannot forget it and can never be one again with the ignorance he left behind. The joys that once filled his soul no longer interest him; the ways in which he once spent his time now seem foolish; it is his own life that divides him from the world. For when one becomes an intelligent worker in the Great Plan, he has new joys and new fears and the wall of mutual interest divides him from the things he once held dear.

In improperly developed candidates, a terrible condition presents itself. They want to go forward and sometimes succeed in passing through the veil, and they place the blue wall between them and the life they have lived. This is because they have forced themselves through ambition or desire to take steps with which the soul was not in tune. They pass beyond the veil not in sweet simplicity and devotion but with the great determination to get there at any price, and their souls are filled with a great longing for the things which they know they should not have. In consciousness, ideal, life, and love, they are tied to earth while by the force of action and mentality they have become citizens of another world. The result is agony, mental, physical, and spiritual, and ultimate insanity.

Man must be a worker with motives, and he should not seek to go on until his whole soul is ready to give all as the price of truth. Otherwise, he must stand like the child before the window of a candy store longing for the thing he cannot have, for the desire is still alive and, he has sought to become one with the greater without giving up the lesser. When he must sit and watch the beefsteak which he longs to eat and knows that he cannot or watch his best girl dissolving in the ethers, the soul of man cannot be very happy. He has not killed the desire, but his vow has removed his ability to satisfy it. By vows most sacred he has renounced the world, and yet he wants the world and the craving for the things he cannot have becomes an obsession and a destroyer. Many have reached a position halfway through the veil of human consciousness; they aspire to heaven while the lower man holds them tightly to earth; a terrible rupture of the organism is the only result of such a path.

Therefore, man must learn renunciation, not of the mind but of the spirit, for until he gives up all things of earth freely and willingly, initiation is hell. For if man lifts himself to the planes of the immortals while every human desire cries out for gratification, he is damned in spirit and in soul. This is one of the most important considerations in the study of occultism; we cannot get away from the thing we really are, and we must build slowly on the solid foundation of harmonized growth. There are thousands of people today studying occultism who will be insane in time; the world is filled with folks who see strange things of all kinds floating through the air and who go around. Imagining they are reincarnations of Napoleon or Joan of Arc. There are dozens of incarnations of Plato, hundreds of Cleopatras, scores of Du Barrys and La Toscas, and enough Julius Caesars to start a Roman Empire, but not one Judas has been found or anyone who wishes to claim his laurels. Slowly, they go crazy one after another. They have honestly and sincerely tried to do that which can never be done by trying, but must be the natural process. Man must willingly and gladly go on because he has honestly ceased to be interested in the things behind. Beauty of spirit, light and truth, and the finer sentiments belong on one side of the veil, the side of the Masters, and the "Do 'em before they do you" type belong on the other, and the consciousness of man cannot be in both places at one time. Many people are spiritually sitting on a beautiful throne playing on a harp, wearing a halo supported by a small brass rod up the back, and all, but at the same time they are trying to stifle a desire for pork chops and to keep their tempers under control. Such a system as this in which man tries to subjugate his desires by strength can never produce any satisfactory result.

We are divided between our ideals and our dispositions and those who seek for initiation and at the same time try to preserve their selfish traits and qualities find that only a hell awaits them if they gain the thing which they seek.

The problem that presents itself is an impossible position if they go forward and self-destruction if they revert. If they seek to go back and satisfy their desires, the organism which they have partly spiritualized is destroyed by the material vibrations. They become insane, idiotic, and completely wreck their being. If they go forward under such conditions, they only pass on to greater sacrifice and more inexplicable agony.

There is only one answer. Before going on, the individual must be through with the thing left behind; he must have worked out, finished, mastered, and completely sealed and dosed the book of the past. No duties shirked, but each thing finished and honestly completed; no love or hate left behind. We cannot go to heaven or to the higher spheres of being carrying with us grudges, likes, dislikes, eccentricities, and diabolical temperaments. In many ways we do these things, and they destroy us; we meditate at night, adorate in the morning and concentrate at midday, and spend the rest of the time in exercising the meanest qualities we possess.

We apply practically nothing and force whatever growth we do make on the power of will. The trouble with most students and occult organizations is that they are fussing and stewing at the same time they are trying to be spiritual. They are trying to cover one side of the wall and also keep a little place on the other. The result is they go forward in an unbalanced way and many really become Aatdepts while still a slave in part to their lower organisms. Heaven looks nice to many people, but so does mince pie — spirituality is nice, but a spree once in a while is not to be depreciated. The result is self-destruction. We cannot split our powers between two such extremes.

This does not mean that we have to be sad, dejected, or what is commonly called super-religious. But it does mean that the destructive qualities must be renounced. We cannot take the power which we are seeking to build on the spiritual planes of nature and use it to settle an account. With the Jones family over last year's lawnmower, or employ our newly evolved powers to digest something we shouldn't have eaten. There are three results in the disobedience of these laws: death, insanity, and idiocy.

Balance, brotherhood, and love are the slow but sure path that leads through the veil of initiation. There are others who dedicate their lives to a more difficult path that they may secure more speedy results. They have taken the great spiritual path of renunciation that they may return later as teachers and benefactors of humanity; but whichever path is taken must be trod with the eyes open and the full realization that the reward of failure is death.

Let us remember this and that the greatest step of life is the one that takes man behind the veil, the blue veil of the gods. Those who cross from one side to the other make the supreme adjustment of life and if they are impure, they take their lives in their hands. Those who wish to be listed with God's messengers among men must be willing to renounce self, ambition, desire, and all things mortal before they seek to become immortal. The only passion of the god is compassion. This is the veil of blue that shrouds the form of Krishna, the veil that divides the earthly from the heavenly. Each must pass through, but each must know the way, the means, and the time; otherwise, all is lost.

ASTROLOGICAL KEYWORD

SIGN OF GEMINI

In this month's edition of the magazine, we are listing a few brief keywords by which it will be possible to give a general delineation of the Gemini temperament. Gemini is the third sign of the Zodiac according to the geo-centric system of Astrology, and as it is symbolized by two children, it is a double sign, and those people who find it either ascending at birth or their sun posited in it should consider well not only the strong and constructive side of the sign but should seek to curb its more undesirable elements. The Wheel of Birth and Death is undoubtedly the great Zodiac of the heavens and so long as man is limited by perverse habits, unconquered tendencies, and destructive expressions of energy, he will be chained to the Wheel of Birth and Death. But there are those who have no rising sign for they have raised themselves above all the limitations of material astrology. They are then above the law because they have so perfected their being that the laws of unbalance neither affect nor sway them.

Man is seeking to become a priest after the Order of Melchizedek who is above the law, and he is only this when his life is above reproach. So round and round the endless circle he must go until finally he has learned and applied all the lessons that it has to teach. When this glorious day comes, he is then above the law, for the celestial impulses have no power over the man who is a power unto himself. Astrology rules the willy-nilly blowing types who know but do not do, while man, when he rules his own organisms, is the master of his planets.

Gemini, the Third Sign of the Zodiac

Gemini is a movable sign.

Airy Speaking, Vernal Fortunate, Hot Bi-corporeal, Sanguine Sweet sign, Moist Ruled by Mercury, Masculine, Human, Barren, Common, Whole, Changeable,

General Characteristics:

Dual in temperament, Exaltation of, the Dragon's, Head, Detriment of, Jupiter, Oriental, Pleasant, Ambitious, Versatile Analytical, Entertaining Self-assertive, Intellectual, Quick-tempered, Artistic Studious, Argumentative Fond of Travel.

Gemini does not always know its own mind. It is changeable in its decisions and contradictory in its attitudes. As it is of a double sign, it is a double nature, usually expressing through two absolute opposites. The thing it likes one minute it will dislike the next; does not keep friends very well; will stand very little domineering; is free in finances but seldom wealthy; quite studious and fond of colors, music, and all artistic pursuits.

Physical Appearance:

Usually tall, Straight in lines, May be either light or dark but usually, light, If dark will have sanguine complexion, Clear skin, Well-shaped, usually long face, Long Arms, Short, fleshy hands and feet, Dark hazel eyes, Dark brown hair, Quick sight, Smart, active, business-like appearance, Well poised before people.

We do not always find full and complete types, nor do the above indications always hold true in their full expression. The reason for this is that the planets and their position in the sign often change the entire shape and form of the body, and also if the ruler of the sign, Mercury, is in bad aspect or the Sun is seriously afflicted the whole organism may be torn down and so changed that it is only recognizable by an expert.

Health:

Gemini is subject to nervous ailments and also to injury to the chest and arms and accidents to those parts of the body. The presence of Neptune in Gemini often points to weak lungs, tuberculosis, pleurisy, and coughs and colds in the bronchials, chest and lungs. It governs the arms, shoulders, lungs, and lower cervicals in the human body. Its diseases have been listed as follows by the ancients:

Brain fever, Nervous impediments, injuries to the arms and shoulders, Bad blood conditions, Stomach trouble, Headaches, Coughs and colds, Mental delusions, Air in the arteries and veins, Fractures, Nervous breakdowns, Melancholia, Injury to the upper ribs, Poor circulation,

Gemini is not always as careful in problems of diet as it might be and must watch carefully that which goes into the system, realizing that food and air make or break the organism.

Domestic Problems:

Gemini is not a domestic sign. It craves independence and self-expression, and usually possesses executive ability to such an extreme degree that it does not blend well with other people. It is not a fruitful sign and unless some very beneficent planet is found they seldom, if ever, raise large families. Gemini usually marries more than once, is seldom happy in matrimony, but usually recovers from any heart-break through which it passes. One of the hardest things to get along with in Gemini people is a peculiar trait that they have of suddenly changing their viewpoint on problems and scolding a person for doing the very things they asked them to do. These temperaments must be mastered and overcome in order that the greatest happiness may come to the Gemini life. Its keynote is duality and diversity, and Gemini is never happy until it unifies the dissenting factions.

Countries Under Influence of Gemini

The Southwest part of England, Eastern third of the United States, Lower Egypt, Flanders, Lombardy, Sardinia, Armenia.

Cities Under the Control of Gemini:

London, Versailles, Brabant, Wittenberg, Nuremberg, Mentz, Bruges, Louvaine, Cordova.

According to Ptolemy the fixed stars in the sign of Gemini are divided in their influence as follows: The stars in the feet of the twins have an influence similar to that of Mercury with a little of Venus. The bright stars in the thighs take the qualities of Saturn and the two great stars, Castor, and Pollux, have the qualities of Mercury and Mars, respectively.

The colors of Gemini are red, white, violet, sometimes orange. Gemini rules from about the 20th of May to the 20th of June, and, according to the ancients, of the twelve orders of Blessed Spirits, it rules the Thrones; of the twelve Angels which rule the twelve signs, it is governed by Ambriel; of the twelve tribes, Judah; of the twelve prophets, Zachariah; of the twelve Apostles, Simon; of the twelve plants, the bending vervain; of the twelve stones it rules the topaz; of the twelve principal parts of the body, the arms; of the twelve degrees of the damned and the devils, it rules the vassals of iniquity. Gemini is a mental sign which seldom finds a great depth of heart sentiment, but when it does make that contact, it is one of the most beautiful signs of the Zodiac.

MAN THE HUMAN VIOLIN - II
Part II - The God of Music

FAR back in the dawn of human consciousness where only myth can reach, there is the legend of Orpheus and his celestial music. We are no longer dealing just with the story but once again with a great Being, a willing instrument in the hands of a still greater, who in his day and age of the world labored to bring to the souls of men a fuller consciousness of the Divine. In Orpheus we see the Initiate and an example for us to follow and within each of us the great Initiates continue their labors, and the great power of Orpheus still seeks to awaken the latent qualities to be evolved within living things.

Orpheus received from his Father, the Sun God, a wondrous lyre and from its strings he brought forth strains of music that charmed all living things, and for ages he has stood as the symbol of those qualities in man which when awakened sound forth from his spiritual nature as celestial harmonies. Man, also has received from his Father, the divine God of Light, a seven-stringed instrument which he is through the ages learning to play. This instrument represents his body, his senses, and organs of consciousness. His life is a wonderful orchestra, its music harmonious or inharmonious according to how he plays upon the strings of his being. Man is eternally working to transmute the discordant sounds into living harmonies which he may offer upon the altar of his gods.

Orpheus, the spirit of harmony in man, is seeking to spiritualize the lower phase of his being with its animal desires and emotions and to lift it from the land of darkness where it has been sent because it has been bitten by the snake of passion, and around this sublime truth has been wound the legend of Orpheus and Eurydice. In the allegory Orpheus stands for the divine principle of truth and harmony in man and the universe, which is seeking to lift the lower expression of itself out of the darkness of Pluto's realm. Orpheus does succeed in saving Eurydice but the lower not yet transmuted to the consciousness of the higher fails, as is shown by the world today because of its lack of trust in the divine, so like humanity it is forced back again into the Great Unknown.

It is said that Orpheus reached so great a position before God and man that the powers of the universe at the time of his death caught up in fingers Invisible his celestial lyre and placed it among the stars where it is still to be seen as a great constellation.

The story is told that Orpheus used to stand and allow javelins and arrows to be thrown at him, but he was so wondrous and the music of his soul was so beautiful that even the weapons fell at his feet charmed by the celestial harmony. This great truth is ever present in our lives. If we are radiating this divine harmony and beauty, the taunts of the world, hate, and anger, the javelins of our brothers, fall harmless at our feet, for nothing can fail to be charmed when within the soul of man harmony and truth prevail.

Through the development of bodies and sense centers man bringing into dynamic power the energies implanted in embryo within him has awakened a wondrous instrument, his vehicle of self-expression. His daily life is the music which he plays upon his enchanted lyre and when the tones are in harmony, the powers of darkness, though they conspire, are unable to injure him. But let this music be drowned or silenced by the powers of emotion and the beings of the astral plane and all of his power is gone, and he is torn limb from limb and his body, and his heart are cast into the river Hebrus or the stream of suffering into which those fall who fail to master responsibilities and conditions.

Of course, the entire legend of Orpheus is an ancient initiative ritual, part of the Greek Mystery School, and as such is a symbol of God, man, and the universe. The seven planetary rays are the seven strings of the celestial lyre, and power is given to each of these strings through Apollo, the Sun-god.

Man has himself centers of consciousness, which are the receiving poles of these planetary rays. If they are awakened and harmonized, he receives only good but when they are unawakened or the ray is impeded, mentally, physically, or spiritually, he must suffer for the unbalance. These seven rays, in various combinations under the direction of the gods, build and create all things. All of these rays are harmonious of themselves and there is not a planet in the entire solar system that is truly malefic. In astronomy, which in ancient times embraced the study of astrology, we find planets which were considered evil because they seemed to injure man with their powers, but in truth this is only so because man has not raised himself to a true knowledge of their powers.

It is well for the student to remember that all these heavenly bodies are one-eyed gods, their rays are neither good nor bad but eternally neutral. It is the adjustment of the receiving pole which causes any inharmony the individual may suffer, for these are all strings on a celestial musical instrument and while they may be out of tune and combined in discords, still each string is perfect if properly played.

Orpheus represents the individual who has mastered this seven-stringed instrument by mastering the qualities and attributes within himself of the seven-stringed lyre of planetary and celestial influxes.

Man consists of two poles which manifest as spirit and matter. Spirit is eternally working with matter, attempting to liberate it and raise it into harmony with itself in order that it may function through and with it in accordance with the plan. Orpheus represents the spirit in each human being who, wandering in the darkness of his lower nature, is seeking to release and transmute the essences imprisoned there which have been forced through ignorance or misuse to serve evil instead of the natural good.

We find that the serpent, which symbolizes perversion while crawling on the ground and mastership when raised, is the cause of the death of Eurydice and all students know that it is the serpent power in man which if misused sends the soul into the land of darkness. The higher man, the spirit, is ever confronted with the eternal problem of lifting the lower nature up from the regions of death into the world of light. In order to do this, Orpheus, the higher powers, took his seven-stringed lyre and, like the Initiate went down into the lower worlds to rescue the one whom he loved. He passed the three-headed dog, the guardian of the threshold, the creature built of his own perversion, and like all the Initiates entered the land of death while still numbered with the living. He implored Pluto, god of the underworld, to return to him the one chained by the powers of darkness. There again we see the spiritual man descending into matter with the lyre of spiritual influx working and striving to lift the lower nature into union with itself.

Orpheus' appeal was so wonderfully expressed and so enhanced by the music of his lyre that even the god of death relented and promised him that if he would take his bride back to the light without once looking back until they reached the outer world, she might have her life. Orpheus failed in this great duty, for like men and women of today he broke the vow of eternal progression, and having taken the path that led to Light he allowed the temptations of the lower to cause him to look back and Eurydice vanished again and the gap between the spirit and the soul was widened instead of becoming narrower. But the work is going on eternally and within each of us it is being slowly carried out until the time will come when we shall raise the lower from the dead and bring it to the surface of the higher worlds without breaking the vows of nature.

The teachings of Orpheus as a great individual are almost unknown, but the result of his work is still obtainable under the allegory of myth and legend. All myths refer to internal as well as external truths and the story of Orpheus is no exception to this rule, and our work is to learn to play this wonderful instrument of the body as Orpheus played his lyre and not to look back once we have taken the path.

The story of Orpheus and Eurydice is the eternal romance, the mystic love story, the basis of all human affections. It is the story of the spirit and the soul which must sometime be united in an everlasting union when man shall have rescued Eurydice from the land of darkness and destruction.

MASONRY
An Appeal for Better Masons

IN THE world in which we live today, there is a great need for which few seem to be willing to study that they may supply the necessary thing. There is nothing more important to the growth of man than the realization of individual responsibility. The average person does not shoulder the duties of his life as he should. He does not live up to the best that he knows; he is not true to the things which he claims to believe, but with selfishness and perversion he desecrates the ideals which he should express in his service and labor.

This is equally true among those whom we call society and that other group who claim to have found a great light or at least to be searchers for it. The average Mason is thoughtless. He is not a criminal nor is he false intentionally to the concepts which he holds, but he is preoccupied, and he feels no responsibility, no individual obligation, in connection with the study of Masonry.

When it comes right down to the truth, the average thirty-second degree Mason knows little or nothing of even the first principles of Masonry because he has not assumed the responsibility and the individual duties which make him one with the spirit of Masonry. When those wondrous rituals are unfolded before him, he is thoughtless; when the lectures are delivered to him, he is thoughtless; as he dons the apron, as he transacts the business of his lodge, he is thoughtless; so, he passes on year after year in close touch with the most beautiful and lofty of human sentiments, yet absolutely blind to both their purpose and meaning.

Why? Because he has failed to take a personal interest or realize an individual responsibility. If the Mason only realized that the spirit of the ancient craft can only live in its craftsmen and that the divine light of Masonry must shine out through the lives of Masons, he would then become worthy of his craft in seeking to glorify Masonry by his own example.

For many years, Masonic candidates have been recruited from various walks of life and various motives have led the seeker to the temple door, yet only about one in a thousand is really seeking either spiritual light or philosophical growth. Business is the usual motive which prompts Masonic affiliation; a desire for social prestige and the privilege of romping around at Shriner's frolics also gathers quite a percentage of individuals who believe that little red fezes will be becoming; still another group joins that they may have an honorable excuse for being away from home one night a week; some are Masons because their fathers were Masons; others because their fathers were not.

This is not malicious nor is it wicked, but it is decidedly unfortunate, for it has absolutely murdered the spirit of Masonry. The ancient mysteries, those glorious temple rites of a people who knew their gods, have been handed down to modern, everyday affairs. In the ancient days the High Priest, that living link between God and man through whose being shone the light of the infinite and who was in truth the incarnation of the rising sun, sat in the eternal East in a glorious chair of light with the wisdom of a god, the compassion of a savior, and the power of a Hercules.

Not being a Mason myself and having taken the "separate look" at the problem on hand, the answer that seems to present itself is this. There is no finer body of men in the world than the members of the ancient and accepted craft, but ninety-nine out of a hundred of them while excellent fellows have not even a dream consciousness of either Masonry or its ideals.

There is only one remedy to this problem for Masonry is probably the most beautiful and most glorious religious philosophy that the world has ever, known. In it there is material for thousands of years of study and consideration. Its sublime allegories and wondrous symbols have behind them truths, which are the answers to the world's problems.

A few Masons realize this. That grand old man of Masonry, Albert Pike, saw what few Masons have ever found. Dr. J. D. Buck, a sainted Masonic soul, found and taught the mystic rites. Frank C. Higgins, with his knowledge of mathematics, geometry, and cabalism, is an honor to the craft. They have found the truth of Masonry, and they are living according to their knowledge of its ideals. But where are all the others?

Just one or two out of a million, where are all the others? They are asleep; they have not lived the Masonic life; they have not dedicated their souls to the answer of the eternal Masonic problem; they have not gone forth in humility and simplicity to search for that which was lost. And the result is that a glorious truth is neglected, a wonderful work has been cast aside, and Masonry which depends upon Masons for expression is retreating again to the silent caves where for ages the illuminated few have guarded the destinies of the ignorant many.

Masons, wake up before it is too late! Your creed and your craft demand the best that is in you, they demand the sanctifying of a life, the regeneration of a body, the purification of a soul, and the ordination of a spirit! You have a glorious opportunity, wake, and grasp it 'ere it passes on to other peoples! Realize that your great privilege is to illuminate the world; not alone the work in your tiled lodge, but in your home, your business, and your association with your fellowmen is the basis of your Masonic power.

Masonry can only be what Masons are, but its spirit is the Wisdom of God. Your temple is a holy place, a sacred place, not to be defamed by material thoughts and dissensions. Drive the money-lenders from your steps, the materialists from your shrines, the schemers from your ranks, or else so live that these shall be regenerated and transmuted while among you. Show your light to the world and as true builders of the Father's house labor for the good of humanity. Forget your robes, your tinsels, and your jewelry and make of your living body and soul ornaments of your lodge. Let not the tinsel drape an empty void, but cover the hearts of noble men.

Editor's note: On 28 June 1954, Hall was initiated as a Freemason into Jewel Lodge No. 374, San Francisco; passed September 20th, 1954; and raised November 22nd, 1954. He took the Scottish Rite Degrees a year later. He later received his 32° in the Valley of San Francisco AASR (SJ). On 8 December 1973 (47 years after writing The Secret Teachings of All Ages), Hall was recognized as a 33° Mason at a ceremony held at the Philosophical Research Society which he founded.

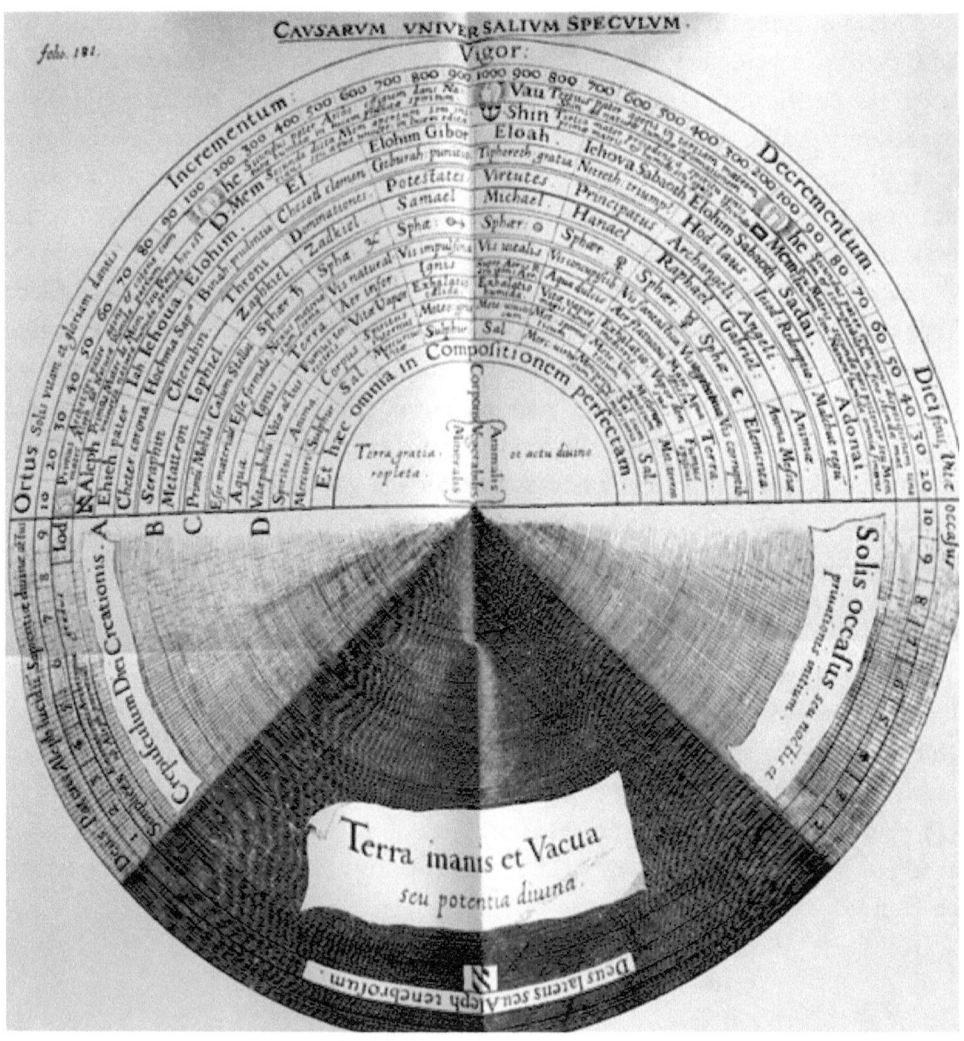

AUTHOR AND MANAGING EDITOR

Darrell Jordan is an acolyte of the August Fraternity, former Noble Grand-IOOF and Freemason. He is also a member of the Theosophical and Philalethes Societies.

BOOKS BY THE AUTHOR

- Illustrations of Masonry
- Surviving Document of the Widow's Son
- The Undiscovered Teachings of Jesus
- The Initiates
- Jefferson's Bible
- Master Masons Handbook
- Forgotten Essays - W.L. Wilmshurst
- Forgotten Essays - Waite
- Forgotten Essays - H. Stanley Redgrove
- The Writings of Sigismond Bacstrom M.D.
- Forgotten Essays — Reincarnation
- Masonic Writings of George Oliver
- Masonic Lectures by Wellins Calcott
- The Fellowcraft Handbook
- Secret Societies
- Vibration and Life
- Key to the Rosicrucian Characters
- The Revelation of John
- Life and the Ideal
- The Philosophical History of Freemasonry
- The Magic of the Middle Ages
- Musings of a Chinese Mystic
- The Life of the Soul
- Christian Mysticism
- Krishna and Orpheus
- The Eleusinian Mysteries & Rites
- The Crucifixion Letter
- The Mystic Key
- You Paid What?
- The Illustrated Pioneer History of the America
- Montana Freemasons 19th Century
- Washington Freemasons 19th Century
- Idaho Freemasons 19th Century
- Rock Metaphysics
- Emblems: Jean Jacque Boissard and Otto van Veen
- Emblems: Nicholas M. Meerfeldt
- Alchemy Art: Manly P. Hall
- Emblems: Manly P. Hall
- Alchemy Art & Symbols
- Splendor Solis

For the latest information, please visit author's book site: Parallel47North.com/collections/esoteric-books

If you have any question, suggestion, or feedback, please contact: info@Parallel47North.com

www.ingramcontent.com/pod-product-compliance
Lightning Source LLC
Chambersburg PA
CBHW020247010526
44107CB00002B/140